CO-AUU-265

ECONOMICS
FOR PLEASURE

BUCHANAN LIBRARY
George Mason University

TO
FRANK KENDON

BUCHANAN LIBRARY
George Mason University

G. L. S. SHACKLE

ECONOMICS
FOR PLEASURE

SECOND EDITION

USED

CAMBRIDGE
AT THE UNIVERSITY PRESS
1971

Published by the Syndics of the Cambridge University Press
Bentley House, 200 Euston Road, London NW1 2DB
American Branch: 32 East 57th Street, New York, N.Y. 10022

© Cambridge University Press 1959

Second edition © Cambridge University Press 1968

ISBN
0 521 06282 9 clothbound
0 521 09507 7 paperback

First edition 1959
First paperback edition 1962
Second edition 1968
Reprinted (with corrections) 1971
Spanish edition published 1962
Dutch edition published 1964
Portuguese edition published 1964
French edition published 1965
Italian edition published 1966
German edition published 1969
Greek edition in preparation
Czech edition in preparation

Printed in Great Britain
at the University Printing House, Cambridge
(Brooke Crutchley, University Printer)

CONTENTS

PREFACE *p.* vii

BOOK I. VALUE

Wants, *p.* 1   Resources, *p.* 5   Scarcity, *p.* 10

Budgets, *p.* 12   Prices, *p.* 19

BOOK II. PRODUCTION

Production, *p.* 24   Specialisation, *p.* 31   Firms, *p.* 35

Activities, *p.* 43   Markets, *p.* 51   Equilibrium, *p.* 61

BOOK III. INCOME

Income, *p.* 68   Outlay, *p.* 72   Circulation, *p.* 78

Price-levels, *p.* 85   Money, *p.* 91

BOOK IV. DISTRIBUTION

Wages, *p.* 99   Bargaining, *p.* 106   Rent, *p.* 110

Profit, *p.* 118   Distribution, *p.* 122

BOOK V. EMPLOYMENT

Saving, *p.* 133   Equipping, *p.* 141   Output, *p.* 152

Demand, *p.* 159   Employment, *p.* 168   Growth, *p.* 176

BOOK VI. FINANCE

Liquidity, *p.* 181   Securities, *p.* 190   Banks, *p.* 197

Living Costs, *p.* 205   Capital, *p.* 211

Contents

BOOK VII. GOVERNMENT

Taxes, *p.* 218   Expenditures, *p.* 225   Deficits, *p.* 227

Debts, *p.* 235   Planning, *p.* 239

BOOK VIII. TRADE

Imports, *p.* 243   Payments, *p.* 247   Currencies, *p.* 254

Tariffs, *p.* 261   Models, *p.* 265

INDEX. *p.* 270

PREFACE TO THE FIRST EDITION

'Some men are so selfish that they read a book or go to a concert for their own sinister pleasure, instead of doing it to improve social conditions, as the good citizen does when drinking cocktails or playing bridge.' JACQUES BARZUN   *The Saturday Evening Post*, 3 May 1958

I could write many weighty paragraphs explaining how useful and indeed essential it is for the leaders of modern life to have some knowledge of economic theory; not only for the politician, the civil servant, the banker and the actuary, but also the schoolmaster, the journalist, the engineer, the agriculturist and many more. But such an assertion would be as dull as it is true. Instead, I want to plead that economics should be read by an even wider circle than those for whom it may be an indispensable means to professional effectiveness; that it should be read because it is interesting and even fascinating, that it should be read for enjoyment. But how can a subject be readable that requires the brain-teasing study of diagrams and equations? For those with a taste for formal geometry and algebra there are many excellent textbooks. *This* book is utterly free from all such apparatus. I would like you to read it, in the words of the Dean of Faculties of Columbia University, 'for your own sinister pleasure'.

1959   G. L. S. SHACKLE

PREFACE TO THE SECOND EDITION

Two new additional chapters have been written for this edition. The new Chapter 9 of this edition seeks to explain the purpose and nature of input–output analysis and activity analysis, though it is not possible to show their detailed methods in a book which avoids algebra. The new Chapter 27 gives an account of the theory of growth originated by Sir Roy Harrod.

I am most grateful to Professor Syed Ahmad of the University of Khartoum for very kindly pointing out to me some passages where my former wording could mislead. Thus on p. 116 I have

Preface

re-written the eleven lines following the reference to Ricardo in the chapter on Rent, and on p. 206 I have re-cast a sentence which referred to the Quantity Theory of Money as tautological. These and the two new chapters are the only substantial additions or changes in the new edition.

1966   G. L. S. SHACKLE

I wish to thank Mrs. E. C. Harris for the endless care she has taken in preparing the typescript and index of this book, and in reading the proofs. I am profoundly grateful to the staff of the Cambridge University Press for the beautiful physical production of the book.

BOOK I. VALUE

Chapter 1. Wants

HATRED, ridicule and contempt, it might be said without much exaggeration, are the lot of the economist, for he is the exponent of what used to be called the dismal science, that is still regarded as dismal if no longer a science. And dismal, in a sense, it is, since it deals with *scarcity*, with not being able to have as much of things as we should like.

Some philosophers have thought that all ends and purposes converge upon one, and can be reduced to the pursuit of the *summum bonum*, the individual's unified, coherent conception of the good life. They have maintained, even, that only by supposing this can we account for our ability to weigh against each other our desire for a little more of this and our desire for a little more of that, an ability which, when one considers it, is quite puzzling when the things are as different as, say, music and mutton. But the economist is not really concerned with this puzzle. There is in any person's world of experience or of imagination a tremendous variety of desirable kinds of thing, plainly distinct from each other. There is also, for each person and for all of us together, a plain impossibility of getting so much of every one of these kinds, all at once, that we could not possibly find any enjoyment in having any more: we cannot have everything to the point of complete satiation. To each person by himself this impossibility presents itself as a lack of money; for all of us taken together it consists in the fact that the quantities in question simply are not there. If everything were free, the shops and showrooms and warehouses would be swept bare in no time, and there would still be disgruntled people who had not got there in time to collect all they would have liked.

What, then? We have to *choose*. Not between having flowers and no chocolates, or chocolates and no flowers, but between different mixtures of both. When we add up the weekly shopping-list, and the total expense comes to more than the weekly house-keeping money, we do not ordinarily cross 'soap' or 'sugar' right off the list: we put 2 lb. instead of 2½ lb., and so on. The choosing consists in deciding at what point to say 'No' to our wish for more of one thing, in order to have a little more elbow room in meeting our wish for something else.

Choose? Decide? These words indicate thought and trouble; why not just reduce a few quantities at random, if the budget will not balance at first? Because, of course, we want to *get the most* comfort, contentment or satisfaction out of the restricted expenditure, and for this some reasonable principle must be applied. The question what this principle is, and why, is much thought about in economics, partly for the understanding it gives of why people behave broadly as they do, and partly for the inferences it enables us to draw about the detailed changes of conduct they would adopt in case of this or that change of circumstances. Businesses, governments and trade unions act upon such knowledge, or upon the intuition or the 'feel of things' that are inferior substitutes for it.

Whether or not, in the last analysis, our wants for all the different sorts of things can be resolved into a single want for the realisation of some specified, coherent plan of life, on the surface at least we seem to experience an immense diversity of wants, as many of them as there are distinct kinds of desirable things within our knowledge or our fancy. Things which we want, which can gratify our wants, are *goods*. Not all goods are things which can be handled. What the doctor or the actor or the cookery demonstrator does for us is a good, just as much as the illumination which comes from an electric lamp, or the weighty groceries in our basket. Indeed it can be argued that what we ultimately want is always some kind of *service*, to be warmed, nourished or entertained, and so on, and that tangible goods are merely a source or a store of such services, able, perhaps, to furnish them continuously or repeatedly through some stretch of time.

Voltaire once reproved his servant for not having cleaned his master's boots. 'They will only get dirty again' said the man.

Wants

'Very well, then it will be no use giving you any dinner, you will only get hungry again.' Most of our wants, and nearly all of those which refer to the necessaries of physical health or comfort, are not 'once for all' wants, but need to be gratified hour by hour or moment by moment. To satisfy them, the shopping expedition must be repeated every day or every week. We speak of a *stock* of sugar or petrol or soap when we mean some quantity existing now or at some other particular moment; if you eat up the sugar in your stock, that is the end of the matter, it is gone. So if we only have a stock of food or fuel or cleaning materials, our wants for these things will not be satisfied for very long. To keep our wants satisfied, we need a *flow*, that is, so-and-so many pounds, pints or what not each day.

Let us be a little more explicit about why most needs are for a flow rather than a stock. Usually the goods, or those qualities of them that matter to us, are destroyed in rendering us satisfaction, they are used up or *consumed*. The want, however often gratified, continually reawakens, and on each occasion a fresh parcel of the goods concerned is needed. These parcels can be imagined, if you like, spread out along a slowly moving conveyor belt, or drifting towards us in a long line of boats on a river, and reaching us one at a time just when needed. They form, indeed, a flowing stream.

What we mean, when we say 'My consumption of tea has increased', is not just that one parcel is bigger but that we have had to decide to have all of them bigger, for at least some appreciable time ahead: the number of ounces *per week* is now bigger. It is the size of the *flow*, measured as so-and-so many units of weight, volume, area, etc., *per unit of time*, that is in question when we speak of an increase or decrease in our consumption of some good. It is when the flow of something, coming to us for us to use up, has got bigger, and promises to go on at its new higher level, that we feel better off.

The bigger the flow of those particular goods that meet some want, the higher the degree to which that want is gratified. To receive five ounces of tea a week is better than to receive four ounces, six ounces is better still, and so on. No doubt it is 'somewhat' better to have a bigger flow than a smaller one. But can we say whether the *difference* made to our feelings of contentment, by having five ounces a week instead of four, is itself 'larger' or 'more noticeable' or 'more important' than the difference made by having six ounces instead of five? Suppose you had, for your own sole use, thirty-two ounces of tea a week. Would you care much if, one week, the parcel was an ounce short? You would not mind, even if you had given away all the surplus tea of past weeks that you had not been able to drink. But suppose each weekly parcel only contained two ounces, and one week it was half empty? That would be a cause for grief, at any rate to me.

If you agree with the general tenor of this last argument, you are accepting the idea that the *extra* gratification or satisfaction or 'utility' furnished by an *extra* weekly ounce, or pint, or whatever it may be, can be said to depend on how many weekly ounces, etc., it is extra to. An ounce of tea a week more or less, on top of or taken away from thirty-two ounces a week, is no matter; but an ounce a week more, or less, when we start from two ounces a week, is a great matter. This is the famous 'law of diminishing marginal utility', an important idea, and, as I believe, true, but by no means as difficult as the length of its name suggests.

The italicised words in this and subsequent chapters are mostly 'technical terms', efficient, like any other tools, only if kept for their proper purpose and used for nothing else. Each such word has a much sharper edge of meaning than those which serve for ordinary conversation, and should be used attentively.

Scarcity prevails whenever we cannot satiate all our wants. An ordinary want cannot be satisfied once for all, but needs a continuing *flow* of the appropriate good. It is an increase or decrease in the size of this flow, measured as so-and-so many physical units per unit of time, that augments or lessens our feelings of contentment. The flow which we use up of any particular good is called our *consumption* of that good. The *extra* contentment or satisfaction or

4

utility due to an *extra* unit flow of consumption of some good is the *marginal* utility of that good to the person concerned. When his consumption goes up by equal small steps, his utility will go up by diminishing small steps. This is the 'law of diminishing marginal utility'. It is only true in general so long as the person's other circumstances do not change when his consumption of one good changes.

Chapter 2. Resources

WE spoke in the previous chapter of warehouses full of goods, but how did the goods get there? It must be confessed, that in conjuring up a picture of shops and storerooms denuded of goods through these goods becoming suddenly free for the taking, we were being very rough and ready in argument. For as we have seen, what matters, for the satisfaction of wants, is not the existence of a once-for-all stock but the assurance of a continuing flow of a suitable size. What is in a shop at any one moment is a stock, and it is of course all the time being depleted by the activities of customers. A flow of fresh supplies into the shop is needed to match the flow that the customers carry away, and these fresh supplies must be produced by the never-ending collaboration of the forces of nature, the hands and brains of people, and the stores, tools, machines and constructed facilities which the people have made in the past and kept for use in the present.

These *resources* are scarce. Between the scarcity of resources and the scarcity of goods ready for consumers to enjoy, there is a curious reciprocal relation. A thing is not scarce unless two conditions are fulfilled: the thing must be wanted and it must be in some degree hard to get. Now resources are not wanted for their own sakes: they are only wanted for the sake of what can be produced by their means. If *consumers' goods* are hard to get, it is because the resources for making them are hard to get, at any rate in the quantities called for by the strong desire for consumers' goods. Resources are, if you like, a sort of unripe consumers' goods. Nobody wants unripe strawberries, only ripe strawberries; but the scarcity of ripe strawberries is due, on one side, to the fewness, earlier, of the unripe strawberries.

There are not, even in a country like the United States, nearly enough resources to produce, in each year, as much of every kind of thing as the people could possibly find any use for. Bounds are set at any time, by nature, geography and the state of technical knowledge, to the productive power of any nation. Yet in spite of this it is true that the different collections of goods, any one of which a nation could, if it chose, produce in a year (given time for preparation) are infinitely various. We in Britain could produce in each year much wheat and little milk, or much milk and little wheat, in infinitely many different proportions, different combinations of quantities, and so with countless other commodities; but to produce appreciably more of one thing we have to produce less of another. We have a freedom of choice about what things to produce in what relative quantities; and the fact that this freedom of choice is ours only within certain bounds, the bounds of our ultimate total power to work with our finite muscular and mental energies, to extract the fruits of fertility from our finite area of soil, and to get service from our finite collection of machines, compels us in exercising this choice to obey certain principles. These principles are a large part of the subject matter of economics.

Productive resources themselves are, in strictness, unlimited in their variety, for no two people, no two fields, no two building sites are exactly alike. But resources fall, nevertheless, into broad classes about which we can say something useful. It is old-fashioned nowadays to speak of 'land, labour and capital' as the three *factors of production*. Yet unskilled labourers are sufficiently alike in their capacities to be treated, for many purposes of discussion, as a uniform type of agent, and thousands of English fields have enough in common, in the qualities of their soil and the character of their climate, to be almost as good, or as poor, as each other for the farmer's various purposes. Two tractors or two railway wagons may, for all that matters, be identical. Thus although it may not do to assume that the factors of production are only two or three, the notion of factors of production itself is a legitimate and a powerful aid to insight.

The reason for grouping the means of production into classes and labelling each class a factor of production is, paradoxically, not the fact that the means differ as widely in their nature and their powers as men do from coalmines, nor because even within a broad group of means, such as 'human labour', there are great differences in effectiveness and competence, but it is the fact that resources which are widely different in technical character can in various degrees act as *substitutes* for one another, can often to some extent do each other's jobs. Because of this substitutability the sharing-out of the results of collaboration of the factors, the sharing-out of the multitude of products considered collectively as a 'national income', depends on the patterns in which the factors are brought together and upon who owns them; or looking at the matter the other way round we can say that the choice of the patterns in which the factors are combined is governed by the various degrees of substitutability, which thus underlie the answer to the question, who gets how much? All this we shall examine later.

For the discussion of some problems it is useful to group the factors of production under headings which virtually bring us back to 'land, labour and capital'. These broad categories, heterogeneous as their contents are, need not for that reason be blurred at the edges. The reason for using these headings gives rise, itself, to definitions which enable us at once to place any particular kind of resource under one or other of the headings. *Land* comprises all the untouched and primal dispositions of nature, the rocks she has laid down, the lakes, rivers and seas she has provided, and the climates with which she has endowed the various regions. Land, that is to say, is what was there before man came and exists and continues independently of his activities. *Labour* means people of any and every kind, with all their various bodily and mental powers and skills. *Capital* means all other 'real' resources ('real', that

7

is, in not being mere tokens, counters or acknowledgments of debt, and so on). Since we have included under 'land' everything that owes nothing to man's efforts, all the kinds of things which come under the heading 'capital' are man-made. Men have, indeed, not only made them; they have done something else which also calls in some degree for self-discipline, purpose and imagination: they have refrained from using all their daily or yearly powers of production to produce immediately consumable things, they have 'gone without' in order to accumulate real wealth.

The context in which these three categories come specially back into their own is that of discussion of how 'under-developed' countries can be made more prosperous. The term 'under-developed' is extremely imprecise. Is Canada, which has 'land' in vast abundance but relatively few people and immense possibilities of using more 'capital', an under-developed country, or do we mean by this expression densely populated India? Or what of Britain and Japan, whose acute shortage is 'land'? For these latter, the most radical kind of 'development', that may ultimately be called for to restore the balance of the categories, would be a negative one, migration.

These broad, mixed collections, what we have called the 'categories' as distinct from the virtually homogeneous *factors of production*, are appropriate for discussing economic needs and policies on the scale of whole countries and subcontinents. Before politicians can set their expert advisers to formulate detailed plans for raising the prosperity of a large region of the earth, they must decide in very broad terms what sort of policy is required. They may decide that the region needs 'capital', because nature's bounty is waiting to be tapped for the benefit of a proliferant population, and set aside so-and-so many billions of dollars for this purpose. For the first definition of their policy, the word 'capital' is precise enough. But for exact theory we must distribute the diverse means of production into classes each internally uniform or homogeneous, such, that is, that any one unit of any such class is a *perfect substitute* for any other unit of that class. Only by assuming that each such class or *factor of production* is homogeneous can we examine the effects of combining the factors in various proportions, and thus study the logic of the sharing-out of income amongst the owners of these factors.

There are two useful ways of sorting the means of production into kinds. The old-fashioned classification under the headings land, labour and capital has gained a new lease of life from the new subjects of 'growth' economics and the study of under-developed economies. To create additional 'capital' there must be a forgoing of some enjoyment which is within reach. Moreover the additional 'capital' must take concrete and specific form as machines, plant, buildings and so on of particular characters in particular places, and the creation of such specific facilities involves action in face of uncertainty. Thus the word 'capital' is needed to express broad policies or fundamental requirements, such as are involved in the 'growth' of an economy or its evolution to a more complex and richly endowed organism.

But the items within each such broad category are far too dissimilar to serve for a theory of productive *recipes*. When it is a question of the effect of mixing the means of production in this set of proportions or that, we need the notion of internally homogeneous factors of production. Whether in reality these would be numbered in their tens of thousands does not matter. The principles on which different factors should be brought together in certain proportions, so as to obtain a given product in the most economical way, can be quite well discussed by supposing only two or three factors, but it is better not to call these land, labour and capital because of the misleading suggestions these words would carry.

Chapter 3. Scarcity

MERE fewness is not the same thing as economic scarcity. What does the fewness of old horse-collars matter if nobody wants them? To be scarce is to be sought after. Nothing is sought after which is not desired, nothing is sought after which presents itself superabundantly without our making any effort to find, collect or fashion it. The early economists were struck by the astounding contrast between the cheapness of such absolute necessities of bare physical existence as air and water, and the dearness of such fripperies as diamonds or ostrich feathers. They perceived that air and water can be had with little or no toil, while gold and precious stones must be laboriously searched for and mined. This misled them into thinking that the value of a thing, its *value in exchange* expressed as the number of units of something else which one of its own units will fetch, was wholly accounted for when we had answered the question: How many times as much effort is required to produce one unit of this thing, as is required to produce a unit of the thing we are going to exchange it for?

This notion, that things exchange for each other in a ratio which reflects[1] the ratio of the quantities of effort or sacrifice which have gone into producing them, seems at first sight most reasonable, and there is a sense in which it is true. But how do we reckon this amount of effort or sacrifice? Do we take the whole annual exertion of the farmer and divide it by the number of bushels of wheat he has grown? If, by working eight hours a day, he has produced 2000 bushels, does it follow that when we ask him to produce, next year, an extra 500 bushels, he can do this by working ten hours a day? Far from it. To produce the 2000 bushels his fields have been working twenty-four hours a day, their response to his extra efforts will be by no means in proportion to the extra hours he works. If he has to work twelve hours a day instead of eight, in

---

[1] 'Reflects' in a more than figurative sense: for one ratio is the inverse, the 'upside-down', of the other.

order to produce 2500 bushels instead of 2000, will he not rightly ascribe to these 500 extra bushels a cost of four hours a day? And will he be willing to produce them unless he is offered, in exchange for each 500 bushels of his wheat, something that he regards as worth four hours of his toil a day for a year?

Now we can see the insufficiency of the notion that exchange-value is proportional to cost. There is a vast question which it leaves unanswered. The relevant cost is the *marginal* cost, the cost of *completing* a given total output by adding to it the final bushels or tons. But this marginal cost will be different when the total output is different. The farmer could perhaps have got 1000 bushels from his land by only working three hours a day, and 500 bushels by only working one hour. Which of these various possible levels of the marginal cost is the one we ought to take? Plainly the one belonging to the output he actually does produce. But then, *what fixes this output*?

Something is missing. We cannot tell what the output will be, merely by knowing the cost of various outputs. We need also to know the *demand*, how badly people want more of the farmer's wheat. For if they very badly want more of it, they may be willing to offer him so much in exchange that he will be willing to work twelve or fourteen hours a day. To ascribe exchange-value to cost alone is like ascribing the tension of an elastic cord to the fact that it is fastened at one end: it will not be under tension unless something is pulling the other end as well.

Thus we come back to the idea that for scarcity of anything to prevail, *two* conditions must be fulfilled: there must be some obstacle to procuring unlimited quantities of this thing, and there must also be some desire to have more of it than can be got without effort.

It is time to refer explicitly to a mathematical idea which is centrally important in economics and every other subject which attempts a logical analysis of relations amongst quantities. It is an idea upon which several of the paths we have been following have converged. In ordinary language, it is that of the *dependence* of the size or measure of one thing on the size or measure of another. But what do we mean by dependence? It is not a question of cause and effect, though where there is dependence in the formal sense with which we are now concerned, we may often think that some relation of cause and effect can, as a separate matter, be reasonably assumed or discerned. For us, however, the dependence of one quantity on another merely means that when the latter quantity is named, as so-and-so many units, the former quantity can then be reckoned as such-and-such another number of its own appropriate units.

Let us take concrete examples. If I know the radius of a circle in inches, I can reckon its area in square inches; the area 'depends on' the radius. No one would claim, however, that the radius 'causes' the circle to have such-and-such an area. Earlier in this chapter we supposed the size of the farmer's crop to depend on the length of his working day. In Chapter 1 we supposed the degree of contentment or comfort felt by the householder to depend on the size of each item in his shopping-list. All of these are illustrations of the idea that one 'variable quantity' is a *function* of another, or of several other, variable quantities.

Chapter 4. *Budgets*

A *budget* is just a shopping-list in which care has been taken to keep the total money cost of all the items within an allotted expenditure. The budget that we are concerned with is the household's daily or weekly shopping-list in which each item names the physical quantity, of some kind of goods, bought per day or per week. We have looked already at the law of diminishing marginal utility, which says that if for every item in the shopping-list, except one, we put down some particular figure to state the number of ounces or pints of that kind of goods that will be bought per unit of time, and if for the one excepted item we write down a series of quantities increasing one ounce (say) at each step, then the difference that successive steps would make to our comfort and contentment diminishes. When we are getting very little tea or butter each week, it matters a great deal whether or not we get an extra ounce a week. When we are receiving two pounds a week, it hardly matters at all.

Does not this suggest that some further condition ought, if we are to manage our affairs well, to be imposed on the shopping-list, besides the condition that its cost, and the allowable expenditure, must balance? If a shilling less could be spent on butter without our noticing the loss of the corresponding quarter-pound, because we are buying such a lot of butter, while an extra shilling spent on tea would meet a craving for two or three extra cups a day, the budget is not as satisfactory as it could be: there is a gain in contentment to be had by spending a shilling less on butter and a shilling more on tea. If this is true of one of the shillings spent on butter, it is likely to be still true of a second shilling, when the first has been transferred to tea; but not as markedly true as it was of the first shilling. Plainly if we go on transferring shilling after shilling from butter to tea, the stage will eventually be reached when we shall be condemning ourselves to eat some of our bread dry,[1] and it will be the tea that is more than sufficient for all our felt needs. Where ought we to have stopped? At the point where there is no gain in comfort to be had by going any further, that is evident. And that point is where the loss of comfort from giving up a shillingsworth of butter is as great as, but not greater than, the gain of comfort from an extra shillingsworth of tea.

No one needs to be told, of course, that this is the principle that should guide the composition of a household budget: everyone follows this plan by intuition or by instinct. But by recognising that this *is* the principle which everyone, with more or less refinement and attention, does apply to his shopping, we can explain

[1] We may allow ourselves, for the sake of simplicity in argument, to abstract from the existence of margarine.

Value

many things that go on in the markets and the commerce of the world. In particular, we can explain the so-called 'law of demand', that a lower price is associated with a larger quantity bought and a higher price with a smaller quantity, which, though we may take it for granted as a description of how markets work, becomes a more satisfying part of our knowledge of the world when we can show it as a consequence of an aspect of human nature.

We have been supposing that a shilling for a quarter of a pound is the price of both tea and butter, and so long as we take this to be the case, we have two ways of expressing the principle which the shopper ought to follow: he will do best for himself, in adjusting his purchases of tea and butter, if he buys these two goods (and every other pair which can be composed out of his entire list) in such quantities that the extra contentment got from spending one extra threepence per week would be the same no matter which of them he spent it on; or if (which comes to the same thing when the prices of butter and tea per ounce are equal) he buys the two goods in such quantities that the extra contentment got from one extra ounce per week is the same no matter whether this is an ounce of tea or an ounce of butter. And we can translate this latter statement into the form that when the shopping-list is right the marginal utility of the two goods will be equal.

But now suppose that instead of butter and tea we were concerned with butter and sugar, and that the price of sugar was threepence for four ounces. Would it still be right to buy butter and sugar in such quantities that an extra ounce of sugar would give as much extra satisfaction as an extra ounce of butter? By giving up an ounce of butter the shopper can get four ounces of sugar. If his 'marginal threepence' is to float freely up and down the columns of his shopping-list, not sticking like a magnet to some one item, it will have to be able to buy the same extra comfort no matter where it settles. For this to be the case, the 'marginal utility,' the extra worthwhileness, of an extra ounce of butter must be equal to that of the quantity of sugar that can be bought for the same price; it must be as great as that of four extra ounces of sugar. The price of butter, we are supposing, is four times that of sugar, and

14

we have just concluded that, in a correctly adjusted shopping-list, the marginal utility of butter will be four times that of sugar. Or to give the principle a form of words which will apply to all the goods in the list, no matter what their prices per physical unit, the well-adjusted shopping-list or household budget has all its items in such quantities that their marginal utilities are *proportional to their prices*.

How are the principles we have been discussing, which govern the correct adjustment of a household budget, connected with the 'law of demand', which says that at a higher price less of any good will be bought in a unit of time, a week or a month, and at a lower price more will be bought?

When the price of butter per quarter pound is four times that of sugar, the budget will be 'right' when the gain or loss of one ounce of butter would make as much difference to the householder's contentment as the gain or loss of four ounces of sugar. Suppose now that the price of an ounce of butter falls so that it is only three times that of an ounce of sugar. How can the 'marginal utility' of butter be reduced so that it only takes three ounces of sugar to compensate for one ounce of butter? The principle of diminishing marginal utility says that the quantity of butter in the budget must be increased: if you want to make the 'marginal' ounce of butter matter less, make it the marginal ounce of a larger weekly quantity of butter.

Now it sounds as though acceptance of the principle of diminishing marginal utility, as a description of how almost everybody feels and acts, would involve us in agreeing that a fall in the price of any commodity must be accompanied, or quickly followed, by a rise in the quantity of it that all the people in the place in question buy in a unit time-interval. Is this necessarily true?

We certainly ought never, in economics, to put forward as universally valid any proposition that declares the size or measure of one thing (here, the quantity of some commodity bought per unit of time) to depend solely on the size or measure of some one other thing. How much electricity did you use last week? Would this amount not have been different if your house had happened to stand several degrees of latitude further north, if the number of rooms in it had been (say) three instead of ten, or if your income had been twice what it is? Must we then never venture to say what the size or other measure of any one thing depends on, without reciting an immense and endless list of influences and factors, immediate and remote, which can at some time affect it? No, for no circumstance (provided it be strictly and correctly identified and defined) can be held to affect the size or measure of anything, so long as it remains itself unchanged. We cannot ascribe the decreased weekly number of bus tickets sold in a certain town to a decrease in the population, if the population has in fact remained constant. We can, at any rate in principle, hold constant or suppose to be held constant all circumstances except one amongst those upon which we believe the size or measure of the thing in question to depend. Thus the list of influences can be shortened to one item, whichever particular one we are for the time being interested in, by simply assuming, explicitly, 'other things remaining unchanged' or *ceteris paribus*. Then, against a background of the constant, unvarying influence of the other factors, we can discuss what difference is made to the dependent quantity when the single factor becomes bigger or smaller, or stronger or weaker, by one unit at a time.

But there is a more special reason why the *demand* for a commodity (the quantity bought per unit of time) cannot be relied on invariably to rise when the price falls. For a community may be so poor that nearly everyone spends a very important part of his income on one single kind of cheap food, say potatoes. If potatoes become much cheaper, while incomes and the prices of other goods, including bread, remain unchanged, everybody will be much better off, for after buying the same quantity of potatoes a week as before, everybody will have more money left to spend on other things. Why not spend some on a better kind of food, say bread? And indeed, why not buy so much bread, now that we are rich enough to afford it, that *less* potatoes need be bought than when they were dearer? This kind of case, which is called the case of 'Giffen' goods, is of more interest as a theoretical nicety than as a practical matter.

There is one more matter for consideration before we go on to sum up all the contents of this Book I under the heading of *prices*: this is the question whether all the goods in the shopping-list are rivals of each other in one and the same sense. Suppose the price of coffee fell to one shilling a pound. I might well decide to have coffee at mid-morning instead of tea, and so put down more coffee and less tea in my budget than before. But how about sugar? I like a lot in my coffee, and if I began to use more coffee I should need more sugar, not less. Tea and coffee, because either of them for many people can meet almost equally well the need for a warming and wakening drink, are good *substitutes* for each other; this means that they are rivals. Coffee and sugar are not rivals in nearly the same degree. On the contrary, they are partners in making up a perfect beverage, they *complement* each other. Which are rivals and which are partners amongst pens, ink, typewriter ribbons, letter-paper, telephones? What happens to the *price* of a good, when the price of a substitute rises? What happens when the price of a complementary good falls?

This chapter has thrown up a number of ideas and expressions which recur again and again in the literature of economics, and which it will be well to pin down at once.

Budget we have defined as a considered list of quantities of goods or services to be bought per unit of time by some one person or institution; a list which is subjected to the double requirement, that the total weekly, annual, etc., cost shall not exceed some named figure, and that some purpose or harmonised group of purposes shall be served and fulfilled to the utmost extent possible within the allowed expenditure. In needing to make budgets, the private individual is on the same footing as governments, the difference is only a matter of scale.

The *law of demand* simply says that in almost all practically important cases, lower prices will be associated with larger quantities bought per time-unit and vice versa, provided that all the other governing and influential circumstances, except the price of the good in question, remain unchanged. We saw that this proposition follows logically from an assumption about human nature, namely the law of diminishing marginal utility. And later we shall see that the whole operation of the so-called 'price-mechanism', the working of markets and the maintenance of balance and order in the entire process of economic life depends on the law of demand as one of its main foundations.

There is an intermediate link between the law of diminishing marginal utility and the law of demand. This link is the proposition that in a successfully adjusted budget the marginal utilities of the various goods will be proportional to their prices: if an ounce of butter costs four times as much as an ounce of sugar, butter and sugar ought to be bought in such quantities each week that the householder would be just, but only just, willing to have an extra ounce of butter in exchange for four ounces less of sugar.

We stated the rule that if we wish to ascribe the whole of some particular change in the size or measure of something, to a change in the size or measure of some one other thing, we must state explicitly that all other possible influences were robbed of all claim to be the causes of the change, by having been constant at the relevant time; we must say *ceteris paribus*.

Lastly, we asked what will happen, say, to the price of petrol if motor-cars become very much cheaper. More motor-cars, more petrol wanted; the price of a good which is *complementary* to motor-cars rises when motor-cars become *cheaper*. And what will happen, say, to the price of coffee, if the price of tea rises very high? We shall not be able to afford so much tea, we shall buy more coffee instead; the price of a *substitute* for tea will tend to rise when tea becomes *dearer*. These propositions can be turned round and used as a definition of what we mean by saying that some pairs of goods are mutual substitutes and some are mutual complements.

Chapter 5. Prices

THERE are in economics a handful of focal words upon which many lines of thought converge, and which in consequence suggest to the economist, when they occur, whole trains of argument and implication. Such a word is *price*. Its formal meaning is simply that of a ratio, the ratio of what you give to what you receive in exchange. What you give and what you receive must of course be expressed in some units, and these units are quite arbitrary, so that we can say the price of coal is £10 a ton or ten shillings a hundredweight. Merely to alter the *units* does not alter the price. But real alterations of price, as from £8 a ton to £10 a ton, bring in their train an army of questions and of consequences. A change of price must have had antecedents which we can, for practical purposes at any rate, refer to as the cause of the change. And the change of price will merely be one link or part of a link in a series of events or of organically meshed situations growing one out of another. All of this, with a host of almost unbidden speculations and suggestions about the particular form which the whole mechanism or process has so far taken and is going to take, are instantly conjured up in the economist's mind by the news of any price-change. Price is the radar of economics.

So far we have spoken as though the numerator, in the fraction expressing price, was always so-and-so many money units, shillings or pounds sterling. In practice this is so. But in a more general and fundamental sense, a price is simply a ratio in which any two goods exchange for one another. It is just as reasonable and meaningful, if a pound of sugar can be bought for eightpence and a pound of butter for forty pence, to say that the price of a pound of butter is five pounds of sugar as to say that it is forty pence. It is convenient to reduce all prices to terms of money, and it is indeed this convenience which is one of the two great services that money renders and which makes the notion of money one of the great discoveries or inventions that have made civilised life possible.

Money's other great convenience, of enabling us to put off making up our minds until we feel better placed to do so, carries very grave and inseparable dangers as well. This we shall see in Chapter 16 (*Money*) and in Books v (*Employment*) and vi (*Finance*).

In this Book I we are concerned mainly with the feelings and consequent actions of householders as such, that is, with consumers or demanders, and with the principles on which it is logical for them to act in an environment of scarcity, an environment in which resources are not enough to satiate all wants. Such resources as there are can, indeed, be used to produce much of this and little of that, or vice versa, and in Book II (*Production*) we shall see the role of prices in this connection. But for the present we will take as given the quantity of each commodity that comes each week into the shops. Then we can say that the price of any commodity, by standing at a suitable level or moving, if necessary, to reach one, does two things: first, it adjusts the quantity per week that people, all taken together, try to buy, to the quantity per week that is there for them to buy; and secondly, it gives the amplest shares of this available quantity to those who, with the incomes they have, would be willing to pay most for *given* quantities of the good. If we think the comparative sizes of incomes are broadly 'fair' we shall have ground for saying that the price of a good, by reaching a suitable level, channels the available quantity of this good towards those who want it most. In claiming this we have to acknowledge that the notion of 'fair' incomes tacitly assumes that we can regard different people as having broadly similar capacities for feeling wants, or at any rate, that there is some sense and some possibility of comparing their capacities in this respect.

But how can price discriminate between the wants of this person and that? Does not everybody pay the *same* price per ounce or pint of any one thing, no matter whether they have a strong taste for it or hardly mind going without it? Yes, but if we ask each of them how much he *would* pay for, say, just one ounce of tea or tobacco or just one pint of beer each week, rather than go without this stuff altogether, we shall get some widely different answers. And any other arbitrary weekly quantities that people were allowed to buy, as when goods are rationed, would find some of them willing to pay far more than others for one extra weekly unit. Our formulation above says that price gives ampler shares to those who would be willing to pay most for *given quantities* of the good. How does it do this? By standing at a height where those with little inclination for this good find that a very small weekly quantity is enough to bring down the utility of the marginal shillingsworth to the right level. They buy this small weekly quantity and so leave larger weekly quantities available for those who really like the stuff in question.

Suppose that a particular painting is being sold by auction. Here, in regard to the quantity available, we have an extreme case, for the painting is unique, and the quantity available is just this one specimen. The demand for the painting has got to be reduced, if matters are to be brought to a conclusion, to a demand for just one specimen; and the bidding will carry the price up to a level sufficient to choke off the potential demand of all but one bidder.

In shops we do not overtly bid for butter and tea, eggs or poultry. But if, at one price, there is not enough each week to go round, the sellers will set a higher price, feeling by trial and error for a price at which only such demands will come forward as can, all taken together, be met from the weekly quantity available.

There is another method of making demand and supply equal, and that is by rationing. Rationing is arbitrary, and hands out prescribed quantities of each good to each person regardless of his tastes, so that the total weekly quantities available give less satisfaction than they might.

This chapter is headed 'prices', but you will often see references to the price-*system* or the price-*mechanism*. This is perhaps the most important idea in the whole of economics. In what sense do prices form a system or an interconnected whole? We have seen, in our discussion of pairs of goods which are mutual substitutes and pairs which are complements, how a change in one price can affect others. Another term for goods which can in some degree take each other's place is *competitive* goods. But do not all consumers' goods of every kind compete with one another for the householder's favour and his money? Prices are like boats on a smooth lake: not a movement of a single boat, however slight, but starts a ripple which will sooner or later affect every other boat. It is only because they do form parts of a web of interpenetrating influences that prices can perform their function of attracting each particular kind of goods towards those who are willing to pay most for it; of attracting factors of production towards the making of those kinds of goods for which there are the strongest demands; and of *balancing* the various pulls and thrusts of desire and cost so that, in a broad sense, and given the fulfilment of certain essential conditions which we shall see later, resources are made to go as far as they can towards satisfying people's needs.

The idea which we made explicit in the second section of Chapter 3 can give us a further insight into the meaning and working of price. It might be that in a small isolated community the number of pence which it would cost a poultry farmer to add a dozen eggs to his weekly output will be greater, the greater this weekly output already is, because, for example, household scraps then provide a smaller proportion of the necessary feed. We should then say that the *marginal cost* of eggs is higher, the larger the number produced per week; or again, that the marginal cost of eggs is an *increasing function* of the output of eggs. Plainly the poultry farmer would not be willing to augment his weekly output by a dozen eggs except on condition that he could sell each dozen eggs that he produces for as many pence as the difference of cost between his existing and his augmented output. Since this difference, the marginal cost, is an increasing function of output, it follows that as the price of eggs rises, the weekly number of eggs that he will be willing to supply will rise also. Householders, on the other hand, would be willing to buy fewer eggs each week at a higher price than at a lower one, and so as the price rose the number of eggs demanded would fall. The only state of affairs in which neither the suppliers nor the demanders would have any incentive to alter the number of eggs offered or asked for, or the price (having regard to the consequences of attempting any such alteration), would be one in which the number of eggs offered at the going price was *equal* to the number asked for at that price. A price which would equalise the supply of and demand for eggs could indeed be found, in all ordinary cases, for if at the going price supply exceeded demand a lower price would cause a curtailment of supply and an increase of demand. If demand exceeded supply, a higher price would likewise tend to curtail demand and increase supply.

Let us turn our attention away from the *actual* price and consider a ladder of possible or imaginable prices, written as a column of numbers, each number being the number of pence per dozen eggs. Beside each of these possible prices, let us suppose two other numbers to be written, one of them giving the number of eggs that would be supplied at that price, the other giving the number that would be demanded at that price. Towards the top of the price column, where prices were relatively high, the 'supply' number would be greater than the 'demand' number. Towards the lowest prices, the supply number would be less than the demand number. Somewhere intermediately the two numbers, of eggs demanded and of eggs supplied at the corresponding price, would be equal. That situation would satisfy both suppliers and demanders, in the sense that none of them would have any reason to do anything within their power to change the situation. That price which balances demand and supply we can call the *equilibrium* price.

BOOK II. PRODUCTION

Chapter 6. Production

PRODUCTION means every kind of operation or process which helps to bring things to the condition, place or time where they are wanted. It thus includes the winning of raw produce from nature by farming, fishing and mining; the treatment, fashioning and construction of materials by manufacture; and the transport, storage and retailing of products which are 'finished' in the sense of being ready to be bought either by the consumer for his sustenance and enjoyment or by the businessman as a rather long-lasting addition to his equipment of tools, machines or buildings. Buying and selling, transportation and storage of partly made things will also be found going on within the general process of manufacture.

What is produced, then, is really always economic value. To produce, in the economist's meaning of the word, is to take some pre-existing things and render them more valuable. The measure of how much has been produced by given operations is how much net addition has been made to the initial value of the collection of materials and tools with which the operations have been performed. It is not always quite obvious, in an economic system where firms supply each other with partly processed materials, how this 'value added' is to be reckoned, and we will construct a simple model to illustrate the point.

Let us imagine an economy whose only *finished* product, ready to be consumed, is bread. The entire economy consists only of the farmer, the miller and the baker, each of whom employs some workpeople. Each year the farmer, the miller, the baker himself and all their workpeople, taken together, buy bread in the bakery to the value of £100, and in exchange for it they hand in £100 over the bakery counter. Of this £100, we may suppose, the baker and his workpeople keep £30 for themselves as pay for their work, and the baker passes on the remaining £70 to the miller as payment for the flour which he supplies to the bakery. Of this £70, the miller and his workpeople keep, let us say, £25 for themselves for their own work and the miller passes on the remaining £45 to the farmer as payment for the grain which he supplies to the mill. This £45 pays the farmer and his workpeople for their work.

Now in answering the question 'What is the total value of production that has taken place in the whole economy during the year?' we might be tempted to add together the £45 paid to the farmer for his grain, the £70 paid to the miller for his flour, and the £100 paid to the baker for his bread, and say that the total of £215 is the total value of goods produced. But plainly this would involve counting the farmer's production three times and the miller's twice: the value of the work done on the farm is embodied in the value of the grain, and the value of the grain is *included*, together with that of the work done in the mill, in the value of the flour, whose value, in turn, is included, together with that of the work done in the bakery, in the value of the bread. The true answer is the total of the three amounts of 'value added' at the three stages of production, and this total is £45 plus £25 plus £30, and is equal to the value of the finished product, the bread. Since everything that is done in the economy is aimed merely at the ultimate production of bread and leads up only to this result, the value of the bread annually produced is the annual value of production in the economy.

At any one moment the world, or the nation, has only so-and-so many people possessing this or that kind or degree of muscular or mental power and skill, so-and-so many acres of this kind of soil or that, so-and-so many cows, sheep, mines, ships, trucks, lathes, looms, furnaces, and so on. This great but definite, limited collection of productive resources is *versatile*: it can be set to produce any one of an infinite variety of different 'national shopping-lists' (or world shopping-lists) of things, that is, different sets of quantities per time-unit of all the various kinds of known product. It cannot, at best, produce nearly enough of everything to satisfy everybody completely; the question is, how to make it go as far as possible in satisfying them. This great question, which embraces all the central core of economic theory, and is indeed the *raison d'être* of our branch of knowledge, contains within itself three distinct kinds of subordinate question, and it is only by answering, one at a time, the type of question representing each of these subordinate levels, that we can in sum answer the great question.

There is, first of all, the technical level. Given that we are to use specified quantities of human effort, natural forces and tools of various kinds to produce a specified kind of product, what techniques, what engineering procedures, will make our given resources yield the largest quantity of product? This is the question how to secure the highest technical efficiency, and in the short-term view it is a question which concerns only the engineer or technologist or natural scientist. (In a longer view, the economist may have to consider how to secure more or better engineers and natural scientists.)

Secondly, there is the economic level, the question of *economic* efficiency. We assume that, whatever set of quantities of physical resources are used, they will be used with the highest technical efficiency. But then comes the question, *what* particular set of quantities of resources, of factors of production, to use in the making of any given kind of product? This question is quite outside the competence of the engineer or technologist as such. He can tell us how best, in the light of existing knowledge, to produce heat from coal, or from oil, or from uranium. But he cannot, *qua* engineer, tell us which of these means is most economical. We have only to consider what would happen to our use of coal, if a huge oilfield were discovered under Britain, yielding petroleum and natural gas at low cost. The engineer's knowledge would be the same, his answers to particular questions, of how to perform specific engineering tasks, would be the same, but the questions he would be asked would concern oil more often than hitherto, and coal less often.

Thirdly, there is the question what kinds of things to produce, and in what quantities. And this question, whose roots so to speak are in the ground of the theory of production, spreads upwards far away into the regions of the theory of consumer's tastes and that of income distribution. It illustrates the principle, of which we can never remind ourselves too often, that in economics no single question can be permanently cut off and isolated from other questions and answered by itself. Every question is interwoven with other questions. *How* to produce depends on what we decide to produce, and *what* to produce depends in return on how various things can be produced, on how easy it is to produce this compared with that. *What* to produce depends also on the answer to, For whom? and For whom? depends on, What method will be used? because the earnings and profits of production will go to those who can contribute productive services of the kinds needed for the particular methods chosen. We can give an answer to each question in turn, but always with the proviso that the exact application of the answer depends on other answers to other questions.

Technology itself, then, we can dismiss. It is not our concern, though general considerations arise from it which are, and one of them we shall study in the next chapter. The sharing of income and the changes in this sharing, and the consequent changes in the leverage it gives to the differing tastes of different householders, we are not yet ready to discuss. This chapter is really concerned with questions at the middle level, that of economic efficiency, and thus with general notions about the consequences of combining the various factors of production in various relative and absolute quantities.

In the principles which must ultimately underlie the businessman's choice of a set of quantities of the factors of production, if he is to be rational, we find a striking parallel to those which must underlie the householder's choice of a set of quantities of consumers' goods to be put down in his shopping-list. Parallel to the principle of diminishing marginal utility there is the principle of diminishing marginal productivity. In the second section of Chapter 2 (*Resources*) and in Chapter 3 (*Scarcity*) we have already touched upon this last. To make the argument concrete we will speak of a dairy farmer, but one who has no access to the complex modern panoply of chemical fertilisers and manufactured feeding-stuffs. Our dairy farmer has available in variable quantities only grazing land, cows and farm workers. Suppose him sitting in his office and pondering the effect of having 12, 13, 14 ... cows upon his present area of farm land and tended by his present number of workers. For each number of cows, he writes down the corresponding daily number of gallons of milk that the farm would produce. Over some range of possible numbers of cows, each number differing from the next by one cow, these outputs might, perhaps, rise by roughly equal steps. But a size of herd will eventually be reached, if he goes steadily on increasing it by one cow at a time, where each cow's share of the sustenance available from the fixed area of land is not enough to enable the cow to give its greatest possible yield of milk. At that stage each extra cow will add less than the previous one to the daily number of gallons of milk. Ultimately, with larger and larger herds on an unchanged area of land, the cows would be so ill-fed that to add yet another would reduce the output of the existing herd by as much as the output of the extra cow, and no net increase of the farm's output would result. Beyond this point still more cows would actually reduce the total output until finally no milk at all was obtained.

A different experiment is possible. With his existing fields and his existing herd, the farmer can consider the effect of employing 2, 3, 4 ... workers to tend the cows and run the dairy. Each extra man, up to a certain number, will find something vitally important, or rather important, or very useful, or fairly useful ... to do. As with the cows, there will be some number of workers beyond which extra men would get in each other's way and actually reduce the output of the farm.

Or it may be that the herd is already too large for his existing fifty acres. Then he can consider using 51, 52, 53 ... acres with his present herd and his present number of workers. The same effect again will reappear. After a time the area of land will be too great to be effectively grazed, and each extra acre will add less and less to the full nourishment of the herd, and to the farm's output of milk.

Now if, in order to add a stated number of gallons of milk to his weekly output, the dairy farmer can use either so-and-so many extra cows or so-and-so many extra acres, it is plain that these two factors of production, cows and grazing land, are in some sense substitutes for each other in the production of milk. Thus when the farmer considers how, in the broadest terms, to conduct his dairy-farming business, one decision he has to take is what particular set of quantities of the various appropriate factors of production to use in obtaining any one stated output of milk. It is here that his problem bears so close a formal resemblance to that of the householder with his shopping-list. The rule for the householder is to make marginal *utilities* proportional to prices. The rule for the producer, the businessman or head of a firm, is to make marginal *productivities* proportional to prices. And the argument is just the same in his case as in that of the householder.

Suppose the dairy farmer finds that, with the numbers of acres, cows and workers that he actually has, one extra cow would increase the daily output of milk by the same amount as he would lose by having three fewer acres. And suppose he also finds that the addition to his total expenses of running the farm, that would be associated with having one extra cow in his herd, is equal to the saving of expense that he could effect by dispensing with only two acres. Then by giving up two of his existing acres, and having an extra cow instead, he can increase his output of milk without increasing the total weekly or yearly expense of keeping his dairy farm going. Alternatively, an adjustment of the relative and absolute quantities of the factors employed would enable him to produce the same output at lower expense. So long as any such profitable adjustment remains unmade, the dairy farmer has not attained that state of affairs where his output (at whatever level it stands) is being produced at least cost. The *economically* most efficient combination of quantities of factors, for producing any given output, is a combination such that an extra £5 a week would add the same number of gallons to the weekly output of milk no matter which factor it was spent on.

We can see, in the light of this argument, the relation of technical efficiency to economic efficiency. The latter subsumes the former. No method of production can attain the highest possible economic efficiency if it does not attain, for a *given* combination of quantities of factors of production, the highest technical efficiency. The economic question can only be answered on the supposition that a great range of technical questions have already been answered. The dairy farmer cannot make his choice between many cows and workers combined with few acres, or many acres and cows combined with few workers, and so on, until he knows the best way to make use of *any given* combined numbers of cows, acres and workers. But the technical answers are not, by themselves, enough. We can at once see why: they say nothing about *prices* of the factors of production. Yet the rule for economic efficiency refers explicitly to prices. If the relative prices of acres and workers change, the best proportions in which to employ acres and workers will change too.

The marginal physical product of a factor of production, in any one firm which uses this factor, is the number of physical units by which the weekly (or monthly or yearly, etc.) output of this firm will be increased when one extra unit of the factor in question is employed, the quantities of all the other factors remaining unchanged. What circumstances, what aspects of the firm's position does the physical marginal productivity, thus defined, of any one factor depend on? Evidently, first, on technical considerations, on the natural qualities and powers of this kind of resource; secondly, as we have seen, on the quantity of this kind of resource employed by the firm; and thirdly, on the quantity of each *other* factor, with given technical powers, associated with the factor we are interested in.

The law of diminishing marginal productivity says that the larger the quantity of one factor combined with given quantities of others, the lower will be the physical marginal product of that factor. The rule for economic efficiency says that the quantity employed of each factor should be such that its marginal physical product stands in the same relation to the price of one unit of that factor, as is the case for every other factor. It follows that when the price per unit of a factor of production goes down, more of this factor should be combined with given quantities of other factors.

Let us remind ourselves what 'marginal' means. A marginal quantity is a *difference* between two levels or sizes of some measurable and changeable thing. Marginal quantities do not tell us anything until two of them, belonging to two things which depend on each other in size or level, are used to form a ratio. Earlier in this chapter we have concrete examples of all these ideas. The number of cows on the dairy-farm is a measurable and changeable thing, so is the number of gallons of milk produced on the farm each week. When everything else about the farm remains constant, we can ascribe any change in the output of milk to an associated change in the number of cows. If, when the number of cows is sixty, the weekly output is 840 gallons, and when the number of cows is sixty-five the weekly output is 910 gallons, we can say that the marginal product of the herd is the *difference* between the two numbers of gallons divided by the *difference* between the two numbers of cows.

Chapter 7. Specialisation

THE best-known passage in the book which many look upon as the foundation-stone of economics describes the advantages of specialisation or 'division of labour'. The principle which Adam Smith explained in *The Wealth of Nations* is timeless and universal in its application. It consists essentially in breaking down into the simplest possible elements the community's total business of providing itself with countless different products each requiring a great many different operations, and of letting each person devote himself wholly to one such element. Thus he can use to the full his natural gifts and improve them by constant practice; he can avoid waste of time and of nervous energy in continually adjusting himself to fresh jobs; and his peculiarly human powers of judgment and thought can be released for tasks which only they can perform, by the taking over of all mechanical tasks and even of routine control by machines.

Sometimes the distinction is made between specialisation by product and specialisation by process, but it is not fundamental. Indeed the complex organisation of modern industry cuts across it in a thousand directions, so that it becomes almost meaningless. A miner, a steel worker, a truck driver, a telephone linesman, a typist, may be helping to make thousands of different consumable goods which will emerge from the immensely complex web of converging and diverging streams of goods-in-process, at each nodal point of which a firm may draw various materials from hundreds of other firms and distribute its own product as material for yet other hundreds of firms to work on. The essential point is that in the ultra-specialised productive system of our day, each worker usually does only 'one kind' of work, and the meaning of 'one kind' has over the last two hundred years become for many people narrower and narrower.

This specialisation has two consequences: first, a measureless increase in the quantities and the variety of goods that can be produced by a given number of people, as compared with what they could produce if each were a Crusoe isolated on his own island; secondly, the necessity for each to exchange with others his specialised kind of service for the diversity of goods needed to satisfy his wide range of wants. So intimately are the two ideas of specialisation and exchange bound up with each other, that they may be said to form together inseparably a single principle underlying the wealth of modern economies. It is from the 'exchange' aspect of the total process that the most central and typical objects of study for economists arise.

Specialisation

It is obvious that these exchanges could not possibly be conducted by direct barter; but this impossibility is only one reason why *indirect* exchange, where a third entity intervenes in the total transaction of giving up one kind of good and ultimately receiving others in exchange, is a necessity of our modern economic life. The other and far more interesting reason is the necessity for *keeping account* of all the transactions in their immense variety and multiplicity, and of enabling every transaction to be related to every other in any time and place by the expression of the values of the exchanged things in terms of a common unit of account.

For although economists still speak of money as a medium of exchange, it would be more illuminating and closer to reality to speak of it as a 'medium of account'. After all, what happens when a person sells a month's work and buys with his month's pay two score or so of different goods needed for the subsistence and comfort of his household? His employer gives him a piece of paper stating a money sum, on sight of which a bank subtracts that sum from the amount which it owes to the employer and adds it on to the amount which it owes the employee. Then the employee in turn writes a dozen cheques, and the total of these is subtracted from the amount the bank owes to him. If he has then spent all his month's salary, the whole business has consisted in keeping account of matters so that, at the relative values, prevailing in the market, of his own services and the goods he has bought, the amount he has put into the common pool of goods, and the amount he has taken out, are equivalent and are in effect *recorded* as having been exchanged against one another.

Things are no different when, instead of a cheque and the corresponding entries in the bank's ledger, there is only the passing of a banknote or a coin from hand to hand. The coin and the banknote are valueless in themselves: they are mere tokens or *counters*, manufactured from the cheapest materials that are sufficiently durable and difficult to imitate. They are counters and they serve for counting up what total value has been exchanged on a series of occasions. In a sense we might say that coins and notes nowadays serve only to *keep account without writing*. A system is perfectly

33

conceivable where we should write a cheque for our bus fare: but it is less troublesome and more economical to write just one cheque for a thousand bus fares, by taking coins in exchange for the cheque and paying them away in small amounts as need arises. When they have all gone, our bank account correctly registers those aspects which are important about the fact that we have exchanged so-and-so much work for so-and-so many miles of bus rides.

What is the total effect of specialisation and exchange? It is that I, a specialist in, let us say, plate-laying or printing or piano-playing, work each day for thousands or millions of other specialists and play a part in enabling them in their great numbers to make railway journeys or read newspapers or hear concerts which, without the tremendous organisation of which we all form a part, would be utterly non-existent and unavailable; while each of them directly or at few or many removes works for me through an immensely complex network of channels, and enables me to enjoy goods and services in a variety and quantity which, if I depended solely on my own *direct* efforts, would be remoter than the rainbow's end.

This network of specialised, interlocking activity stretches literally to the ends of the earth, and related elements of it are often separated in time by years or decades. How could a copper miner in Rhodesia exchange his labour for the books which are printed, years later, by machines which perhaps his copper has helped to build, without a universal accounting system able to reduce the value of everything, everywhere, at all times, to a common scale? Money's purpose is to provide such a scale and such a system of accounting. It does not do so in perfection: no human arrangements or institutions can give perfect *foresight*, and unexpected changes of price can cause the reward for productive efforts to be less, or more, than the suppliers of them hoped for. But it is money which puts all producer-consumers the world over potentially in touch with each other.

Chapter 8. Firms

BETWEEN private people in their capacity as consumers and demanders of goods, and those same people in their capacity as owners and suppliers of factors of production, there intervenes the firm, which buys and brings together the factors and seeks to sell the resulting goods for more than the factors have cost it. In doing this it serves the general interest as well as its own, for provided there is sufficiently unimpeded competition and that every one has enough income to be comfortable according to his own standards, the firm's endeavour to produce a given quantity of a given good with such a set of quantities of the factors of production as fetches least in the open market results in our getting that product with the least possible sacrifice of other satisfactions. Factors of production, like other goods, are cheap when nobody badly wants them. But factors of production which nobody else badly wants are ones that are not much use for producing anything except what our own firm intends to make. In seeking to produce at lowest money cost and thus enlarging its own profit, the firm automatically seeks to produce at lowest real sacrifice of the kinds of other goods that the community most wants and is accordingly willing to pay most for. Moreover, our firm will be most successful in making its own profit, if the kind of good it produces is one which people very much want and are willing to pay well for. Thus in seeking to maximise its own profit, the firm is led naturally to produce something that is much wanted at the smallest possible sacrifice of other much wanted things.

The firm's essential function is to take decisions. It must decide what commodity to produce; what quantities of factors to use, according to what technique, in making this commodity; and how much of this commodity to put on the market in each unit of time. In this list of its problems we have said nothing of price. Does it not have to decide how much to charge for its product? Whether or not this question arises depends on how far the chosen

35

product is looked upon by all the potential buyers as something standardised which can be obtained indifferently from any one of a great number of rival suppliers. If this condition is perfectly fulfilled, if there is 'perfect competition', then the price which each firm charges for a unit (an ounce, a ton, a gallon, etc.) of its own product cannot be more, and need not be less, than that charged by the other firms. For no customer will pay a higher price than he knows is being charged elsewhere for a good which he regards as identical. Thus a uniform price must prevail amongst all the firms, and to each of them it will appear that this price, from which there appears to be no escape, is a *datum*, a fact imposed upon it by circumstances.

In Chapter 6 (*Production*) we established the rule which the firm must obey in order to produce at the lowest possible expense any stated output of any particular product. In order to apply that rule, the firm needs to know how many money units it would have to pay for one man-week of unskilled labour, one acre-week of land of a specified kind, one tractor-week or one truck-week of the services of a certain kind of machine, and so on. By a man-week or an acre-week we mean, of course, the packet of services which one man or one acre can furnish in a week. These prices of productive factors may be different when the quantity of the factor which the firm requires is different. To allow for all possibilities, we ought to recognise that in general the price of a week's or a year's use of each acre of land will depend on ('be a function of') the number of acres the firm wishes to use. On a small and crowded island, the firm would no doubt find itself facing an increasing reluctance on the part of owners of land, and of other potential users of land, to let it take over for its own purposes a larger and larger proportion of the available land, a reluctance which would find practical expression in a price per acre-week which rose as the number of acres demanded increased. This means that in order to answer the next question facing it, *how much* to produce, the firm would need to know what the price of each factor would be at each different possible level of the firm's demand for this factor. The firm would need to know, for example, what the weekly

wage of unskilled labourers would be if it decided to employ one
hundred of them, and if it decided to employ one hundred and
fifty of them, two hundred of them, and so on.

This is the most general frame of assumptions in which we can
study the firm's problems, the frame which allows for all possibilities. But, just as we can reasonably assume that in selling its
product in competition with a great many other firms all offering
what is, in the estimation of buyers, precisely the same commodity,
the firm will take the market price of its product as a datum, so we
can plausibly suppose that the firm will ignore any possible rise
in, for example, the wages of unskilled labourers which might
accompany an increase in the number of them which it employs.
We shall, that is to say, assume perfect competition in the firm's
factor market as well as in its *product market*.

By what test, on these assumptions, should the firm select its
output, the number of physical units of product which it shall turn
out per unit of time? To see what this test must be, we need to
consider the consequences to the firm of selecting smaller or larger
outputs.

The principle of equi-marginal productivity can only be fully
applied provided the firm is free to choose any combination of
factor-quantities whatever. But it will only have this freedom in
perfection when two conditions are satisfied. First, it must be
possible for the firm to alter by as little as it likes the quantity it
employs of each and every factor of production; and secondly, it
must be possible for the firm to make such adjustments of quantities without any delay. For suppose the first condition is not
satisfied, and that there is some factor which cannot be 'cut up
small' but must be taken in large lumps. Then in the first place it
will be difficult to say just what we mean by the marginal product
of this factor, though it may still be possible to tell whether the
firm should use one, two, three ... 'lumps' of this factor. But in
the second place, when the firm is using, say, one 'lump' of the
lumpy factor, the output which can then be produced at the lowest
cost per unit will very likely be determined at one particular level.
To produce a somewhat larger, or a somewhat smaller, output than

this may mean a higher cost per ton or gallon of the product. For the lowest cost per unit of the product can only be achieved by an ideal combination of quantities of the factors of production, and when the quantity of one of these factors is 'stuck', any other output than that to which one 'lump' of the lumpy factor best lends itself can only be achieved by distorting the proportions of the factor-quantities away from what is economically most efficient. Now there is no reason why the buyers, all taken together, should happen to be best suited by just that output which, given the prices of the non-lumpy factors, can be produced more cheaply than any other by one lump of the lumpy factor, and it follows that sometimes the community may have to put up with a less efficient combination of factors than the ideal, and pay more for the product.

We say that a factor of production which can be cut up into as small pieces as desired is perfectly 'divisible', and lumpiness of a factor is called 'an indivisibility'. Examples of lumpiness are easy to think of. If our dairy farmer is operating on a small scale, his herd of cows is a lumpy factor, since it can only be increased or diminished by one cow at a time. A fleet of ships is a lumpy factor, since ships for technical reasons are large, and to increase his tonnage a shipowner may have to order an extra 20,000 tons. An example which will make one effect of lumpiness clear is that of an hotel. Suppose the manager has a building with accommodation for one hundred guests. If he has one hundred guests, all is well, and he can adjust the numbers of his kitchen staff, his waiters and chambermaids so as to provide just the service needed. But suppose he has only fifty guests? He will still need a chef and a boiler-man, a receptionist and an accountant, and the wages of these will (so long as the hotel stays open) be on the same footing as the rent, rates and repair bill of the building itself. We can call all these 'overhead expenses'. They do not diminish as the number of guests diminishes, and this means that the weekly cost *per guest* increases as the number of guests falls below one hundred. A different effect of lumpiness is illustrated by the case of a shipbuilding berth. The speed of building each ship could no doubt be increased by employing more men on and around the ship under construction, but as their numbers grew so would the difficulty of finding useful tasks and room to work, and above a certain number, each extra man would effect a smaller and smaller reduction in the total construction time.

The effect of changing the proportions in which factors are combined is, of course, a *technical* phenomenon, and if the change is pushed far enough, the result can fairly be described as a disproportion between the factors. Beyond the point where, for example, the cows on a given acreage are so many that an extra cow makes no difference to the total output of milk, it is unmistakable that there are too many cows, in an absolute sense, combined with the given acreage. But we must beware of thinking that technical facts alone can always tell us that the quantities of factors are badly proportioned to each other. Over all that range where an extra unit of one factor, combined with fixed quantities of the other factors, makes *some* net addition to output, it is possible for any particular proportion to be right at *appropriate relative prices of the factors*.

Now what of our second condition for the full efficacy of the principle of equi-marginal productivity? This condition is, that adjustment of the quantities employed of the factors must be possible *without delay*. The point scarcely needs explaining. If the attainment of the lowest possible cost per unit of product requires an adjustment of factor-proportions, then so long as this adjustment has not taken place, the lowest unit cost will not have been attained. Now the lumpiness of some factors of production may not be inherent and essential in their technical nature, but may be only temporary, and such that *if time is allowed*, the quantity of the factor can be adjusted as finely as can be desired. This will not be true in every case. The traffic between two small islands may be insufficient to make full use of even the smallest ship which is big enough to be seaworthy. But in other cases a factor may be 'lumpy' only for so long as it takes to wear out a machine of unsuitable size and replace it with a somewhat bigger or smaller one. We said 'if time is allowed'. This is of course the crucial point. There will in all such cases be some length of time which is *too short* to allow of the complete adjustment to each other of the quantities employed of all the factors. Such a time is called 'the short period'. If, in the short period, one or more factors used by the firm are lumpy, then during this period there may be only one particular level of the firm's output which will allow unit cost to be the lowest possible. To increase its output beyond this, the firm will have to make larger and larger additions to the quantities employed of other factors in order to make successive *unit* increases of output.

All that *extra* expense, which is entailed by increasing a given total output by one unit, is called the *marginal cost* of that output. Now we are supposing our firm to be operating under perfect competition in its product market, and this means, as we have seen, that it can sell as much or as little of its own product in a week or a month as it likes without being either compelled or able to alter the price per unit. This means that the extra sale-proceeds or *revenue*, the extra money taken in per week or per month 'over the counter' in exchange for the firm's product, due to its selling one extra unit of output, will be simply the *price* of a unit of product. This extra revenue, due to one unit of extra output, we call the firm's *marginal revenue*. What happens to marginal cost, and what happens to marginal revenue, which, under perfect competition, is equal to price, as the firm passes in review a succession of possible short period outputs, each one bigger than the last by one unit of product? Marginal cost, as we have seen, will increase, at any rate when output exceeds a certain level. Price, by definition of perfect competition, will stay the same. (Let us remind ourselves that we are not considering a series of output-levels actually attained one after the other at a series of different historical dates, but a series of different *possible levels* amongst which the firm is free to choose, and will choose as a consequence of its present deliberations, undertaken with the actual present price in view as a datum.) It follows that at some particular output, marginal cost will be equal to price. To add yet one more unit to that output would carry marginal cost *above* price, and thus actually *reduce* somewhat the excess of total revenue over total cost. To allow output to fall short of this level would be to forgo some possible profit; for when marginal cost is below price, extra output will add more to total revenue than to total cost.

This, then, is the answer to our question, what test will select the firm's most profitable output? Profit, or *net revenue*, will be the greatest possible, for a firm operating in perfect competition with other sellers of the same commodity, when its output is such as to make the cost of the marginal unit equal to the market price of a unit.

In this chapter we have again seen the role of price as a warning system, telling would-be users of resources what level of sacrifice of other productive possibilities their particular proposed employment of these means of production would entail. The obstacles which price interposes against wasteful use of resources are not, in a free and competitive economy, the result of arbitrary dictation, but they are a putting into figures, a numerical expression, of the fact of scarcity, the fact of the 'parsimony of nature' and of the insistent competing demands of other people and other purposes.

In this chapter we have seen in detail how the price per unit which people all taken together are willing to pay for a commodity marks the limit beyond which the output of that commodity should not be pushed, because to do so would take away from people other things which they value more than the extra output of this commodity. We have seen, too, that provided this commodity is sold in a perfectly competitive market, there is an automatic mechanism by which the output of it will in fact tend to be pushed up to, but not beyond, the level where its marginal cost is equal to its price; and we have seen that this mechanism, which serves the *general* interest, is driven by the *private* interest of firms which seek to maximise their own net revenue. In reaching these conclusions we have built up a formal apparatus of ideas, those of total, marginal, and average cost, and total and average revenue (this last being the same thing as price per unit) which it may now be worthwhile to examine again briefly as a whole.

Production

There are usually certain expenses which a firm cannot avoid if it is to remain in business at all, but which are constant in total amount regardless of whether the output is large or small. These *overhead expenses* are rightly considered as part of the cost of whatever output, greater than zero, is chosen, for only a zero output would avoid them. But since their amount is fixed, the share of these overheads to be borne by each unit of output will be smaller the larger the output. So much for overhead costs. The *direct costs* or *prime costs* of output are those expenses whose total amount depends upon output and is 'an increasing function' of it. They include the costs of materials, power, labour and wear and tear of machines; everything directly involved in the process of manufacture. The result of adding together the overhead costs and the prime costs of any output is the total cost of that output. When we divide this total by the output (the *number* of physical units produced per time-unit) we get the *average unit cost*. This will be made up of two components, the unit overhead cost, which gets smaller as output gets larger, and the unit prime cost, which is likely over some range of outputs to be much the same for all these outputs, but, because of the short-period lumpiness of some factors, will begin to increase when output rises above some particular level. The combined effect of these two tendencies is that up to a certain level of output the average unit cost may decrease as output increases, but that beyond that level the average unit cost will increase as output increases. At that particular output where the change-over from decreasing to increasing unit cost occurs, the unit cost will be the lowest possible to this firm in the short period.

Moreover, just at that output where the change-over occurs, the unit cost will be neither decreasing nor increasing, it will be constant. What score does a batsman have to make in any completed innings, if his batting average is to remain unchanged? His new score must be *equal* to his previous average. If it is less, his average will go down, if it is greater, his average will go up. So his *marginal* score, as it were, must be equal to his *average* score if the latter is to remain constant. Just so, at any output where the firm's average cost is constant, marginal cost is bound, by mere arithmetic, to be equal to it. Thus when average cost is the lowest possible, marginal cost and average cost are equal.

We know that the firm will be maximising its net revenue if it produces that output at which marginal cost equals price. It will be possible for the firm to stay in business provided total cost is not greater than total revenue, for then the necessary expenses of continuing production are being covered by the incomings from the sale of what is produced. We get average unit cost by dividing total cost by output, and we get average unit revenue, which is the same thing as price, by dividing total revenue by output. So equality of total cost and total revenue means the same thing as equality of average cost and average revenue. When we put all these ideas together, we see that a position is quite possible where the following three things are true:

> Marginal cost equals average cost   (i)
> Average cost equals price   (ii)
> Marginal cost equals price   (iii)

The firm will then be making the biggest net revenue that it can; this is shown by (iii). This net revenue will in fact be zero, as is shown by (ii). But the firm can continue in business, and we can presume that it will, because amongst costs we include the necessary reward of *all* factors of production, including the work of the organiser and manager of the firm. It will then also be producing at the lowest possible cost per unit of output, as is shown by (i), and this is desirable in the general interest. In Chapter 10 we shall see the full significance of such a position of the firm.

Chapter 9. Activities

Prefatory Note

WE seek here to give the reader by purely verbal means some view of the nature and purpose of two modern economic methods. The claim of these methods to be highly regarded is their fusing of realism, measurement and theoretical depth; in a word, their exemplification of *econometrics* at its best. Input–output analysis is a main tool for understanding the problems and needs of developing countries and those, like Britain, with a need for modernisation. It has been applied by governments or powerful institutions in some dozens of countries. Linear programming has proved valuable on a smaller scale to individual firms and industries. Both are mathematical techniques which, in application, cannot possibly dispense with their proper formal notation. However, it seems feasible to make their essential nature understandable in words. If the reader finds these rather intricate matters distasteful, he is urged not to let them deter him from the rest of the book, but to omit this chapter or read it in the spirit of one who explores and savours rather than studies.

The thing produced and sold by one firm or industry can be a means of production bought and used by another. Each firm or industry is a centre upon which many streams of various goods converge, to be used in conjunction with each other in making a product which is then distributed by many divergent streams to other firms. The number of physical units of its product, which is annually demanded from a given firm, thus depends not only on how many units are bought from it each year by consumers directly, but also upon how many units are bought by them indirectly, in the form of other goods which this firm's product has helped, directly or via yet other products, to make. The picture of general production as a whole is thus a web of activities where, except on its fringes which sell to consumers' markets, every activity is linked closely or remotely with almost every other. The mines produce ore and coal which produce iron which enters, via steel, into countless engineering products, helping to make nearly every other thing, including machinery for mining ore and coal and for making machinery. Electricity enters into the fabricating, transporting and selling of everything conceivable, including itself. Examples can be multiplied without limit. But it is still true that if the public comes to spend relatively more on petrol and less on beer, various industries will gain or suffer in varying degree. How then are we to calculate the effect of a shift of consumers' desires from one kind of good to another, upon the demand experienced by a producer buried deep in the network of intersecting channels of supply? *Input-output analysis* is the means invented by Wassily Leontief in the 1930's for solving this type of problem for all industries together in one general and inclusive operation. At its full strength, the problem we have stated is too complex to be solved. Its typical datum is the number of value-units of product i used in making a given number of value-units of product j. If there are a thousand distinct products, there will be a million such ratios. But such a number would make calculation too expensive. Instead of considering pure, uniform products, each divisible into specimens alike in all respects, we gather products into classes, each defined by some broad similarities of nature, origin or use amongst the items. We suppose that in each firm, all that goes on contributes to the making of one such class of products only, and we gather all the firms which help to make one class of products into an *industry* or *sector*. The number of such industries or sectors has thus to be a compromise between two opposing aims. To ease calculation, we desire few sectors. But in order to find some meaning and consistency in the co-efficients which show how much, or what value, of sector i's product is needed by sector j, we desire a fine classification requiring many sectors. In the general theory of production, we suppose that the proportions in which various materials and services are combined in making a given product can be varied according to the prices and technical powers of these means of production, so as to produce the product at lowest unit cost. But this supposition of variable technical co-efficients would greatly complicate the input-output problem, where, therefore, we assume that, at given prices, the value of product of sector i (or, equivalently, the physical quantity) used per unit value (or unit quantity) of the product of sector j is fixed and unchanging for each particular pair (i, j) of sectors.

45

Production

Book-keeping records, gathered into a statistical table, can show us for each industry a row of entries, each stating the value (at given prices) of this industry's product annually used as a means of production by some one of the entire list of industries including itself. Let us call this industry i, and let us use j as a general label which can be tied on any one of the whole list of industries including industry i. If now we divide the entry showing the value of product i annually used in making product j, by the total value annually produced of product j, we get the value of i required *per unit value* of j. This answer will be a proper fraction (some number between zero and one) because the value of an ingredient must not exceed the value of the cake. We shall call each such answer an *input co-efficient*. Let us now write down a new row of entries, replacing each former entry j by its equivalent, namely the input co-efficient obtained from it, multiplied by the total annual output of product j. Each such entry will express, just like the former entry, the value of product i annually used in making product j. Now at the end of this new row of entries for industry i, let us write a final entry showing the annual value of product i demanded by final users (typically, consumers). The entire row of new entries thus completed will amount to, and account for, the whole value produced in a year of product i. This completed row of entries can be looked on as the right-hand side of an equation whose left-hand side is the total value produced in a year of product i. In this equation, the total value annually produced of product i is shown as depending on the *total* quantity annually produced of *each* product j, and upon the final demand for product i. But what we should like to know is how the total value annually produced of product i depends, not on the *total value annually produced* of each product j, but on the value which *final users annually demand* of each of these products. We should like (that is to say) to transform the equations of this first type (one for each industry i) into a new set where, instead of total annual quantities multiplied by input co-efficients, we should have letters of the alphabet, each standing for the final demand for some product *j*, and each multiplied by a new, appropriate co-efficient. Having this new set of equations, we could replace the letters of the alphabet in any one such equation *i* by actual numbers, namely, the annual values required for final use; multiply each such number by its co-efficient; and add together all the resulting terms. This would give us the total annual value of product *i* needing to be produced in order to satisfy the final demand for *i and the final demands for all the other products*, and this total annual requirement of *i* would be expressed as a number standing by itself on the left-hand side of the equation. Thus the whole set of new equations, written one below the other, would have on its left-hand side a column of total annual requirements of the various products, and on its right-hand side the expressions of the dependence of each of these totals on the set of final demands for all the products. By filling in these final demands as actual numbers instead of letters of the alphabet, we could calculate the column of *total* annual amounts needing to be produced.

The reader who is not on easy terms with algebraic modes of thinking will have done well to follow us so far. But now we can at least remove one or two puzzling features of our account, which arise from the conventions adopted by algebraists as a convenient notation or *language*. The reader will have noticed that we sometimes referred to 'the set of industries *j*' and also sometimes to 'the set of industries *i*'. But plainly, since we are in both cases speaking of the entire list of all the industries into which we have divided production as a whole, the two sets, *j* and *i*, must be one and the same set. And this is the case. What we achieve by having two different labels, each of which is deemed to point out any one industry at a time from the whole list of industries, is to indicate which of two opposed viewpoints we are using when speaking of the list. An industry labelled *i* is seen as *selling* parts of its output *to* other industries; one labelled *j* is seen as *buying* parts of their outputs *from* other industries. This conception can be made vivid and helpful by the admirable device of the square *array* or square *matrix*. We list our industries in one and the same sequence, first in a column, where they stand as the names of a ladder of *rows* of entries, and secondly, in a row, where they stand as the names of a series of *columns* of the very same entries, each of which thus finds itself in both a row and a column of the pattern. The square array, or matrix, of entries is thus like the square elevation of a house, whose windows can be thought of as arranged both in horizontal rows and in vertical columns, so that any particular window can be given an identity by calling it the ith window from the top and the jth window from the left. The beauty of this arrangement is that every entry (every 'window') declares instantly by its position in the array which two industries it is concerned with. And more than this: there can be no risk of writing down, for example, different numbers for the value of goods sold in a given year by industry i to industry j, and the value bought by industry j from industry i, for a single entry serves both purposes. Nor can there be any danger that our accounts will show a different total of goods bought as means of production, and goods sold as means of production: for again, both these calculations will use the very same set of entries. Internal consistency, one of the prime purposes and requirements of any system of account-keeping, is very efficiently and powerfully served by this scheme. However, its main value and meaning lies in its convenience for algebraic manipulation.

As we have seen, the central and essential operation of input-output analysis is the transformation of a set of facts given in one form into a set given in another form, without these facts themselves, in their essence, being changed at all. (Mathematical manipulation cannot *add* to the underlying information fed into it, but only reveal and interpret that information.) We obtain directly from our statistics the quantity (i.e. value at given prices) of good i needed per unit of good j. These co-efficients, each shown as multiplied by its corresponding total quantity produced of j, constitute a set of equations where the total output of each good i is distributed amongst its various destinations: some to each of the various industries, some to final users. But these are not the equations which we ultimately want, for they express the total output of i as depending on the *total outputs* of all the j's, whereas we need to have the total output of i expressed as a requirement depending on the quantities of the j's *demanded for final use*. Therefore, the original set of equations must be solved to obtain the second set. To solve an equation is nothing more nor less than to perform upon it some re-arrangement of what it tells us. An equation which tells us that a times x is equal to b, can be solved to tell us that x is equal to b divided by a. Matrix algebra enables us to express very concisely the series of operations by which our initial set of equations can be transformed into our desired set. The actual solving of the first set of equations to get the second (the finding of an 'inverse matrix', corresponding to the finding of the reciprocal of a in our equation $ax = b$ to get $x = b/a$) is not itself made any simpler by matrix expression. When the number of industries is several hundred, solution even by computer is costly, and by any other means, impossible. The advantage of matrix notation is to express the whole problem, and the operations (manipulations) needed for its solution, in a highly compact, synoptical and self-evidently coherent form.

In purpose and essential principle, the Leontief scheme is simple. It is the immense diversity and multiplicity of detail presented by its field of operation that renders the application of the scheme intricate and difficult. In order to cope with this intricacy, the scheme deliberately and drastically simplifies its problem and approach. Thus it assumes that for each product there is one, and only one, industry or *sector*, and that for each sector there is one, and only one, product. This is remote indeed from reality. Each sector uses inputs of primary or produced means of production (that is, of natural and human forces and of products used as materials or tools for further production) in fixed proportions. Since, therefore, each product comes from only one sector and each sector uses only one 'recipe' or set of input-proportions, there is no freedom to choose a different productive method in order to take advantage, for example, of a change of relative input prices. We can, of course, build a number of Leontief models, each using a different set of technologies. But the Leontief analysis itself is concerned with discovering the properties of some one such model, after it has been selected, designed or derived from an examination of real statistics. The input-output scheme in itself does not concern itself with choice of method of production. Nor does it concern itself with the basis of choice of the 'bill of goods for final use', that is, the list of respective annual quantities of products to be made available to consumers or others, such as the government, who will use them to satisfy ultimate human wants. And in especial, this choice of the bill of goods for final use is not linked, within the input-output analysis itself, with the outcome of that analysis. We can of course say to ourselves: Let us see what would be involved by choosing this or that bill of goods, and then we will decide which one to choose. But the aim of such a procedure can be attained more directly, within a more general frame of thought referred to below. Finally, we do not, within the input-output scheme, concern ourselves about the adequacy of supplies of primary factors, labour and land, or of supplies of the services of durable equipment, which equipment, for the 'short period' purpose envisaged by the scheme, we assimilate to land. The input-output scheme is really concerned with relative, rather than absolute, outputs of goods, and its practicable overall scale is a matter for separate investigation.

Now choice is in a sense the heart of economics: choice limited by scarcity and therefore guided by relative prices. The typical economic problem is how to make as large as possible (how to maximise) some performance or result which depends on things whose supply is scarce; or how to make as small as possible the sacrifice involved in achieving some given end. When the basic notion of inter-meaningful, inter-determined and mutually supporting activities is liberated from the special simplifying assumptions and concrete meanings which the input-output scheme itself adopts, and embodied in a scheme of reasoning and calculation where maximising or minimising, in a word 'economising', is the central and ultimate goal, we have *activity analysis*, of which the best known and most practical form is *linear programming*. Activity analysis is a very general and abstract scheme which can be filled with any of an unlimited range of different subject-matter. A *commodity* is anything which, if it were scarce, the economist would call a good, no matter whether it consists of wares[1] or services. When such commodities in a fixed list of quantities per time-unit are transformed or exchanged in any manner into a fixed list of quantities of other such commodities, we have an *activity*. Since the inputs and outputs of an activity are fixed in relative amount, any one of them can measure the *activity level*. Activities and their levels are to be so chosen that some desired result, expressed as a mathematical function of these levels, that is, as quantitatively bound up with and depending on them, is attained to the greatest degree compatible with given quantities available per time-unit of the *primary inputs*, that is, commodities not produced within the system of activities. When the dependence of the *criterion* or *objective function*, that is, the measure of the desired result, on the activity levels is such that a given increment in some activity always yields one constant increment in the criterion, we have *linear programming*. Under our rule of eschewing algebra and diagrams, this outline is as far as we can go in explaining its nature.

Chapter 10. Markets

W E defined perfect competition as a state of affairs where a large number of firms are selling to a large number of buyers a commodity every specimen of which is exactly the same in all respects as every other, in the eyes of every one of the buyers, no matter

[1] It was, I believe, Professor E. H. Phelps Brown who adopted this very useful word to mean tangible goods as distinct from valued performances.

which firm supplies it; and where all prices asked, offered or accepted are at once known to all sellers and all buyers. This was a sufficient definition for our purpose, which was to discover how a firm in perfect competition can detect or 'determine' the output which maximises its net revenue. But in this chapter we have something to add to this definition.

We say, in the economist's conventional language, that the firm in perfect competition is 'in equilibrium' when it is producing an output at which marginal cost equals price; for there is then nothing that the firm can do, so long as technical knowledge and the prices of factors and of the product remain unchanged, to improve its position and make its net revenue greater. The firm, having no incentive to do otherwise, will continue to produce the same output, and in this sense will remain at rest.

What will happen if the price of the product rises? The firm will no longer be in equilibrium at its old output, for at an unchanged output the marginal cost will also be unchanged and the new, higher price will therefore be above it. To reach a new equilibrium the firm must increase its marginal cost; not, of course, for the sake of incurring extra costs, but because the new, higher price *makes room* for extra units of output which will now add more to total revenue than they do to total cost. So the firm, to take advantage of the new higher price, must increase its output and so push the marginal cost of output up to equality with the new price. So we reach a part of the explanation of a very important idea, namely that a rise of price of a product elicits an increase of supply, an increase of the number of physical units of this good produced in each unit of time. But there is a further important part of the explanation. At a higher price, as we have seen, each firm will produce a larger output. The total cost of the old output has not increased, but the sale-proceeds of the old output, the revenue due to it, have increased, because of the higher price which each unit of that output now fetches. Moreover there are now the extra units of output, each (except the very marginal one of all) bringing in a rather greater addition to revenue than its own addition to total cost. Thus for two reasons when we subtract the firm's total costs of producing its output from its total revenue from selling that output, the excess or *net revenue* will be greater in the firm's new position, when it has adjusted its output to the new price, than it was in the old position. Even if in the old position the firm was only just covering its costs, in the new position it will therefore be making a net revenue greater than zero, a positive profit. Businessmen who are not yet producers of this good will see the opportunity to make similar profits for themselves by setting up new firms in this industry. When these new firms start production, their output will make an addition to the industry's output, and in this way also the higher price will have encouraged a growth of the aggregate supply of the good in question.

We come now to one of those seeming paradoxes that arise, not from the reality of the economic world, but rather from that method of analysing it which was made explicit for economists by Alfred Marshall, the founder of the 'Cambridge school' whose ways of thought have become part of the fabric of our subject. Marshall, differing in this from his contemporaries on the Continent, declared that economic reality is too complex for its whole mechanism of interacting pressures and impulses to be comprehended in a single picture. We have to examine 'a bit at a time', by treating the rest of the economic world either as not affected by what goes on in this bit, or at any rate as not offering a sufficiently good 'reflector' for the effects to be thrown back so as to disturb the adjustment that the forces arising inside the isolated portion that we are examining would achieve among themselves. But, of course, we cannot be content merely with examining one bit at a time. As Marshall himself insisted, the task of assembly must be faced in the end. One aspect of it is that what could occur in one bit of the economic system without much affecting other bits may occur in very many bits simultaneously through some influence common to all the bits. In such a case the combined effect of all these occurrences may pervade the whole economic system and change its state very markedly.

Now, we have seen that in perfect competition any one firm can alter its own output to any extent that is likely to be within its power, without affecting the market price of the good. This is far from saying that if all the firms in the industry alter their outputs together, there will be no effect on the price. A ten per cent increase of output, by a firm which supplies only one-thousandth of the whole output of the industry, will make a difference of only one ten-thousandth to the industry's total output. But a ten per cent increase of output by *every* firm in the industry will mean a ten per cent increase of the quantity which buyers, all taken together, are invited to buy in one unit of time, and we have seen that they will not ordinarily respond unless tempted by a reduction of price.

It follows that as new firms are added to the industry in the hope that they will earn profits similar to those which existing firms are making, the resulting growth of the industry's output will gradually bring down the price of the product and so reduce the profit of each firm. Where will this process stop? It is here that we need to extend the meaning of perfect competition. We include in it also the idea that factors of production of all sorts are, as it were, frictionless in their movement from one industry to another, so that as long as the smallest difference of profitability between two industries remains, offering a gain to anyone who moves factors from one to the other, this movement will take place. With this perfect freedom of movement, the process of setting up new firms in the exceptionally profitable industry will only cease when those exceptional profits have been eliminated by the price fall which the process of growth of the industry itself brings about. Indeed, provided we include amongst the firm's costs a reward for the organiser and manager of the firm just sufficient to induce him to stay in this industry, we can say that the industry will grow until the net revenue of each firm is zero. In that state of affairs, each firm, having access to the best technical knowledge and having had time enough to adapt its own equipment of buildings and machines to the right size, will be producing the same output at the same total cost and the same total revenue as every other firm. Not only each firm, but the whole industry, will then be in long-period equilibrium, the complete and perfect adjustment which, in the frictionless economic system we are assuming, will eventually come about, provided the non-economic governing conditions of tastes, technique, population and resources remain unchanged for long enough.

Before going on to make our model more realistic by considering conditions other than perfect, frictionless competition, let us bring together into one formula the two conditions we have found to be necessary for equilibrium of the industry. In order that there may be no tendency for the industry to grow or decline in number of firms, each firm must be operating with no profit over and above what is just sufficient to induce the organiser and manager of this firm to remain in the industry rather than set up a firm in another industry; that is, net revenue of each firm must be zero. Now net revenue is the difference obtained by subtracting total costs from total revenue, and so zero net revenue means equality between total costs and total revenue. If, now, we divide total revenue by output, we get *average unit revenue*, the number of money units which each unit of output fetches when sold on the market. Another name for this is of course *price* per unit. Further, if we divide total costs by output we get *average unit cost*. If, then, total revenue and total cost are equal in each firm, that is the same as saying that average unit cost is equal to price. But we have already seen that for equilibrium of the firm (as distinct from that of the industry) *marginal* cost must be equal to price. It follows that for complete equilibrium of the industry as a whole and every firm in it, we must have marginal cost equal to average cost and equal to price.

This conclusion is exceedingly important, for it means that when the industry producing any good has achieved perfectly competitive equilibrium, the total revenue being received by that industry from the sale of its product is just and only just sufficient to pay for the factors of production needed to produce its existing output of that product. The people of the economic system are then getting the existing output of the product for the least possible price: economic efficiency in this industry has been brought to its highest pitch.

In the real world, we do not find perfect frictionless competition. Factors of production are not induced to move out of one industry into another by the smallest difference in the profitability of these industries. People like to stay at the same kind of job, and even more, they like to go on living in the same place. When we come to machines designed for a particular purpose, the only way to move to a different industry the resources they represent is to let these machines wear themselves out in the industry for which they were designed, and carefully reserve enough of their earnings to replace them with a quite different sort of machine suitable for the other industry. We can see in this example what is meant by 'the long period'.

But the central idea of perfect competition is that, because there are many firms whose products the buyers regard as in every respect identical, no one firm by altering its own output can affect the price of this homogeneous product. Any firm in a perfectly competitive industry which sought to charge more than its competitors would immediately lose all its buyers, while to offer the good at a lower price than the other firms would merely cause it an unnecessary loss of revenue, since it can dispose of all the output it wants to without any such undercutting. It is with this aspect of perfect competition that the real world so often shows a striking and important contrast.

Over all that part of industry and commerce where one firm's product can be distinguished from another's, because of small or large difference of design, quality, packaging, manner of selling, location of business, use of a trade mark and so on, we can no longer say that the products of two firms are homogeneous. They are, indeed, no longer the same product. Two different makes of motor-car are two different products, so are two brands of cigarettes, even superficially identical packets of sugar from two different grocers whose shops are in different places or whose assistants have different personalities. Some of these differences may seem to the buyers concerned very important and some only trifling, but every one of them means that, strictly speaking, the situation over much of the economic system is *one* firm to each product, the very opposite of the perfectly competitive situation of many firms to each product. Now if one firm makes the whole of the output of one product, it can no longer expect to sell as much or as little as it likes of this product without affecting the price. Because there are no *perfect* substitutes for the product of firm *A*, it will not lose all its customers if it somewhat raises its price. The products of other firms may be closely similar, and many of those who have been buying from firm *A* will decide that the difference between *A*'s product and *B*'s is not enough to make up for the higher price per physical unit of *A*'s product. But some customers will remain faithful to *A*. Correspondingly if firm *A* lowers its price, it will not thereby capture all the customers of firms *B*, *C*, *D*, ... for firm *A* is not offering precisely the same good as firm *B*, or as firm *C*, or any other firm.

Firms which offer products as much alike as two makes of motor-scooter or of television receiver or two kinds of chocolates or of whisky are evidently not selling in isolation, but, on the contrary, they are strongly competing with one another. Yet in a sense each is the sole seller of his own distinctive product. A firm which is the sole seller of some commodity is called a monopolist. Thus to the firms which sell distinguishable but highly substitutable products in competition with one another we give the name of *monopolistic competitors*, or we say that such firms are selling under *imperfect competition*. What distinguishes a firm in imperfect competition from one in perfect competition? It is that the former has to lower his price in order to sell a larger output, and can raise his price on condition of selling a smaller output, while the latter has no control over price and can simply choose his output. The perfectly competitive firm's saleable output is independent of price, but the monopolistic competitor's saleable output is a *function* of the price he charges. How can we pin down more precisely the character of this linkage of price and output?

Some price changes will make a big difference to the quantity per week of the product that can be sold, some only a small difference. 'Ah, yes', you may say, 'naturally a small price change will have less effect than a large price change'. But what is a small price change? Is 5p per unit a small price change? When applied to a pair of shoes, yes, but when it refers to a box of matches, it constitutes a trebling of price. Here we have the clue. A trebling or doubling of price, or even a fifty per cent increase, is in an obvious sense 'large'. But to add 5p to a price which starts at £5 is to add one per cent, a trifling change. So what we are concerned with is not the absolute amount of change in the price of an arbitrary physical unit of some good (suppose coal were sold by the ounce, would an extra penny be a small change of price?) but the *proportionate* or *percentage* change in the price of no matter what unit. And in just the same way, the effect on the weekly quantity sold must be measured as a proportion or a percentage. So we arrive at an idea which plays an important part throughout economic theory, the idea of *elasticity*.

The elasticity of demand for a particular good is a measure of the sensitiveness of response of the weekly (monthly, yearly, etc.) quantity sold of this good to changes of its price. If a five per cent reduction of price is followed by a twenty-five per cent increase of the weekly quantity sold, we say that the elasticity of demand is five. If reduction of price by five per cent only increases the weekly quantity sold by one per cent, we say that the elasticity of demand is one-fifth. The idea is simple in itself, and the possibility of expressing it in a complicated-looking formula does not destroy this fact.

Now let us see the bearing of this on the distinction between perfect and imperfect competition, and on the monopolistic competitor's problem of policy, which can be expressed either as 'How much shall I make and sell?' or 'How much shall I charge per unit?' but does not give him freedom to ask both questions at once. What is the elasticity of demand for the product of a firm selling in perfect competition? The smallest lowering of its price will bring, in effect, an indefinitely great increase of demand: the elasticity is *infinite*. The monopolistic competitor, by contrast, will find that the response to a one per cent lowering of price is only a *finite* increase in the weekly quantity sold: some particular, nameable number of percentage points by which this quantity goes up.

Will it pay him to make this change of price with its determinate accompanying change in quantity sold?

Let us suppose at first that the firm is already committed to a fixed weekly expenditure on factors of production, and that without any additional expense at all it can produce an output larger than there is likely to be any demand for, even at a zero price. By this assumption we reduce marginal cost to zero for all relevant outputs. What test can the firm apply to any proposal for a price reduction? Suppose that a one per cent reduction from its existing price would elicit a one per cent increase in the weekly number of units bought. Then sale-proceeds at the old price can be represented by one hundred multiplied by one hundred, while at the new price sale-proceeds will be represented by one hundred and one (the larger quantity) multiplied by ninety-nine (the lower price). The first answer comes to 10,000, the second to 9999. But this apparent difference, small as it is, would be much smaller still if we spoke of a reduction of price and increase of quantity sold by one-thousandth, and yet smaller if we considered a reduction of price by one ten-thousandth leading to an increase of quantity sold by one ten-thousandth (where the difference between the two answers is only one in a hundred million), and so on. We can see, therefore, that the difference between the two answers is not of the essence of the matter; it arises from our having to speak in terms of finite reductions and increases. The essence of the matter is that if a reduction of price by some given small proportion increases demand by that same small proportion, virtually no net difference is made to sale-proceeds. This, then, is a very special and critical level of elasticity, it is a sort of watershed between those elasticities which imply that a small price-reduction will increase sale-proceeds and those which imply that a small price-reduction will reduce sale-proceeds. We say that the former elasticities are 'greater than one' or 'greater than unity', the latter are 'less than one' or 'less than unity'. That elasticity in which the proportions are *equal*, so that quantity sold is increased in the same proportion as price is reduced, is called *unit elasticity*.

For elasticity is just a ratio, and we can write it like a vulgar fraction with a numerator (the percentage change of quantity) and a denominator (the percentage change of price). When we divide the 'upstairs' part of the fraction (its numerator) by the 'downstairs' part (its denominator), and find that the latter goes exactly once into the former, it is natural to give this vulgar fraction the value *one*, and say that the elasticity it represents is *one* or *unity*.

Now for our firm's problem, whether or not it will pay it to lower its price. If the elasticity of demand is greater than one, a lowering of price by a given small percentage will increase demand by a larger percentage, and so will increase sale-proceeds or revenue. Since we have assumed that marginal cost is zero, this increase of revenue will mean an increase also of *net* revenue or profit. If elasticity is less than one, the decrease of price will bring a decrease of revenue and of net revenue.

In this chapter we have extended the equilibrium analysis from the single firm to the industry, and in the next chapter we shall extend it to the economic system as a whole. The notion of *equilibrium* is that of a state of affairs arrived at when a great number of individuals each seeking his own interest give away to each other what they can best spare in exchange for what they most desire. It arises from bargains freely struck between, as the lawyers say, willing buyers and willing sellers, and is for each person the *best* situation he can attain by this free bargaining and exchange, consonant with the right and freedom of every other person to pursue his own interest by the same method.

In this chapter we have seen the paradox of profit: that where there is perfect factor mobility, and perfect 'freedom of entry' of new firms into an industry, which perfect competition assumes, the pursuit by each actual or potential firm of maximum profit will lead to a universal levelling-down of profit to that point where only the necessary minimum reward is being earned by the enterprising organisers of production, to induce them to continue in the industry.

But we have also seen that the conditions of perfect competition are rarely fulfilled in the actual world. Not only are factors never perfectly mobile, but only in the case of raw materials or primary products is it at all common for buyers to be quite indifferent which of many sources of supply they get the commodity from. If they prefer one firm to another, the products of the two firms, however technically similar, cannot strictly be regarded as the same commodity. A firm whose product is unique is a *monopolist* of that product, and a given percentage change in the firm's output is fully and precisely reflected in the output of the commodity, strictly defined. In consequence a larger output will only be saleable at a lower price, and a smaller output will make it possible to charge a higher price: or as we can say, for the monopolist or the monopolistic competitor, output is a decreasing function of price, and price is a decreasing function of output.

This idea, that the quantity sold per unit of time responds to changes in price per unit, can be rendered quantitative by means of the idea of *elasticity of demand*, namely, percentage change in weekly number of physical units sold, divided by the percentage change in price per unit which called forth this change in quantity sold. Elasticity of demand is said to be *unity* if the two percentages are equal, for then the answer to the division sum is *one*. When the elasticity of demand is unity, a small change of price, together with the consequential change in weekly quantity sold, makes no difference to total revenue. When elasticity of demand for the firm's output is infinite, the firm is selling its product in a perfectly competitive market.

Chapter 11. *Equilibrium*

THERE is a logic of how to make the best of things, of how to attain the position of greatest comfort and contentment in spite of our human circumstances of scarcity, of not having as much of things as we could use. Economics is the subject which studies this

logic. Each of us strives to attain such a 'best' position for himself
or his family or some larger unit with which he identifies himself.
For *given* conduct on the part of each other person, there is some
principle of conduct for me which will make my position as good
as it can be made; the same holds for each person in the economy.
When every person simultaneously tries to make his own position
(or that of his family or other unit) as good as possible, there is a
total adjustment in which the 'best position subject to the constraints of circumstance' is realised by everyone at once: in which
for every person at once it is true that for him, given the conduct
of *A*, of *B*, of *C*, ... right through the list of people in the economy,
his own position could not be bettered. This total adjustment,
which plainly has some right to be called the optimum position of
the economy as a whole, is called *general equilibrium*. Such a position is interesting for two reasons: first, because of its being in
some sense a *general* best position, and secondly, because the drive
of human nature for greater comfort and scope of activity gives
some reason to believe that this position is always tending to be
approached. Some might say there is a third reason: that when
once attained, such a position will be one of rest where the economy
can permanently remain, so long as the framework of governing
conditions within which economic forces work, the tastes, technical
knowledge, resources, political institutions and laws of the people,
remain unchanged. However, the very life of a modern economy
is borne on a stream of ceaseless change: the restless rivalry,
curiosity and desire to do new things for the sake of their novelty
seems to be as essential to prosperity as forward movement is to
maintain an aircraft in flight. If growth of knowledge, population
and productive facilities were to cease, it may be that a stagnant
economy would be unable to furnish anything like the same standards of material comfort, except by some radical change of our
economic institutions. The reasons for supposing that this may be
so will be examined in Book v (*Employment*). In this light, the
proposition that if the governing conditions remained fixed, we
might attain and retain a particular position of general optimum
or equilibrium, seems to me of little interest. It is the tendency

for such a position to be approached, and in consequence to be always partially and approximately realised, while the governing conditions change slowly or rapidly and continually shift the target, that is interesting and important. Nevertheless it is useful and illuminating to make a complete picture and to list all the conditions whose simultaneous fulfilment would constitute a state of general equilibrium.

Amongst the governing conditions, upon whose constancy the maintenance of a *given* equilibrium position depends, we have listed 'resources'. By this we mean not only that the total quantity of each kind of resource, available to the economic system as a whole, must remain constant, but that the quantity at the disposal of each individual person must be unchanging. For otherwise, the growth or decline of the leverage with which people of differing tastes could bring their desires to bear upon the settling of outputs and prices would change the equilibrium and destroy the state of rest. Now one kind of resource is the tools and other productive facilities that a man owns, and these he can build up by spending less than the whole of his income on consumption. Thus equilibrium requires us to suppose that each person spends the whole of his income, neither more nor less, on goods and services for immediate consumption.

In the simplified model of the economy which we are building up, there are in effect three kinds of economic agents, or more exactly, there are three economic roles, of which every flesh-and-blood person who takes a full part in the economic process fulfils at least two. Everyone is a consumer, most of us are also suppliers of productive services, a few of us are organisers of production and managers of firms. The conditions whose simultaneous fulfilment would constitute general equilibrium can be considered in three groups corresponding to these three types of agent.

In his capacity as a consumer, or demander of goods for present consumption, each person will be in equilibrium (that is, in a position which, with *given* conduct on the part of other people, he cannot improve on) when an extra sixpence a month would bring him the same amount of extra comfort no matter which good it was spent on: that is, when marginal utility divided by price, or 'weighted' marginal utility, is the same for every good. This principle will ensure his getting the most comfort out of any given income. But what settles the size of this income?

We are supposing that as a consumer he buys in a perfect market where prices are independent of the weekly quantity that any individual demands. Equally reasonably we can assume that in his other capacity, as an owner of productive factors, he again has a perfect market in which to sell the services of these factors, so that their prices are independent of the weekly quantity that any one owner offers. For simplicity let us suppose that he supplies only one kind of service, for example his own labour. Then his income will depend on the weekly number of hours he works multiplied by the market price per hour of labour of that kind. To work means to forgo ease and leisure, the opportunity for pleasurable activities and the freshness of mind and muscle to enjoy them, and the longer the weekly hours of work the more irksome will an extra weekly hour become. The work itself in moderation may be pleasurable, but even then there will be a point beyond which increasing fatigue makes it distressing. Thus there will be some number of weekly hours such that one extra hour beyond that number would cost more in ease forgone and effort made than would be compensated by the extra goods that the earnings of that hour could purchase. To work fewer hours than this would be to sacrifice more income than the extra leisure was worth; to work more hours than this would be to sacrifice more leisure than the extra income was worth. This point, at which the marginal utility of leisure and of income are equal, or as we might more accurately say, where the marginal utility of time is the same no matter whether we use the borderline half-hour for work or play, will give him greater all-round satisfaction than any other way of dividing up the 168 hours of his week: it gives his equilibrium number of weekly hours of work.

Now for the firms and the industries in which they are grouped. In long-period equilibrium these firms and industries will be producing consumers' goods of all sorts in such outputs, and by such combinations of quantities of factors, that any increase of one output and corresponding decrease of another would entail the substitution of a less-wanted for a more-wanted stream of goods, as judged by the price that will be paid on the market for streams each equally expensive to produce. Within each firm, factors of production will be combined in such proportions that, given their prices and their interacting and interdependent technical powers, so far as these are known in the given state of technology, the average unit cost of the product is the lowest possible. If, through the presence of some inherently indivisible factor of production, an output somewhat smaller and also one somewhat larger than the actual output would each entail a rather higher average unit cost of the product, then the marginal cost of the actual output will be equal to the average unit cost of this output. This average unit cost, which includes just sufficient reward for the organiser and manager of the firm to induce him to remain in his present industry, will be just, but only just, covered by the unit price which the product of this industry fetches on the market. That is to say, there will be no profit over and above the minimum incomings necessary to pay for the cheapest set of factors of production which can produce the actual output of the firm.

Because, in this perfectly competitive equilibrium of the firm, marginal cost equals price, there will be no incentive for the firm to change its output. And because in this equilibrium of the industry average cost equals price, there will be no temptation for any new firm to be set up in the industry nor for any old firm to leave it. Thus there will be no tendency for the output of all the firms in the industry taken together, that is, for the whole quantity of the product in question produced per unit of time, to change.

Since, under those conditions of perfect mobility of factors between all firms and industries, which are part of the assumptions of perfect competition, no factor will sell its services to one firm for a lower price than is being paid for identical services by another firm, it follows that each factor of production will be receiving the same price per unit of its services in all the different firms and industries which employ it. Since, moreover, each firm, in order to maximise its net revenue, will employ such a quantity of each factor that the marginal product of that factor is worth just enough to cover the cost of employing the marginal unit of that factor, it follows that in the general equilibrium the value of the marginal product of any factor will be the same in every firm of every industry, and there will be no possibility of getting a more valuable product by transferring some units of this factor to a different industry.

Such is *general equilibrium*, a pattern of use of all resources such that, in a free economy, any shift away from this pattern could and would be successfully resisted by some or all people, who in case of such a shift would find their own productive powers and resources providing them with less comfort than before.

The aspect of general equilibrium into which it is hardest to gain imaginative insight, and which is hardest to convey in words, is the idea of completely general mutual interdependence of all the economic quantities, an interdependence which implies that if any one of these quantities were altered from the size which it has in the general equilibrium, every other quantity in the pattern would also be disturbed more or less. Any attempt to explain this *simultaneous* mutual dependence in a series of verbal sentences makes the argument sound circular and endless: *A* depends on *B* and *B* on *C* and *C* on *A*, we seem to be saying; where do we ever reach a resting-point in such an account of things? It is for this reason that economists resort in this matter to the mathematical conception of a system of simultaneous equations. The idea is familiar to many of us, for we come across it in school algebra books. Such problems as the following involve and illustrate the idea. We are told that a man is four times as old as his son, and that his son is thirty years younger than himself. What are the ages of the two people? Here it appears at first sight that if we knew the son's age we could reckon the father's, and if we knew the father's age we could reckon the son's, but that since we are given neither of their ages, we are at a stand. Each of the 'unknowns' depends on the other, and the same sort of circularity seems to be present as we thought ourselves faced with in the account of general equilibrium.

However, if we adopt some symbol, x, for the son's age, and another symbol, y, for the father's age, we can say that y is four times x, and from this it follows that if we subtract x from y, the difference will be three times x. Now we know that this difference is thirty years, and so we can conclude that x is ten years. From this we can tell that y is forty years. The problem is solvable, and in the vastly more complicated case that we should meet with if we tried to represent a general equilibrium of an entire economic system as a system of simultaneous equations, similar problems also turn out to be in principle solvable. We therefore say that such general equilibria are 'determinate', meaning that for every one of the inputs, outputs, prices and incomes involved, there is one, or at most a finite (definite, not boundless) number, of possible sizes compatible with the sizes of the other quantities.

In reflecting on this idea of a general equilibrium, we ought to remind ourselves that to prove the 'existence' (the logical possibility or non-self-contradictoriness) of a set of 'sizes' or levels of all the economic quantities, which would be self-consistent and have no inherent tendency to change, is not at all the same thing as to show how such a state of affairs could ever, in practice, be attained.

BOOK III. INCOME

Chapter 12. Income

IMAGINE a map in which each dot represents, not a town, but a firm, and each line joining two firms represents, instead of a road or railway, an imaginary channel along which flows some one particular kind of good or service, supplied by one firm to the other to help the latter to carry on some productive operation. Besides the dots representing firms we will have others standing for private people in their double capacity of consumers and of suppliers of productive services. Each of these person-dots will be converged upon by a host of lines from all sorts of firms which supply his diverse consumption needs, and from it at least one line will lead back to a firm which employs him. Such a map can be looked upon equally well as showing the paths, not of 'real' goods and services useful in themselves and wanted for their own sakes, but of the money which is exchanged for them. These money streams will, of course, flow in the opposite direction from that of the real goods and services which they are paying for. For example, the work performed for a firm by a private person will be thought of as going from him to the firm, while the wages he gets in exchange will flow from the firm to him. The goods supplied for his consumption will flow from shops to him, while the money he pays for them will flow from him to the shops; and so on.

Such a map would be immensely more complicated than an ordinary geographical map, and one might feel that an impression of the complexity of the economic system is almost all that it would really convey to us. But it can be vastly and illuminatingly simplified.

The means of simplifying will consist in classifying and grouping the streams flowing between individual persons and firms, and summarising each group in some sort of total. Now it is plain that we cannot add together half a pint of milk, a loaf of bread, a news-paper and a pair of shoes to get any economically meaningful total. We can only combine a variety of different objects into a sensible total by finding some common measure for all of them. Their total weight or volume would tell us little. The measure of their *economic* significance is their market values, their *prices*, and these are avail-able in our imaginary map ready made: they are to be found simply by looking, not at the 'real' stream flowing, in each particular case, in one direction but at the money stream flowing in the opposite direction. Once we have grouped the money streams according to any particular scheme of classification, we can at once add up the total of each group. So we come to the problem of what scheme of classification will make most sense and throw most light on how the economic process works.

One scheme that suggests itself is to separate the private indi-viduals from the firms and treat the individuals as a group, and further, to look at this group twice, first in the people's capacity as demanders of goods and secondly in their capacity as suppliers of productive services. It is when we take this second view that we get a group of many streams all running *towards* the individuals, as the counterparts of the streams of productive services that are flowing away from them. These money streams going into their pockets and their bank accounts together make up, of course, their aggregate income.

In subsequent chapters we shall subdivide this group of *all incomes* into classes of incomes according to the kind of productive service for which they are paid, so finding a place in our analytical scheme for such traditional words as wages, rent and profits. But first we need a definition covering incomes of all sorts. One definition which admirably combines in brief compass the everyday meaning of the word with what the economist has in mind, is that 'Income is what you can part with and not thereby be made worse off than before'. This form of words raises a number of questions and sug-gestions. First, it intimately connects with income the idea of out-lay of money. And after all, something must happen to every penny of income that comes in: it must all be disposed of or accounted for in some way. So if we can find another class, or a few classes, of transactions (money payments) which together carry off the whole of income and dispose of it, we shall have found an alternative method of measuring the total of incomes. *Outlay*, defined as the equal counterpart of income, will be the subject of our next chapter. But meanwhile we have to consider what is to be meant by 'not being made worse off'.

One of our 'categories' of means of production (we used 'category' to mean a class of things having some one or more common characteristics but not being homogeneous in *all* respects which bear on their productive usefulness and powers) is well enough named by the old-fashioned word 'capital'. This comprises things serving as instruments or aids in the production of other goods. When 'capital' consists simply of bins of raw or partly processed substances waiting to be passed through a new stage of manufacture, there is little danger that the need to replenish these bins as the stuff in them is used up will escape the notice of those who are reckoning up the cost of the manufacturing operations. The cost of the wheat that becomes flour and later becomes bread obviously must be counted as part of the ultimate cost of the loaf. Any particular 'packet' of wheat can contribute only once to the making of a loaf, since it becomes embodied in the loaf and is carried away in it. The case is quite different, however, when the instruments are *durable*, when they are long-lasting tools, machines or buildings, and when, therefore, each of them can render the same sort of service repeatedly through months or years, contributing something to the making of a great many distinct 'packets' of product. For then it might easily escape notice that the use of these instruments costs anything at all. The truck which has today conveyed a load from the mine to the factory or from the factory to the market looks the same as it did yesterday. Yet in rendering service it has progressed another stage towards that time when it will be worn out and fit only for the scrap-heap. Against the moment when it will be no more use and will have to be replaced by a new truck, the owner must set aside out of the daily value of its services a sufficient sum to mount up, by the end of the truck's useful life, to enough to buy a new truck. Only so will he avoid 'becoming worse off'. Thus if the truck-owner draws his whole income from the haulage services he renders by means of his truck, he must not count as *income* the whole difference between what is paid him for these services and what it costs him to buy fuel, lubricant, tyres and running repairs for his truck. He must, in addition to these costs, also deduct a *depreciation allowance*.

In this chapter we began by taking a bird's-eye view of the economic system or machine as a whole, and we separated out one of the working parts of this machine and called it income. Then looking more closely, we saw that, obviously, not all of the money going into a shop to buy goods over the counter is income *for the people who work in the shop*. Some of this money must be passed on to other people who, at one or other stage of manufacture, help to fashion or assemble the goods to be eventually sold in this shop. As we look behind the retail shop to the successive ranks of other firms, the nearer ones simply assembling what remoter ones have shaped, fabricated or even dug from the ground, we can see that eventually all the money paid at retail will have become somebody's income; what we must be careful over is to include amongst the 'somebodies' *everybody* whose contribution is needed to keep the entire process, through all its interwoven stages, going continuously; the baker buys flour, the miller buys wheat, but both of them also from time to time buy durable tools and machines, some fractions of whose cost must be charged to each of the loaves sold over the counter.

Though the reasonableness and necessity in principle of making continuous provision for the perhaps rather discontinuous and spasmodic replacement of pieces of durable equipment, and of replacing them when the time comes, is unmistakable, it may not be so easy in practice to know how much to set aside in each year. Nor may it be possible to show unequivocally how much of the price of a newly bought machine represents replacement of an old machine which has been scrapped, and how much represents a net augmentation or improvement of the firm's equipment; for the new machine, though perhaps able to be paid for by the depreciation fund accumulated from the earnings of the old machine, may be an improved model of much higher efficiency and power. But such difficulties are part of the nature of economics, and do not mean that we should abandon the concepts in which they inhere.

Chapter 13. Outlay

ON our imaginary map of the economic system, income was the total of all those money streams which flow from firms to individual suppliers of productive services. All this money is necessarily disposed of in some way by its recipients. Some of it they part with in exchange for things to eat and drink, burn for warmth or otherwise use up and destroy in the act of obtaining sustenance and enjoyment from them. This money simply goes back, directly or via other firms, to the firms which produce these goods. If the steady, even-paced production and equal consumption of goods for immediate sustenance and enjoyment were the whole of the economic process, so that we had what the economists call a 'stationary state', closely analogous (though very much earlier invented) to what the cosmologists have recently begun to call the 'steady-state cosmos,' where matter is continuously created and replaces other matter which as continuously vanishes beyond human ken, then the money circulation would be a very simple affair. As the equal counterpart of income we would have outlay on consumption-goods, and our whole story could be told in a simple picture of two concentric, circular canals by both of which two lakes were linked. One complete ring would represent the circuit of 'real goods and services', and in it consumption-goods would flow from the lake representing the firms to the other lake, on the opposite limb of the ring, representing private individuals.

Outlay

If we imagine the firms' lake at the south of the ring and the individuals' lake at the north of the ring then the flow of consumption-goods would occupy, let us say, the eastern half of the ring. The western half of the ring would be occupied by the stream of real productive services flowing from the individuals' lake to the firms' lake. Thus we would have one complete circuit of 'real' goods.

The other ring would represent the circuit of money. Money-income would flow from firms to individuals and its stream would occupy the western half of the ring; money outlay on consumption would flow from individuals to firms and occupy the eastern half. Thus the money could be thought of as going round and round, equal in value and opposite in direction of flow to the fresh goods and services for which it was endlessly exchanged.

Already in Chapter 6 (*Production*), however, we have come across the idea that some income, in a modern progressive economic system, is withheld from consumption-spending and used instead to build up the economy's equipment of tools, machines and buildings. But what do we mean precisely when we speak of 'income being used' to improve and augment equipment? Four quite distinct aspects are involved. First, any tool or machine which is to become an extra item in the economy's list of equipment must be produced. This requires the use of real productive resources. Secondly, this item will not count as a *net* augmentation of the list if, at the same time as this item is added, the concurrent wear and tear of other items reduces the total value and effectiveness of the equipment by as great an amount as it is increased by this item. So there must be a forgoing of possible consumption. This item could have been applied simply to make good some of the wear and tear involved in the current production of consumers' goods. In that case there would have been no sacrifice of consumption. But if it is to constitute a net addition, it must not be offset in that way. These two first aspects, production of equipment items and non-consumption of their equivalent, are the two 'real' aspects of the process of building up equipment. Matching these there are the two money aspects, and these are most conveniently considered in reverse order.

First, then, part of the aggregate of all incomes must be left unspent on goods for immediate consumption. Why? Because all money-income is the counterpart of real production. If, therefore, all money-income is spent on immediate consumption, there can be no excess of production over consumption to provide a net addition to the stock of real wealth. Secondly, the firms which are creating this net addition to the stock of real wealth, being unable to recover the money they are paying out for this purpose by selling the goods to consumers, must nevertheless replenish their coffers in some way or all their reserve of cash will drain away and leave them unable to continue operations. How can these firms as a group get back the money which they have paid away in producing goods to keep as distinct from goods to sell to consumers? By borrowing it, and so in some form and in some greater or less degree taking some of the individual suppliers of productive services into partnership, as shareholders or perhaps as lenders of long-term loans.

Thus we have a second money stream flowing back from the individuals to the firms: a stream of *saving-and-lending*. The effect of its existence is that individuals are receiving some part of the goods which their work and other productive services are creating, not in the form of immediately consumable goods but in the form of ownership of equipment or of claims to some part of the future earnings of equipment.

Think now of a storage tank with water flowing in by one pipe and out by another. The inflow represents the production of goods, the outflow represents the consumption, that is, the using-up or destruction, of goods, and the body of water which at any moment is in the tank represents the stock of goods of all sorts existing in the whole economy at some one moment. The actual identified objects composing this stock will of course change from moment to moment, one loaf being eaten while another takes its place upon the shelf, but the size of the stock as a whole, measured by its money value, could remain constant by virtue of equality between the pace of depletion and the pace of production. There is no reason, however, why these two processes should be equal, and if, for example, production exceeds consumption the stock of goods will be growing. Thus we can say: production equals consumption plus accumulation. This means no more than that all the excess of goods produced, over and above what is needed to replace those that are at the same time consumed, must necessarily be added to stock.

To the 'real' processes of consumption and accumulation there correspond the two monetary processes (*a*) of spending on consumption-goods, and (*b*) of saving-and-lending, and it would be quite legitimate to say that outlay consists of just these two classes of money transactions. However, not all spending and not all saving is done by private individuals or by the firms which they own as partners or shareholders. The central government and the local governments take upon themselves the tasks of providing, for example, defence, police, justice, medical care, education and roads and the support of the sick, elderly, unemployed and destitute. The payments which a government makes for some of these purposes can be looked on simply as a substitute for private consumption-spending on the same sorts of objects, and when we are dividing the whole outlay of the economic system into consumption-spending and saving-lending, this class of government payments will come under the heading of consumption-spending. The rest of the total expenditure of governments, which will be on such things as roads, school buildings, hospital buildings and airfields, will have the same effect as private saving-lending, in that it will bring about the building-up of material equipment. Thus it is perfectly possible to regard governments simply as agents of the private individual income-disposer, and not as a separate kind of economic entity. However, this view leaves us with a sense of unreality and blurs our analysis in an important respect, and it is preferable to treat 'government' as a third force, in addition to persons and firms.

The great difference between the direct outlay of private individuals, and the outlay made on their behalf by governments, lies of course in the method and the closeness of the control which the individuals can exercise in the two cases. When they buy things for themselves their control is perfect; when the government buys things, private people can influence the choice of these things only at the long intervals of parliamentary elections, and then only by casting a vote for (or against) a large bundle of very diverse and often incongruous vaguely expressed policies which there is no guarantee that the elected government will try to carry out, even if this government turns out to be the one they voted for. 'Government', therefore, must be looked on as an independent economic agent, and the individual's outlay will comprise, in addition to consumption-spending and saving-lending, a third component consisting of payments to governments under the heading of *taxation*.

Both in the scale and in the arbitrariness of its economic actions the government is a monstrous intruder into the sensitively organised world of private competitive demand and production, yet there is no longer an unmistakably located definite line between government and enterprise. Through the nationalised industries, the public boards and the Post Office, the government organises production and sells the product to the individuals. It augments and improves the economy's stock of 'capital goods', both through the nationalised industries and more directly through its own departments. For this purpose it draws off from time to time a large part of the stream of private saving-and-lending. Yet it may use such loans to buy goods for somebody's immediate consumption, and there is no clear-cut correspondence between government borrowing and government-sponsored creation of equipment.

In one more way the government's operations complicate our picture of 'outlay'. Some taxes are 'direct', like income tax and surtax and local rates. But a very important part of the central government's revenue is still gathered in by using the shopkeeper as a tax collector. Part of what the consumer pays over the counter for some goods does not become income for the suppliers of the productive services which have made those goods, but is handed on, instead, to the government. These goods are thus made artificially expensive, and the whole pattern of demand for goods is made different from what it would be if there were no such commodity taxes. Customs and excise and purchase tax fall under this head, and their existence means that not all of what, from the viewpoint of private individuals in their capacity as outlayers of income, looks like consumption-spending, is *factor-income* from the viewpoint of these individuals in their capacity as suppliers of productive services. The threads are crossed: some income is spent on consumables by those who do not help to make consumables but, instead, work for the government or are the recipients of its bounty; some of the money spent on consumables goes, not to those who make these consumables, but to those who are paid by the government.

If we can say what we mean by the income, and by the outlay, of an economic system as a whole, can we not put a figure on these equal magnitudes for any particular economy in any particular year? In practice any such attempt will have to grapple with all the complexities of the real business world. Information will have to be sought from several kinds of source, will have to be carefully interpreted and then pieced together into a total which, at best, will have no claim to be *the* correct figure or to have a perfectly unequivocal meaning. Amongst these practical difficulties there is one outstanding obstacle which has usually led statisticians to abandon any claim to calculate the 'national income' in the sense which we have given to income in this chapter, and to be content with what they call the 'gross national product', usually abbreviated to GNP. This difficulty lies in knowing what figure to put down for the depreciation, the wear and tear and loss of value and effectiveness, of the economy's durable equipment of all kinds, including, for example, buildings and civil engineering works. The range of figures for each of which a case could be made out is too wide. So the statisticians simply ask themselves what the figure would be if depreciation of equipment were zero, and this figure they call the gross national product. It is evidently likely to vary in the same direction as national income *stricto sensu* and perhaps by a not very different amount, and for many purposes, in view of the blurred outlines, both in interpretation and magnitude, of any such figure, the GNP is a good substitute for national income.

Chapter 14. Circulation

IN this chapter we have merely to bring together the ideas of income and outlay, elaborate a little on the 'double circular canal' model which we suggested in Chapter 13, and consider how the working of the system of circulating money is affected by the possibility that money may accumulate in reservoirs which can afterwards pour out again into the general stream, and how it is affected by changes in the amount of money circulating in the system as a whole. These two last questions we shall only briefly consider, because Chapter 15 (*Price-levels* and 16 (*Money*) and the whole of Book VI (*Finance*) will be very largely concerned with them.

In a self-contained economic system with no government, where the stock of equipment is not being augmented or depleted, we could say simply that money-income flows from firms to individuals and money-outlay flows back from individuals to firms, the whole purpose of this circulation being to keep account of the 'real' flows of goods and services moving in the opposite direction to the money. Even in this case, if we suppose that there is a stock of equipment which has to be maintained in an unchanging state, it will be helpful to add corresponding features to our model of the circulation system. Thus instead of simply having one part of our picture (one 'lake') standing for the group of individuals and another part standing for the group of firms, we shall divide this second part (or 'lake') into two, one part for the firms in their capacity as producers and sellers of consumers' goods, the other for the firms in their capacity as producers of equipment, which we must think of them as selling to themselves. When they sell equipment to themselves, a stream of money must flow from that part of the picture which represents the firms in their consumers' goods capacity to that part which represents the firms in their capacity of equipment builders. All this will sound simpler if, instead of talking about firms as a body acting in two capacities, we talk about two kinds of firms, the consumers' goods firms and the machine-

Circulation

building firms. Then if we assume that every time a unit of money reaches any one of the three 'lakes' which our picture now contains, another unit is thence despatched on its way to some other 'lake', so that in each of the three 'lakes' the number of money-units arriving in any unit time-interval is equal to the number departing in that interval, the working of our economy might be represented by the following table, in which the figure in any row and any column is the number of money-units (say, of £1 million each) going *from* the part of the system named at the end of the row *to* the part of the system named at the head of the column.

	Individuals	Consumers' goods firms	Machine-building firms	Totals of rows
Individuals	0	13	0	13
Consumers' goods firms	10	0	3	13
Machine-building firms	3	0	0	3
Totals of columns	13	13	3	29

In this table, the total of the first column and the total of the top row, it will be seen, are equal, and these are respectively the income and the outlay of the individuals. Also the total of the second column and the total of the second row are equal to each other, these being the revenue and expenditure of the group of consumers' goods firms. And the total of the third column and the total of the third row are equal to each other, these being the revenue and the expenditure of the machine-building firms. The three units of money flowing (per unit of time) from the consumers' goods firms to the machine-building firms is the *depreciation allowance*.

Now let us make on similar lines a picture of an economy (still without a government) which is steadily building up its stock of equipment. Here we shall have to include a stream of saving-lending, and it will be convenient to make the picture a little more explicit by showing the group of consumers' goods firms in two capacities, as producers and as 'financiers'. In their capacity as financiers they will accept a depreciation allowance from themselves in their capacity as producers, and also the saving-lending flow

from the individuals, and as an equal counterpart to these combined
incoming flows they will pay away to the machine-building firms
the total cost of all the machines needed both for making good
depreciation (wear and tear) and for augmenting the stock of
machines.

	Individuals	Consumers' goods firms, production	Consumers' goods firms, finance	Machine builders	Totals of rows
Individuals	0	13	2	0	15
Consumers' goods firms, production	10	0	3	0	13
Consumers' goods firms, finance	0	0	0	5	5
Machine builders	5	0	0	0	5
Totals of columns	15	13	5	5	38

Before we take the final step to achieve a broad realism for our
picture, by including a government sector in it, let us consider
what is the meaning of one feature of this table, namely the equality
at each part or sector of it, of the total inflowing and total out-
flowing streams. This feature is a consequence of our using money
flows to reflect explicitly, precisely and continuously the 'real'
processes of creation, consumption and accumulation of goods.
The creation of goods is reflected by the payment of incomes by
the firms (of both kinds) to the individuals, and we exclude from
the essential design of our picture the possibility that goods might
be created without the corresponding money-incomes being paid.
The consumption of goods is likewise represented by the stream
of money payments which buy these goods from the firms, and
we exclude from the inherent meaning of our picture the possibility of any divergence between the value of goods consumed in
any unit time-interval and the value of consumers' goods bought
in that interval. And again we intend the flow of depreciation allowance, and the flow of saving-lending, to reflect exactly at all
moments the production of equipment for maintaining or extending the economy's total stock of equipment. Our definitions, the
meanings we thus assign to the money-flows, compel us to show

the total incomings of the individuals equal to their total outgoings, for this is a system of *accounting*; we are concerned with money as a 'tell-tale' of the real processes, and not really with money 'in the flesh'. This is the place, however, to ask whether there cannot be a divergence between the actual money stream that individuals, for example, receive and the money stream they part with. May they not have reserves or idle stocks of money, out of which they can spend more than they are currently earning? Or may not the machine-building firms build machines for which payment out of the saving of the individuals or the depreciation allowances of the consumers' goods firms is not at once forthcoming?

Plainly such things can happen, and it is important to realise that the essential condition which must be simultaneously fulfilled if in any short time-interval the economy's stock of equipment is to be augmented, is not that some part of the money which in that interval is received as income should be handed back to firms by way of loans or the purchase price of newly issued shares in the firms, but that in that interval less should be spent on consumption than is received as income. (In expressing the matter thus, we are taking the purchase of consumer-goods as the same thing as actual physical consumption.) If some people do £1000 worth of work in a week, and only destroy £900 worth of goods by consuming them, then £100 worth of goods has been added to the stock, no matter whether the £100 of unspent income has been lent back to the firms or whether it has merely been put into a bank account or a cash box. (We must beware of the fallacy that money put into a bank account is 'available to be lent' to other people. Money standing to the credit of a person or a firm in an ordinary bank is part of the nation's stock of money, and far the greater part of this stock has been brought into existence by the banks' own lending operations, which ordinarily they will already have pushed as far as their cash reserves allow; but more about this in the next chapter.)

Plainly, however, no single firm, nor the body of firms all taken together, can continue indefinitely to part with more money than they are receiving from all sources. If the firms, taken together, are augmenting their stock of machines and at the same time depleting their stock of money, this does not mean that they are becoming essentially insolvent, but merely that they are getting the proportions of their various kinds of possessions or assets into an inconvenient state. One way of looking at the situation is to say that the individuals as a body, who have now got the money which the firms as a body have parted with, have in effect *lent goods* to the firms; for if the individuals had chosen to exercise the purchasing-power which their stocks of money represent, they could have possessed themselves of goods which, instead, have remained in the hands of the firms. One way, perhaps the most obvious and natural way, for such a situation to be adjusted, or rather, prevented from arising, will be for the individuals to lend the money to the firms, or else to become partners or shareholders in the firms. In the latter case, the individuals will become explicit owners of a share of the equipment and goodwill of particular firms. In saying that if the individuals build up stocks of money by spending on consumption less than their income, they are in effect lending goods to the firms, we are choosing to look on money as a kind of acknowledgment of a claim to goods, and this in a sense is what shares in a firm are: they acknowledge the shareholder as part-owner of the firm's goods.

Money, however, is intended to serve as a circulating medium, and so it is better for savers to become explicit creditors or shareholders of firms, rather than pile up in the form of money a hoard of unexercised general purchasing power. The existence of market rates of interest is, as we shall see, an inducement to the individuals to lend rather than hoard their savings.

What would have to happen, if savers did not let themselves be induced to lend back to the firms the money representing income which they do not wish to spend on consumption? The firms would have continually to borrow more money from the banks, and this process would evidently imply a continual increase in the total stock of money in the hands of individuals and firms all taken together. This growth of the stock of money in the economic system as a whole would have very important implications, which we shall begin to consider in the next two chapters.

Circulation

Now we must make our summary picture of the economic circulation complete by bringing in a sector labelled 'government'. We shall do this in two stages. First we shall suppose that the only source of government revenue is direct taxes levied on individuals, and that the government uses its revenue to employ individuals directly. In this case our picture will look somewhat as in the table.

	Individuals	Consumers' goods firms, production	Consumers' goods firms, finance	Machine builders	Government	Totals of rows
Individuals	0	10	2	0	3	15
Consumers' goods firms, production	7	0	3	0	0	10
Consumers' goods firms, finance	0	0	0	5	0	5
Machine builders	5	0	0	0	0	5
Government	3	0	0	0	0	3
Totals of columns	15	10	5	5	3	38

Here we see that individuals earn a total income of fifteen money-units per unit of time, and that seven units of this total is earned by services which they render to firms which make consumers' goods, five units by services to machine-building firms, and three units by services to the government. Out of this total income of fifteen units, individuals spend ten units on consumption, save two units, and pay three units in taxes. Out of their revenue of ten units, consumers' goods firms pay away seven units to individuals for their productive services and three units to their own 'finance' sector for depreciation allowance on their equipment. The 'finance' sector of the consumers' goods firms has an inflow of five units, three from the depreciation allowances and two from new net savings, and it hands on the whole of this to the machine-building firms, which pay it out for the productive services of individuals. The government derives a revenue of three units from *all* the individuals as a body, and it uses this to pay for the services of certain individuals (namely the Civil Servants and the members of police forces and armed forces, the schoolteachers, the doctors and so on).

Income

Not all of those who receive incomes from the government are necessarily rendering services in return. We count as a service the lending of money to the government, and interest on such loans comes under payment for services. But the old-age pensioners and recipients of unemployment or sickness pay cannot reasonably be regarded as rendering productive services. Their incomes are known as 'transfer incomes', since they are in effect created by one set of people and transferred to another set to be spent. The only modification our latest table would need in order to include transfer incomes would be an extra row and column labelled 'Pensioners, etc.', and the splitting of the government's total outlay between (productive) 'Individuals' and 'Pensioners, etc.', together with a figure, equal to the transfer incomes, showing that these incomes are spent on consumers' goods.

As a final stage in the elaboration of our picture, we will suppose that of the government's total income of three units, one unit is obtained by direct taxation of individuals and two units by taxing commodities. Then our final picture (which we leave for the reader to draw if he desires) would show a figure of one instead of three as the payment by individuals to the government, and a figure of two instead of nought as the payment by the consumers' goods firms to the government. The payment by individuals to the firms will now be twelve units instead of ten, two units of this being 'indirect' taxation which will be handed on by the firms to the government. We shall see in Book VII (*Government*) that we are here rather over-simplifying the matter of indirect taxation. Indeed it is plain that when the consumers' goods firms try to recoup themselves, for the tax payments they must make to the government, by raising the prices of their goods to individuals, there will be effects on the quantity sold per unit of time, and the repercussions will spread throughout the whole economic system, leading to an entire new equilibrium. But this does not concern us in our study of circulation as a way of looking at the economic process.

The reader can most conveniently review this chapter by considering again the meaning and structure of the three tables. They show in a sense the physiology of the economic system, indicating how its vital processes support each other, each remaining in being only by the aid of other processes which in turn it helps to maintain. Thus men work in order to produce goods, and they consume these goods in order to give themselves strength to continue working. The interlocking flows which make up the whole pattern of the 'real' circulation are necessary to each other. Money's prime purpose is to register these flows by equal and opposite flows of its own, but like a great river basin the monetary system is subject to floods, droughts and tides. Money in its modern forms has properties of great subtlety and complexity which radically affect the whole character of the economic system. We shall take a first view of these in the next two chapters, but our main study of them will be in Books V and VI.

Chapter 15. *Price-levels*

IN Chapter 11 (*Equilibrium*) we met with the idea that a number of measurable things, each of which, by itself, can yield at different times a different answer to the act of measurement, and which are therefore called variable quantities or simply variables, may all depend on or mutually influence each other in regard to the measurements they yield. Sometimes in such cases the thing in question is only a 'variable' in the sense that we do not know, until we have solved the problem, what its size or measurement or 'value' is, and when its variability is merely another name for our ignorance of its actual size, it is better to call it an 'unknown'. We illustrated the idea of two unknowns which fix each other by an example of a man and his son, whose ages at some one date were to be found out from two independent relationships between them. We showed that in this case the appearance of 'circularity' in the pair of statements giving these relationships is illusory, and that *taken together* they do give a definite answer.

This idea, that the 'unknown' respective sizes or levels of a set of things, which are linked with each other in regard to these sizes, can all be found out if we have enough independent pieces of information about the linkages, is the basis of the idea of a determinate (that is, unique and discoverable) general equilibrium position of an economic system. In a general economic equilibrium, the unknowns are the outputs and market exchange ratios of different goods and kinds of productive service, and the linkages are, for example, the respective degrees of extra comfort which each particular individual would get from consuming a small extra weekly quantity of some one good, if this weekly quantity was increased step-by-step while his weekly quantities of all other things remained fixed. Now for all 'real' commodities and services desired for their own sakes and capable of yielding satisfaction directly, this satisfaction or comfort is something quite separate, distinct and independent of the possibility of exchanging the commodity in question for something else. And in the system of information about linkages between outputs, prices, incomes and so on, so long as only 'real' goods and services are involved, there is no circularity.

But as soon as we try to introduce into this system *money* in the sense of something desired *only* because it can be exchanged for other things, and not capable of directly furnishing any satisfaction, the case is quite altered. For now if we ask 'How much of this good or that will a person in such and such a situation give for a unit of money?' the answer depends on what he is going to be able to get in exchange for the unit of money, since to exchange it is the only possible use for it. And *these* two answers quite plainly *are* circular. They amount to saying 'The exchange value of a unit of money depends on its exchange value', and this tells us nothing.

We claimed that our general equilibrium was a *determinate* position, that is, a definite position settled by the tastes and resources of the individual people in the system (no other position being compatible with all these tastes and given quantities of resources at once), and capable of being found out from a knowledge of these tastes and resources. And now we discover that it is only determinate up to that point where we introduce money in the sense of a pure exchange medium or pure accounting medium. The ratios in which real goods exchange for one another are determinate. But the ratios in which they exchange for 'pure' money are *not* determinate, except in the sense that the ratio between the money prices of two goods must reflect the ratio of the quantities of these goods which exchange against each other. (For example, if an ounce of butter exchanges for four ounces of sugar, then the money price of an ounce of butter must be four times the money price of an ounce of sugar.) For if at a given moment *all* money prices were, say, doubled, and if at this same moment everybody's stock of money were also doubled, everything would go on just as before, nobody would have any reason to behave differently as everyone would be exactly as well off as before. (The price of his own services having doubled, his money-income would also have doubled, but each unit of it would only buy half as much of anything as before.) So we are faced with the fact that there is a great gap in our theoretical model: it contains as yet no means for determining the *general level of money prices*.

We have been careful in the foregoing part of the chapter to speak of 'pure' money, by which we mean money serving *only* as a medium of exchange or of account. For money serves other purposes and has other qualities, which indeed cannot really be separated, even conceptually, from its use in exchange. These other qualities and roles have the effect of putting money back into the class of 'things desired for their own sake', and the conclusion we shall reach in Book vi (*Finance*) as a consequence of studying these other properties, is that after all the general level of money prices is determinate. But we cannot simply include money along with other goods and treat it as though it were not money. It is a very special entity indeed, and an elaborate analysis will be required. In the next chapter we shall get a glimpse of this analysis, but first we have to ask: what do we mean by the general level of money prices, and why does it interest us?

A price, we have seen, is simply a ratio between two quantities, the quantity of *A* and the quantity of *B* which exchange for each other on a market. There is evidently no fundamental or *a priori* reason for putting either the quantity of *A* or the quantity of *B* as the numerator or upstairs part of the ratio. If it takes five units of *A* to buy one unit of *B*, the price of *B* is (five *divided by* one) units of *A*, and the price of *A* is (one *divided by* five) units of *B*. When one of the two goods is money, we are nearly always interested in the money price of the other good: money is the numerator of the fraction. But when we are considering what style of living can be managed on a particular money-income, we are concerned with the price of money, or as we usually say, the value of money, the question of what so-and-so much money will buy. Now in such a case it is no use expressing the 'price of money' in terms of *one* other good, for a money income has got to buy a collection of all sorts of goods. Moreover, this collection is not just a list of different kinds of goods, but a list giving the quantity of each good. When we call such a list of quantities 'one unit of goods' and use it as the denominator of a fraction whose numerator is the number of money-units needed to buy this collection of goods, we have the idea of the 'price-level of goods in general'. The 'price-level of goods in general' can be thought of, at a first approach, as simply the result of turning upside-down, or taking the reciprocal of, the fraction giving the value of money in terms of a collection of goods of fixed quantitative composition.

Now we are interested not merely in finding what set of quantities of goods so-and-so much money will buy at one particular date, but, even more, in comparing the purchasing power of money at two or more different dates. One way of doing this is simply to take some particular set of quantities of named goods and find out the money price of this collection at each of the two dates. If the money price in June 1955 was one-and-a-half times as high as it had been in June 1947, and if the relative quantities of the goods in this collection were just those which appear in the household budgets of a certain group of people, we can say with a clear meaning that the 'cost of living' of that group of people rose to half as much again between June 1947 and June 1955.

One essential feature of such a proceeding is suggested by the fact that the goods in the list are not just names but are quantities, and that, moreover, these quantities are chosen because they properly represent what people, in some context, actually spend their money on. If any other procedure is to be used for the same sort of purpose, it must, in some way or other, reproduce the essence of this feature if it is to give us a sensible and meaningful result. What difference, then, would be made to the result if, in the kind of calculation we have outlined above, the quantity of some one good were made many times greater while those of others remained unchanged or were reduced? The effect would evidently be to give any price-change undergone by this good, between the two dates, a more powerful voice in saying what the change between those dates had been in the 'general' price-level. For, to take an exaggerated case, suppose one such list comprised one hundred loaves of bread and one ton of coal, while the other comprised one thousand loaves of bread and one ton of coal, and suppose the price of a loaf of bread were initially one shilling and finally two shillings, while that of a ton of coal remained unchanged at £10. Then the change in the price of the first list would be from £15 to £20 while that of the second list would be from £60 to £110. Thus one list would make out that the general price-level had increased, between the two dates, by about thirty-three per cent, while the other would make out that it had increased by more than eighty-three per cent.

Which answer would be the right one, or the best one? The one derived from that collection of goods which was most *relevant* to the purpose for which we need to know about the change in the price-level. If this purpose concerns the kind of person who buys more nearly 1000 loaves for every ton of coal than one hundred loaves for every ton of coal, the second answer has more claim to be accepted than the first one. But its validity arises merely from the particular circumstances, and in speaking, as we have done until now, of *the* general price-level, we have been making some use of the economist's indispensable licence to be occasionally imprecise. There is no one procedure or calculation which will give us a uniquely correct answer to the question how 'prices in general' moved between two particular dates.

The idea we have been leading up to is that of an index-number of prices. To construct such an index-number, we choose some particular historical date and declare that the prices which prevailed at that date for a particular set of carefully specified commodities shall be taken as our basis of comparison. This we call the 'base-date'. Next we ask ourselves whether, in judging the movement of prices of this set of goods as a whole, a ten per cent increase (for example) in the price of any one of them ought to count for just as much, or for twice as much, and so on, as a similar increase in the price of any other. The criterion for such a decision may be, for example, that at the base-date the group of people interested in this price-level spent twice as much each week on good A as on good B. In that case we count any change in the price of good A twice for each once that we count any change in the price of good B. In doing this we are said to assign twice as much *weight* to good A as to good B. In our example of coal and bread, with their initial prices, our first list in effect counted coal twice for bread once, because the £10 for one ton of coal is twice the £5 for one hundred loaves of bread; while our second list counted bread five times for coal once, because the £50 for 1000 loaves of bread is five times the £10 for a ton of coal. In practice the weights in any two index-numbers intended to answer the same question would of course never differ to such an extent as this.

When we have chosen our base-date, our list of commodities and our scheme of relative weights, there still remain a number of technical questions to be settled, especially that of the methods by which the diverse price changes of the various goods should be calculated and then averaged. These, however, are matters which lie outside the scope of this book. The final result of our calculations will be a series of numbers, each belonging to some one calendar date, and representing, by its ratio to one hundred, the ratio which the price-level on that date bore to the price-level on the base-date. Thus in effect we say: 'The set of prices prevailing at the base-date, taken as a whole, shall be represented by 100; the corresponding set of prices at any other date, if it appears from our calculations to be half as high again as those at the base-date, shall be represented by 150'; and so on.

Let us end with a problem. Suppose that an index-number of the prices of consumers' goods stands today at 200; what is the value of money today, according to this index-number, compared with the value it had at the base-date?

Chapter 16. Money

MONEY is exchanged and held in stock, but it is not consumed and it does not wear out. There is thus no need to produce it, except when the total quantity in existence is to be augmented. As soon as it has been received by one person from another, it is ready to be handed on again. There might appear at first sight to be no limit to the number of times each unit of money is handed on from one person to another in a year, and so it might seem that if a list could be made of every transaction in which money passed from one owner to another during a year, stating the number of money units involved in each such transaction, and if the total of all these numbers of money units was added up, there would be nothing to limit the size of this total, no matter how small was the number of money units *existing* at each moment during this year. If this were so, it would mean that the total value, reckoned in money, of all the goods exchanged against money during a year would also be quite unconnected with either the quantity of money existing or with the quantities of goods changing hands. Given quantities of goods exchanged would have an unlimited money value, or in other words, the general level of prices could rise to any height, no matter what limitation was placed on the size of the total *stock* of money. For this stock of money could flow through the channels of the economic system indefinitely fast, and perform in a given time any number of transactions no matter how big. What is it, then, which in fact puts a brake on the *velocity of circulation* of a given stock of money, the number of times that each unit of it, on the average over all units, changes hands per year? For if there were no such brake, we have just seen that there would not in principle be any limit to the general level of prices, no matter whether the total *stock* of money in existence at each moment were large or small.

The velocity of circulation will be slowed down if each person who receives some money from another person keeps it a little while; the longer he keeps each such packet of money, the slower will be the average velocity of circulation, and the lower, other things equal, will be the general level of prices. What is it, then, we are ultimately led to ask, which tempts a man to keep for a time each packet of money he receives instead of immediately spending it?

If a person receives a packet of money and does not immediately spend it, he has, for the time being, a larger stock of money, in his bank account or his till or his pocket, than before. Thus the desire to have at all times a certain stock of money, or the desire to have at certain times a larger stock of money, would be a motive for retaining unspent for a certain time each packet of money received. So our question about what limits the velocity of circulation of money comes to this: What inducements are there for a person to keep in his possession a certain stock of money? What considerations will he have in mind in deciding how large this stock of money should be?

Let us begin by turning the question back to its earlier form, and asking why a person who receives, let us say, his weekly or monthly pay does not immediately spend it. One fundamental part of the answer to this question is that he does not want to make up his mind, all at once, what to buy. As a householder he does not want the trouble of thinking out in detail the whole week's or month's purchases in advance, and he does not want the feeling of constraint and risk that would arise from his committing himself to take just such-and-such quantities of particular goods to meet the needs of a considerable stretch of future time. The same principle applies to firms and governments. People prefer to commit their incomes to particular uses as needs arise, or rather as they crystallise and take definite shape and insistent urgency. Now if I receive my pay cheque on the last day of the month and spend it evenly over the ensuing thirty days, I shall have *on the average over these days* half a month's pay in my bank account. But in this statement we already have a clue to the second of the questions posed at the end of the preceding paragraph.

That question was: What things will a man look at, in deciding how many money units to keep in stock, in his bank account or pocket, on the average over all days? Or if we regard his consultation of those indicators as unconscious rather than deliberate, still we can ask, what things do in fact settle the size of his average bank balance? The clue we have come across is the notion that this average balance will be related to the person's income, or to the firm's revenue, amongst other things.

It is upon this idea that one of the most compact and simple accounts of how the general level of prices comes to be at any time what it is, has been based. This theory is associated with Alfred Marshall and the Cambridge tradition. We shall approach it rather indirectly. Let us imagine an economic system where the only form of money consists of £1 notes, there being no banks or bank deposits, and where by law everyone who receives such a note from someone else must sign his name, with the date, on the back of the note. Let us also suppose that the number of notes in existence is fixed and unchanging. Now if at the end of the year the total number of signatures with dates falling in that year were counted up, this would tell us the total money value which had passed from one person to another during the year. If we further suppose that the only things given in exchange for money, in this economic system, are real goods and services of kinds whose prices we wish to include in our notion of the general price-level, it follows that the total money value of the goods and services of these kinds, exchanged against money during a year, will also be given by the total number of all the signatures. The price of each 'packet' of such goods and services, on the average over all 'packets', evidently depends on two things: How many packets there are, and how many signatures there are. The physical quantities of these goods and services, and so the number of 'packets', being supposed fixed, any change in the average price per packet must arise from a change in the number of signatures, and that number, in turn, can be thought of as depending on two things: the number of banknotes in existence, and the number of signatures, on the average over all banknotes, found on the back of each note, that is, the number of times the average note changes hands during the year. Thus we can write out the following *truism*:

> Number of notes *times* velocity of circulation *equals* number of packets of goods *times* average price per packet.

This is just the same thing as saying:

> Number of notes
> *equals* total annual value of goods exchanged *divided by* velocity of circulation of money.

Now when we say that the total annual value of goods exchanged is to be divided by some number, we are in effect saying that a certain fraction or proportion (not necessarily a fraction smaller than one) of this total annual value is to be taken. This particular proportion, which the Cambridge economists have habitually represented by the letter k, is the factor on which we concentrate attention when we seek to explain according to their theory the mechanism by which the general level of prices is pushed to or held at a certain height in comparison with where it stood at other dates. We can now rewrite the truistical formula in yet a third shape:

> Number of notes *equals* total annual value of goods exchanged *times* k.

Since we are assuming that the number of notes in existence

is fixed and unchanging, and that the same is true of the number
of packets to be exchanged in a year, it follows that any change
in the average money price per packet of goods (the general
level of prices) must be associated with a change in k. If k goes
down to, say, three-quarters of its former level, then the average
price-level must go up to four-thirds of its former level, because
otherwise the results of multiplying these two and the given
number of packets all together would not be equal, as it logically
must, to the number of notes in existence. Thus we reach a provi-
sional result: The number of packets of goods to be exchanged
being given, the average price per packet of goods exchanged
depends, when the size of the stock of money is fixed, on the ratio
which people, all taken together, want that stock to bear to the
total annual value of their purchases of goods.

All the notes in the economic system's total stock of notes must
at each moment be in the possession of particular persons, firms,
etc., and if such a person feels, at that moment, that his stock of
money is not as big as he would find convenient, he will refrain
from handing on the next packet of money he receives and will
add it to his stock. His action in refraining from spending his
money will reduce, *pro tanto*, the total annual value of goods
bought, and thus will influence the size of k, the ratio of the number
of money-units in existence to the total value of exchanges of
money-units for goods occurring in a year; and in doing so it will
influence the general level of prices.

To sum up this stage of the argument, the Cambridge theory
says that, *given* the size of the economy's stock of money, the
general level of prices depends on the proportion k which people
all taken together want this stock to represent of the annual value
of goods exchanged; or *given* the proportion k, the general level
of prices depends on the size of the stock of money.

Now there are several further things to be said about this theory.
First, there is no reason why we should include in the list of money
transactions that we take account of, every kind of transaction in
which money is exchanged against goods and services. We might
confine the class of transactions considered to those in which

people receive and dispose of their incomes, thus excluding all those inter-firm transactions in which, for example, the baker buys flour from the miller and the miller buys wheat from the farmer. If we do so, we must re-express our formula thus: The general level of prices of services by which income is earned, and of goods on which it is spent, depends on the quantity of money in existence and on the ratio in which income-earners and disposers wish this quantity to stand to their total annual incomes.

This theory satisfies a test to which all economic theories ought to be submitted: the test of whether it rests ultimately on human tastes and decisions. The ratio k is evidently the resultant of the decisions of all the individuals in the economic system into whose possession money comes. By deciding whether to keep a larger or smaller balance of money in his own bank account, each person contributes to making this ratio settle at some particular number; and in giving effect to his decision, he gives an upward or a downward push to the general level of prices. The factors, the thoughts and feelings which influence his decision can be analysed in far greater depth and detail than we have here attempted, the mechanism by which his decisions can be supposed to bear on the general level of prices can be greatly elaborated. These developments we shall explain in Books v (*Employment*) and vi (*Finance*). But even without them, we can plainly claim that the theory makes human reactions central in its explanation.

What we have done, earlier in this chapter, is to outline one version of the so-called Quantity Theory of Money. There is another version, associated with the name of the American economist Irving Fisher, which consists in elaborating, by means of additional assumptions, the first of the two identities, or truisms, we gave on p. 94. The Fisher theory is less satisfactory than the Cambridge theory for two reasons. First, it does not pass nearly so well the test of depending essentially on human tastes, beliefs, reactions and decisions. The most the Fisher theory can do is to invoke *habits*, such business habits as that of paying wages weekly and salaries monthly and rents quarterly. From the constancy of these habits is deduced a constancy in the velocity of circulation of that portion of the total money stock which is used in the paying-out and spending of money-incomes and in the purchase of real goods by one firm from another. Let us call this portion the 'real transactions' stock of money. When the velocity of this portion is taken to be constant, any changes in the general price-level of goods and services must be associated either with a change in the quantities of the goods and services annually being exchanged against money, or else in the quantity of money in the 'real transactions' portion of the total stock. If, by assuming that all productive resources are fully employed, and are also in the short period constant in amount, we take the exchanged quantities of goods and services to be also constant, we are left with changes in the size of the 'real transactions' stock of money as the sole explanation of changes in the price-level.

One weakness of this theory is that it fails to explain why the ratio of the 'real transactions' portion of the total money stock to that stock itself should not vary widely from time to time. Such variation could be understood either as a change in the size of the 'real transactions' portion of the total stock of money, or as a change in the velocity of circulation of that stock as a whole. In either view, the basis of the theory would be undermined.

The second reason why we claim superiority for the Cambridge version is that it forms a natural approach to that account of the general price-level given by John Maynard Keynes in his *General Theory of Employment, Interest and Money*, the book which, in 1936, added almost a new dimension to economic theory. This account we shall discuss in Books v and vi.

Meanwhile there is another matter on which this chapter must touch. If the general level of prices depends, other things being equal, on the existing quantity of money, on what does this quantity itself depend or how is it settled? The detail of this matter will be discussed in Book vi. Much the greater part of the stock of money in a modern advanced economy, we shall there show, has been brought into existence by the banks by making loans to some of their customers. These borrowing customers, who may be private individuals or firms or even governments, have paid away the money they have borrowed from the banks to other customers of the banks who have deposited this money in their bank accounts, where it stands to their credit, that is to say, it is shown in the ledgers of the banks as owed *by* the banks to this second set of customers. Thus in Britain thousands of millions of pounds are owed *to* the banks by one set of people and *by* the banks to another set of people. Most of this money never gets into the open as notes and coin at all: it is simply transferred from one person's or firm's account to another's, in the same or, more often, a different bank. However, not all payments, as we saw earlier, are made by cheque. Wages are paid and shopping is largely done by means of tangible money, banknotes and coins. The total daily value of these cash transactions bears some fairly stable relation to the total value of all payments, and that again is related, as we have seen, to the quantity of money in existence. Thus when the banks create extra money by making extra loans, they are exposing themselves to a demand for extra cash, which some of their customers will want to take away in exchange for a reduction in the amount the bank owes them, or in exchange for an increase in the amount they owe the bank. Now the total quantity in existence of these notes is controlled by the central government through the Bank of England, and by convention as well as proper caution, the ordinary banks do not let their total deposits, that is, the amounts they owe to some of their customers, grow larger than a ratio of one hundred to eight of their available cash. Thus it is ultimately the government which, in Britain nowadays, controls the size of the nation's stock of money.

BOOK IV. DISTRIBUTION

Chapter 17. Wages

T HE writer and the reader of this book could have excused themselves the labour of studying 'distribution', the sharing of income, as a separate branch of theory, on the ground that a clear-cut account of the principles on which this sharing proceeds can be given only for a rather abstract and heroically simplified model of the economic system, and that in this model the sharing of income amongst those who provide the productive services which generate that income is simply a reflection of the general pricing process and of the fact that each person is able and willing, in given circumstances, to furnish a certain quantity of a certain kind of service. Nonetheless the mechanism at work in such a system is also at work in more realistic economic systems and even in the real world itself, however much obscured by other kinds of interplay of forces, and it can still be claimed that an understanding of distribution in the purely competitive static system, such as we have, after all, mainly had in mind in previous chapters, is the best starting-point for our exploration.

When an unskilled labourer finds that an hour's work of the kind he can do adds 25p to the value of the hourly output of a firm to which he attaches himself, and that the firm is in consequence just willing to pay him 25p an hour; and if when he has worked eight hours in one day he feels that the irksomeness of going on for a ninth hour, missing the ease and leisure he would have enjoyed in it, would not be compensated by the *extra* goods he could buy with an *extra* 25p, over and above those that £2 a day would provide him with; then he will settle down to working an eight-hour day for an income of £2 a day. On similar lines, so long as we confine ourselves to an economic system where each individual person and firm is free to make any contract that

Distribution

another party will agree to, without regard to the feelings or requirements of 'third parties', of other institutions or organisations, we
can explain the income of every supplier of any kind of productive
service. One question only, but a difficult and basic one, will
then confront us, so long as we are content with our abstract
system: when all such incomes are added together, will they add
up to more or to less than the total value of production, out of
which they must of course be paid, or will they in sum just equal
this value of production and precisely exhaust it, leaving no part
of it unaccounted for, that is, 'undistributed', and leaving no
individual without a source of just the amount of income
that the process 'imputes' to him? This is the famous 'adding-up
problem', and we shall study it in Chapter 21 (*Distribution*).
But first let us look more closely at the idea of imputation,
of a principle by which, when so many identical units of some
factor of production are employed by some firm, the value of
the services of this quantity of this factor to this firm can be
reckoned.

Suppose the number of units of this factor, let us say workers,
employed by this firm is at first one hundred. And then suppose
that, without any change in the quantities employed by the firm of
any other factors of production, the number is reduced to ninety-
nine. The effect will be to reduce the weekly number of gallons,
tons, therms, square feet or what not of the firm's output, and also
to change the money value of this weekly quantity produced. If
the firm is selling its product in a perfectly competitive market,
where the firm itself is a mere drop in an ocean of other firms all
producing a commodity which is in all respects, as judged by the
buyers of it, exactly the same, and where all the firms and all the
buyers know all the time what prices are being asked, offered and
accepted, then these two changes, of the physical quantity of output
and of its money value, will be very closely linked. For in a perfectly competitive market, each firm can sell any output within its
practicable range at the going market price, and thus to change
its physical output by one unit is to change the value of its output
by the value of one physical unit.

Wages

Suppose, then, that each physical unit, each gallon or ton, of our firm's product is worth £2 in the market, over and above the expense for materials, wear and tear of machines, and so on, which its manufacture entails, so that each physical unit represents £2 of 'value added' in the sense explained in Chapter 6. And suppose that when the number of workers is reduced from one hundred to ninety-nine, the physical weekly output is reduced by five units. Then we can see that the marginal worker makes a difference of £10 to the value of the firm's weekly output, when it is employing one hundred men. It will just be worth the firm's while to employ one hundred men if it can hire them for £10 a week each. If it can only get them for £12 a week each it must so arrange matters that the marginal man adds £12 to the value of the firm's weekly output. How can it do this? By employing fewer men in collaboration with unchanged quantities of the other factors of production. For, as we saw in Chapter 6, the various factors are not perfect substitutes for one another, and as more and more land, animals, tools or machines are employed in conjunction with each man, the importance and value of the marginal man continually rises. Suppose, instead, that the firm can get men for £8 a week each. Then it must increase their number until the addition or subtraction of one man makes a difference of only £8 to the value of the firm's weekly output. In short, it must employ that number of men which, against a *given* background of quantities of other productive resources, will have a *marginal physical product* whose value is equal to the money wage. This holds for a firm selling its product in a perfectly competitive market.

The 'given background of quantities of other productive resources' is of course only an analytical device, a stage in our bit-at-a-time procedure of building up the whole picture. The firm can be supposed to try out, first, various quantities of labour against one 'given background', and then these same various quantities against a *different* 'given background', and so on. Each factor in turn can be treated as the variable one, and varied over and over while the others are 'shifted' between each set of variations. We need not elaborate further. In equilibrium in perfect competition the firm will be paying *each* factor a reward equal to the value of the marginal physical product of that factor.

This result is but the beginning. We have to recall yet again, and we can never recall too often, that in the economic system everything depends on and influences everything else. A worker who can add £12 to the weekly value of firm *B*'s output will not be content to stay in the service of firm *A* for £10 a week, nor will firm *B* be content to let him. If every firm knew precisely what size of output would result from each given combination of quantities of factors of production, and if every worker knew just what wage each firm would offer him, and if there were no difficulties or drawbacks for any worker in transferring himself from one firm to another, all workers of a given type and quality of skill would be paid the same wage no matter which firm they served. Thus we can say that in an economy in perfect competition, where every firm knows just how many men it can profitably employ at each supposed wage-rate, and where each man knows what each firm is offering and can freely move without cost from one firm to another, it is legitimate to speak of *the* value of the marginal physical product of labour; for this value will in equilibrium (that is, when every man and every firm has done the best he can for himself) be the same in every firm and in every industry throughout the economy; and every man's wage for an hour's work will be equal to the difference one extra man makes to the value of each firm's hourly output.

'In equilibrium': by this we must evidently mean a *general* equilibrium of all outputs, prices and employed quantities of factors in all firms throughout the economic system. A firm will not be doing the best it can for itself, will not be making its net revenue as large as possible, until it is employing the various factors of production in just such quantities, for any chosen output of its product, that the marginal £2 expended weekly on any one factor adds exactly the same extra value to output as the marginal £2 expended weekly on any other factor; and until, in perfect competition, the firm has chosen the best level of output, where the marginal weekly £2 worth of each factor will be adding £2 to the weekly value of output.

So much for the demand side of the labour market, as far as it can be isolated from the supply side. What of the latter? In a perfect 'atomistic' market, where each man would consult only his own feelings without constraint or support from any Trade Union or law, the number of man-hours of work supplied would be a function of the hourly wage. Beyond a few daily hours each man would find it increasingly irksome to extend his working day to a fifth, a sixth, etc., hour. With any *given* hourly money wage and any *given* set of money prices of goods, each extra daily hour would secure a less badly wanted basket of goods than that purchased with the previous hour's pay. A low income would provide him with necessaries, a rather larger one would add modest comforts, then luxuries and in the end mere superfluities. In short, the marginal disutility of daily work would be an increasing function of the number of daily hours worked; the marginal utility of daily earnings would be a decreasing function of their amount, and this amount itself would increase with the daily hours of work. There would be for each man some length of working day at which the utility of a half-hour's extra earnings and the disutility of a half-hour's extra work would just balance each other. By working each day for just that number of hours he would get the most satisfaction out of life.

We have seen, for a perfectly competitive economy, how much labour of some particular kind will be *demanded* at a given wage-rate: it will be that quantity which will make the value of the marginal hour's physical product of this kind of labour equal to the hourly wage; it will be a number of weekly man-hours such that an extra weekly man-hour, in whatever firm it was applied, would yield extra weekly product of a value just equal to the wage for one man-hour. We have also seen, for a perfectly competitive economy, how much labour will be *supplied* at a given wage-rate: it will be that quantity at which the marginal disutility of labour is just but only just compensated, for every individual worker, by the marginal utility of earnings; at the given hourly wage, some men will work five hours and some twelve, in order to equalise the disutility and the utility of working and earning; and when the hours contributed by all of them in a week are added together, this will be the weekly supply of labour at the given wage-rate. Thus the supply of labour will be such that, if any single worker were asked to furnish one extra half-hour, he would find himself barely induced to do so by the prospect of a half-hour's extra earnings. Before we are tempted to wind up the argument quickly by saying that the wage-rate and the number of hours worked will mutually determine each other at levels where demand and supply of labour are equal, let us once more remind ourselves of the interdependence of things. Men have differing tastes and differing skills. If there is a strong widespread taste for a particular commodity which men with some particular skill are specially well-fitted to make, those men will tend to have high wages. High wages give to the tastes of those who earn them an exceptional power to influence the use of resources, to cause those things to be made which the highly paid workers wish for. A *complete, general* equilibrium is one in which all the mutual influences have settled down into balance with each other.

So far we have been considering how wages would be determined in an economy in which perfect competition prevailed in both the product market and the factor market. But in these days when wages are largely settled by 'collective bargaining' between a Trade Union on one side and an employers' organisation on the other, the picture which the perfect competition model gives of the supply side of the labour market is no longer realistic. We have to turn instead, as we shall do in the next chapter, to a study of the bargaining process, in which, instead of a balance achieved automatically and impersonally by the pressures of thousands of individual workers and firms, we see a diplomatic contest between two parties only.

The demand side, on the other hand, remains essentially what our foregoing picture showed. In the long run, it will not pay any firm to employ so much of any factor that the marginal unit of this factor adds less to revenue than to cost. It remains for us in this section to broaden a little the idea of the 'marginal productivity' of a factor of production.

Suppose that instead of being one firm among thousands all selling a product which is uniform to all consumers, none caring from which firm his own supply comes, a firm has a distinctive product of its own. This product may differ technically, in its material form or constitution, from all similar products; or it may differ in the location of the source of supply, the factory or shop which sells it; or it may differ in the personality of those who sell it, a pound of sugar sold by a genial grocer being different from a pound sold by a sour one; or it may differ merely by bearing a brand name or a trade mark. So long as it differs at all, in any respect which marks it out in some buyers' minds as distinctive, the firm which makes it will have a *monopoly* of the supply of this particular product, strictly defined. Not, indeed, a monopoly which will enable the firm to charge any price it likes; for if one brand of tea or tobacco rose sharply in price many people would turn to other brands; but for a moderate rise in price, not all buyers will desert the firm, it will retain some faithful customers; and for a moderate fall in price not all the customers of other firms will desert them and rush to this one.

The consequence of this is that in a market where 'imperfect' or 'monopolistic' competition prevails, a firm has not an unlimited market in which it can sell no matter how large an output, within its practicable range, at a going market price; to sell appreciably more, it will have to lower its price, and if it markedly reduces its output, it will be able to charge a higher price. This situation modifies in an important way what we mean by the 'value productivity' of a marginal unit of a factor of production. For suppose that by taking on one extra man a firm can increase its weekly output from 100 units to 105 units, but that in order to sell 105 units the price must be lowered from £1 to 19s. 6d. The output of 100 units selling at £1 each brought in a weekly revenue of £100. The output of 105 units selling at 19s. 6d. each will bring in a weekly revenue of £102. 7s. 6d. The difference made by one extra man to the value of weekly output is no longer the same thing as the value of the difference he makes to physical weekly output. The former is £102. 7s. 6d. less £100, that is, £2. 7s. 6d. The latter is the £4. 17s. 6d. for which five units sell when 105 units are being sold each week altogether. It is, of course, the £2. 7s. 6d. which matters to the firm in this case. This *marginal value product* is what the firm can afford, in this situation, to pay the marginal man. Only if men could be hired for a weekly wage of £2. 7s. 6d. would it pay the firm to employ so many of them in conjunction with its present equipment of buildings and machines.

Chapter 18. Bargaining

SUPPOSE that I am the possessor of a certain painting by an artist of whose pictures you, amongst all the wealthy collectors, are by far the warmest admirer. You wish to buy my picture and I am willing, in principle, to part with it. But how can the price be settled? There is here no question of price emerging ready-made from the impersonal forces of a perfectly competitive market. There is, by assumption, no effective competition amongst buyers, for you, wealthy and enthusiastic, are able and willing to ignore rivals. There is no competition at all amongst sellers, for the painting is unique, and I am the sole possessor of it. This situation, where a single potential seller confronts a single potential buyer, is usually known (not very felicitously) as 'bilateral monopoly'. It is at a far extreme from perfect competition, for instead of a great swarm of sellers and buyers, each of whom treats all the others as part of an impersonal environment which cannot be influenced by himself, we have two men face-to-face, each addressing his offers to the other alone, each having the other's gaze concentrated, as it were, upon himself.

There will be some level below which any price for the painting would at best buy things which I value less than I value the painting for its own sake. This will be the very lowest price I shall in any circumstances accept, an absolute minimum. And there will be some level above which any price would buy for you things which you would rather have than the painting. This will be the very highest price which you will in any circumstances give, an absolute maximum. If it becomes apparent that my lowest price is higher than your highest price, there is an end of the matter. No deal can be done. If it should appear that, by a remarkable coincidence, my lowest price and your highest price are equal, we can agree there and then without ado. But suppose my lowest price is lower than your highest price. Then there is what F. Y. Edgeworth named a *contract zone*, a range of possible prices affording room for *bargaining*.

Now Edgeworth declared that when there is a contract zone, the price in bilateral monopoly is 'indeterminate'. Since we often observe that in such situations a bargain is actually struck, and necessarily at some particular price, how are we to interpret Edgeworth's assertion? It can be understood to mean that if we possess only such information as is properly the concern of the economist, namely facts about the tastes and the resources of each of the two parties, we cannot deduce what the agreed price will turn out to be. The question which then presents itself is whether it is reasonable to draw the boundary of economics where it excludes the facts needed to show why and how a particular price is arrived at. What kind of extra information would make the price deducible or 'determinate'?

Plainly the seller would like the price to be as high as possible and the buyer would like it to be as low as possible; and since it is not in the grip of an impersonal and inexorable market, there is in the abstract the possibility for one or other of them to push the price in the direction he desires. However, if the buyer, for example, knows what is the ultimate lowest price that the seller will accept, and if the seller by contrast can find out nothing about the buyer's absolute maximum price, the latter will be able to secure the picture at the seller's minimum. The one bargainer's advantage in such a case (it might just as easily belong to the seller) lies in his adversary's ignorance, in his own success in concealing his own real extreme price.

It seems plain, then, that the third category of information that we need, besides facts about the two bargainers' tastes and resources, is facts about their knowledge or beliefs. If we knew what each man believes about the other's tastes, intentions and beliefs, then we might perhaps have some ground for claiming that the price that would ultimately emerge from the series of offers and counter-offers that compose the actual bargaining process, would be capable of being deduced.

'The price that will emerge....' But is it certain that some price will actually be agreed on? There is another possible outcome of a bargaining process, namely its breakdown and abandonment, one or both parties 'walking out'. In what circumstances will this happen? We might be inclined to say: only when the process of offer and counter-offer reveals the absence of any contract zone. For surely, if the buyer's maximum price is higher than the seller's minimum price, it will be advantageous to both of them to agree on some price within the zone? This is the answer which Edgeworth and many others seem to imply; yet we cannot accept it.

If each of the two bargainers knew that he would never again be engaged in a negotiation, then the gain or loss to be had from the present particular negotiation might consist solely in the securing of a high price for the painting or the painting for a low price. But when a bargainer thinks it possible that the present instance of bargaining will be followed by others in the future, he must bring into his reckoning of gain or loss the effect that his present 'toughness' or its opposite will have on his reputation as a negotiator, and thus on his success in future negotiations. If we suppose that, before he begins the interchange of bids, the seller, for example, makes a plan for the conduct of his side of the negotiations, this plan may specify the price that he will initially ask for his painting and also the lowest price he will accept. In selecting these two prices, the seller may have regard to the largest descent he can make from one to the other without injuring his prestige and reputation, without 'loss of face' as a bargainer. To make a larger descent than this would stamp him, he may suppose, as one who does not mean what he says. The buyer, too, may have a plan prescribing his initial bid and his maximum ascent from it. The initial offers will sometimes be designed to give scope for a possible concessiveness on the part of the other bargainer: the seller, for example, cannot hope to get a higher price than the one he first suggests, and so he will have an inducement to start with a high asking price. Thus the two initial prices may be far apart, and too far for the largest concessions, which the bargainers are respectively willing to make, to bring about an overlap and an *effective* contract zone.

In sum, it may be claimed that when economics takes account of the knowledge and expectations in the minds of bargainers, and of their reactions to the uncertainty bound up with those expectations, the outcome of a bargaining situation is no longer, in principle, indeterminate; and when economics takes account of the bargainers' desire not to lose prestige and reputation through making too great and too easy concessions in the process of probing each other's minds for knowledge of their contents, it is no longer plain that the existence of a contract zone guarantees that a bargain will actually be struck; the negotiation may, instead, break down.

If we were bold enough to try to re-express Edgeworth's attitude to bilateral monopoly in terms acceptable (though all too vague) to the economist of eighty years after, we might say that bilateral monopoly does not fit into the frame of static analysis. It belongs to a scheme of thought involving *time* in other than a purely passive, empty, unreal and nominal sense. Here we must speak of the *expectations* of the bargainers, their thoughts looking to the future and forming of it images which are mutually contradictory and amongst which they cannot choose with certainty. We must discuss the *successive moves* by which they seek to explore each other's minds. We are concerned with time in each of two quite different senses, neither of them 'empty': time as expectation-space, and time as event-space. Time in both these senses is foreign to the conception of static analysis, which studies attained states of affairs and not the process of attaining them.

Chapter 19. Rent

WHEN we look to the factor market for a theory of the distribution of income, we find its demand side dominated by a single principle, which tells a firm exactly where to stop when passing in review successively larger possible quantities, which it might employ, of some factor of production. When that quantity is reached, at which one extra unit of the factor would increase total cost by more than it would increase total revenue (sale-proceeds of output), that is the right quantity to employ. Plainly there is more to be said about the rule. Are revenue and cost to be measured per week or per year or over the whole expected life of the firm? But when such questions have been settled so as to agree with the particular meaning of 'net revenue' or 'profit' which the businessman has in mind as the thing he wishes to maximise, we have a cast-iron upper limit to the quantity of any factor which any firm, in given circumstances, will employ; or alternatively, a cast-iron upper limit to the price per unit of the factor which the firm will pay when it is employing a given quantity.

On the supply side the picture is not quite so easily summarised, for we find amongst the various categories of means of production great differences in the effectiveness of price increases in eliciting a larger supply. The effect of an increase in the hourly pay of workers is, on the one hand, to increase the quantities of goods which, at given prices of these goods, a man can buy with his marginal hour's earnings. But on the other hand it has the effect of increasing the earnings he gets from any given weekly number of hours' work, so that even if this number of hours is unchanged, the worker finds himself able to buy larger weekly quantities of goods. The marginal utility to him of goods whose weekly quantity has increased will be smaller than before, and so the utility of the marginal shilling of earnings of any given weekly number of hours will now be smaller than before. Will the increase of his hourly pay make him more eager or less eager than before to earn an extra hour's pay? An extra hour will now bring in more shillings than it would formerly have done, but each shilling now matters less. The upshot of these considerations is that we sometimes find a rise in the hourly wage-rate of a particular kind of worker actually reducing the number of weekly hours they are willing to work. This happens especially when some kind of workers have an habitual and settled pattern of life which they find fully satisfying. As soon as they have earned enough to afford, in addition to bare subsistence, the particular comforts and forms of entertainment that it consists of, they are little interested in earning more.

Whether they respond with a larger or a smaller supply of work to the offer of a higher wage, workers are at any rate not wholly insensitive to change of price. But nature is. However far men's ingenuity may go in adapting, reorganising, improving and exploiting what nature has provided, this ultimate provision will plainly always be indispensable. The most obvious of nature's gifts are comprised in the terrestrial planet as a habitable place. The earth's crust provides room for men's doings on its surface; chemical and biological powers in its soil, its streams and oceans and in the atmosphere and sunlight above it; and sources of minerals and of water-power. These things compose the chief part of what the economist means by 'land', those ultimate potentialities which only nature can furnish. Now nature disdains payment. To mankind as a whole, 'land' is by definition a pure gift. It is provided and maintained by nature free of all cost, and whether men would be willing to pay much or little for the use of any of the great variety of factors of production comprised in it, the quantity available (perhaps 'available' only to strenuous effort) of each such factor will remain unchanged. Why, then, should it be necessary for anyone to pay anything for the use of 'land'?

The reason is that, through a natural and universal human instinct tending to preserve the individual, the family and the race, land has been appropriated, and cannot legally be used except with the consent of its owners. A firm which has access to land, and can employ it in conjunction with materials, labour and machines, can produce goods which will sell for more than the sum of the payments which the firm has to make in order to get its materials, hire its labour and run and maintain its machines. The sale-proceeds or revenue from the firm's weekly or yearly output exceed its weekly or yearly expense for its factors of production other than land. This excess of market value of output over cost of output can only be secured provided the firm has access to land, to nature's powers which human beings have appropriated. The owners of the land can therefore hold the firms to ransom: they can demand a part or the whole of the surplus, as a condition of enabling the firm to earn the rest of its revenue. This payment to the landowners is rent.

There is much more to be said about rent, but before we proceed let us disclaim any intention of putting landowners in a pillory. To own land and to receive a rent for it is no more unnatural than to be a portrait painter of outstanding skill who can charge his clients £1000 for his paintings of them. His performance may cost him no more in time and nervous energy than the daubs of an amateur cost that amateur, so why should he get £1000 for his work while the other can get nothing? It is a rent. The large incomes which a rapturous public pays with overflowing goodwill to Menuhin, Markova or Olivier are largely rent, *rent of ability*, rent for gifts of nature or Providence which no pressure of demand can create or increase in supply.

Now this last sentence will raise in the reader's mind a query which we must deal with at once. Is it true that the available quantity of things falling under the heading 'land' cannot be increased? Cannot land in the literal geographical sense be reclaimed from sea or marsh or desert? Yes, but only in so far as there is something to reclaim. The gift of nature is the earth itself, with a surface partly dry and partly covered by water. These materials can by human effort be rearranged, and in so far as the result of such re-arrangement is more valuable than what we began with, the extra value can be ascribed to men's efforts and not nature's. In other words, the result of reclamation is only partly 'land' in the economist's sense. For the rest, it is man-made *equipment*. Anything that humanity produces for itself is not in the relevant sense a gift of nature. To extend the practical reach of the mind by electronic computers or to reclaim the desert by irrigation is to *replace* nature's efforts by men's own.

It is, then, the unresponsiveness of the total available quantity of some factor of production, to the offer of a higher price per unit, which accounts for the kind of income called rent. Rent must be paid by those who wish to use some of this factor, since those who own the factor will make it available to the highest bidder; and thus the would-be users must compete amongst themselves, offering such a price, and each securing such a quantity, that the marginal value product of this quantity is equal to the marginal cost of employing this quantity.

In the foregoing chapters for the most part we have assumed that firms *sell* their product in perfect competition with each other. To say that perfect competition prevails is to say that the number of competing firms, all selling a product uniform in every sense, is so large, and the proportion which any one firm represents of the whole industry is so small, that no firm can appreciably affect the size of the industry's total output by making any practicable change in its own output. In such circumstances any firm can sell as much of the product per time unit as it can possibly make and still it will not affect the price: price to the firm is given on the market and is independent of the firm's own output. Under perfect competition, then, the difference made to the value of the firm's output by increasing that output by one physical unit of product (sold per unit of time) is simply the market price of one unit of product. *Marginal product of value* and *value of the marginal physical product* are then equal. But suppose that the firm is one of only a few which compose the industry, or makes a product which is in some way distinctive and different from those of all other firms. Then in order to sell more the firm must lower its price, and the effect of increasing output by one unit will be, on the one hand, to add the value of this extra unit, at the new price, to the total value of output, and on the other to *reduce* the total value of output by the difference between the old and new prices multiplied by the old output. In this case the *marginal product of value* will be less than the *value of the marginal physical product*.

So much for the term 'marginal value product', 'marginal product of value', or 'marginal revenue product'. Whether or not it is equal to the value of the marginal physical product of a factor, the firm will only employ that factor in such quantity that the extra total cost due to employing the marginal unit of the factor is equal to the marginal value product of the factor. What will this extra cost consist of? If the factor in question is in *perfectly elastic supply*, that is to say, if the firm can obtain extra units of it at the same price per unit as it has hitherto been paying for a smaller quantity, then the marginal cost of the factor will simply be this prevailing, constant price per unit. But if the factor is in *imperfectly elastic supply*, if extra units can only be secured by paying a higher price per unit for all units employed, then the extra cost which must be laid at the door of the employment of these extra units will consist, not only of the price of these units themselves, but also of the difference between the new and old price of all the formerly employed units. Now if the firm produces only a small fraction of the total output of its product, it will also demand only a small fraction of the total supply of each necessary factor, and will thus be able to draw to itself extra units of this factor by a very small increase in the price per unit that it offers; but if the firm bulks large in an industry which is the sole user of the factor, it will have to offer a higher price in order to overcome the reluctance of the rest of the industry to part with some of the factor, which, when it is some kind of 'land', is by definition in perfectly inelastic total supply.

In either case we can formulate a general rule as follows: In equilibrium, every unit will be receiving one and the same rent; and this rent will be such that the *extra total rent*, which each firm pays because of the marginal unit of the factor that it employs, is just equal to that factor's marginal product of value.

Let us sum up as follows, using, for simplicity of wording without the loss of anything essential to our point, the assumption that all the firms are selling their products under perfect competition: When one of the necessary factors of production is some gift of nature, some form of 'land', whose total available quantity cannot be increased, it will command a price sufficient to make the firms that need it, all taken together, content with the amount which exists; content, because when they offer their product at a price equal to the resulting marginal cost of this product, the consuming public is content with the corresponding supply of the product.

If this particular kind of land is superabundant, the price it can command will be *nil*. But if it is 'scarce', if there is not enough in existence to serve every possible purpose completely, then it will command a price greater than zero, and this price, because the factor in question is provided and maintained in existence by nature without any human care or effort or expense, will be a rent.

Any factor of production belonging to the category 'land' will be needed by many different industries; that is to say, for the making of many different commodities. The rent which the owners of this factor receive will therefore serve a double purpose. It will equalise the quantity of this factor which all industries taken together demand, with the quantity of it which exists; and it will share out this existing quantity amongst the industries and amongst the firms in such a way that, with perfect competition in the product and factor markets, the existing quantity makes the most valuable contribution possible to the stream of goods of all kinds being produced by the economic system as a whole.

Amongst the factors of production, each strictly homogeneous, needed by the firms producing some commodity, there may be more than one whose total existing quantity is given and is quite unresponsive to changes in the price which the market will pay for it. Several such factors may together compose what we have called a 'category' of productive resources. For the farmer's purposes some types of land will be better than others. When all of the best land is in use any further increase of output of its product will cause the rent of this best land to rise, and ultimately, instead of securing a share of this best land for his own use by paying this high rent, a farmer will find it just as cheap to use a poorer quality of land from each acre of which given quantities of labour, machine services and fertiliser can only extract a comparatively small crop. So long as this 'second best' land is superabundant its owners can exact no rent for it; but the high price of the product, which has made even this poor land worth cultivating, will mean that the better land, each acre of which with given quantities of collaborating factors yields a large crop, and therefore, so far as the expense of those factors is concerned, a relatively cheap one, will command a rent greater than zero, a 'rent of differential fertility'. David Ricardo, writing in the years immediately after Waterloo, showed that it is not the high quality of the best land, but its limited quantity, which enables it to earn a rent. Soil so poor that the cost of cultivation is barely covered by any crop that can be raised on it earns no rent. Between the best land of all, and the worst which is just worth cultivating, there can be many grades earning various levels of rent. The price of the crop will stand at a level where the quantity annually demanded at that price can be supplied by land worth cultivating at that price. Thus the stronger the demand, the poorer will be the land just worth cultivating at a zero rent and the higher the rent on better land.

The two essential characteristics of rent are:

(1) The factor of production, whose owners receive rent, would exist and continue to exist even if no rent were paid. Rent is a payment not necessary to maintain this factor of production in existence.

(2) Rent can be exacted because the existing quantity of this factor of production does not increase in response to the offer of higher pay per unit employed, and because this existing quantity

Rent

is insufficient to meet all the needs that would appear if the factor were available free.

The category of factors of production whose owners receive rent is called *land*. The reason is plain: land in the ordinary sense offers the most obvious examples of factors of production whose supply is inelastic to changes in their price. Of what category of factors exclusively is this total unresponsiveness true by definition? It is true only of gifts of nature. Anything that man has a hand in may be influenced by price: nature alone is impervious to payment.

None the less there are some man-made productive facilities whose total existing quantity can only be increased with long delay. In the short period, before there has been time to increase these facilities, their existing quantity will remain unchanged in spite of price rises. Thus in the short period their owners will be able to exact a sort of rent, what Alfred Marshall called *quasi-rent*. Machines, buildings and engineering works which take a long time to construct fall into this class, and part at least of the 'profit' obtained by their use is quasi-rent in this sense.

From the point of view of the individual employer of factors of production, rent is not an important idea. It is a payment which he cannot escape if he wishes to employ certain quantities of certain factors. In this it is on the same footing as wages or as interest on borrowed money. The quantity of 'land' of this kind or that which it will pay him to employ will be determined in just the same way as the optimal quantity of labour.

The idea of rent is only important from the point of view of the economy as a whole. If those who have political power declare the receipt of rent to be unjust, they can impose a tax on this form of income, and by the nature of rent those who receive this income will not be able to escape the tax. For rent does not help to keep any factor of production in existence. In so far as the landlord's income is payment for the use of facilities he himself maintains in existence, the farm buildings, the drainage of the fields, the shelter provided by belts of trees, it is *not* rent. Tax *that* income away, and he will let the farm buildings fall into ruin, the drains silt up, the trees be cut down and sold. Rent is linked only with the gifts of nature.

Chapter 20. Profit

IN Alfred Marshall's day it was perfectly easy to see profit as a natural and essential element of the competitive mechanism by which a free-enterprise economy allocated resources according to tastes so as to maximise satisfaction. It was not even necessary to ask 'Whose satisfaction?' Profits were made by those enterprises which most efficiently, exactly and imaginatively served the needs of the people as a whole. The people as a whole had the power to confer or withhold profit, because they had the income to spend. They spent it where they could most cheaply obtain the goods they most ardently desired, and it was the firms who supplied these goods at least cost who made, for a time, the high profits. Only for a time, for it was part of the role of profit to attract more resources into a high-profit industry so that the people as a whole could have more of the goods they desired and have them more cheaply still. The entry of additional firms into the industry increased the output and reduced the price, thus benefiting the people as a whole, and if in the process these firms were able to reap some temporary gains, over and above the minimum needed to induce them to *stay* in the industry, they had deserved these gains, which might very likely be 'ploughed back' into the industry to help enlarge it.

If anyone invented a new technique by which an existing commodity could be produced more cheaply than before, he also made, and deserved, a temporary high profit, for until fresh investment had enabled all the firms in the industry to be equipped with the new machines, he could undersell them.

In short, profit steered resources where they were wanted, or were going to be wanted, and at the same time rewarded those whose special foresight or energy had put them in the vanguard of the movement to satisfy a growing want, or to satisfy an existing want better, or even to create a new want. And it also rewarded those whose luck had placed them in this favourable position; and this also was a deserved reward, for to be ready to trust one's capital to luck was again part of the free-enterprise system; without such readiness, resources would have been far less mobile, there would have been far less 'enterprise' or none at all. Luck, too, was a factor of production.

So profit, in Marshallian economics, was the reward of a factor of production, or of a bundle of factors collected under the name of enterprise. Along with land, labour and capital there was a need for all that 'enterprise' stood for: imagination, daring, ambition, energy, organising power, managerial capacity, and patience. These, successfully applied, earned profit; and the fact that they had been successful meant that they had served a need of the community as a whole. They had enabled *somebody* to be given what he wanted; and even if what he wanted was diamonds and champagne, with which the greater part of mankind are not concerned, still, the fact that he could afford these things meant that he had supplied other people with what *they* wanted, so that, at one remove, the original profit was serving the economy well.

The chief analytical defect of this conception of profit is its failure to distinguish between what is expected or hopefully imagined, and what is realised in recorded fact. It is not the recorded profit itself of an interval already past that directly induces a business man to invest his capital in buying the equipment to start a new firm or to extend or modernise an existing one. If he decides thus to invest his capital rather than keep it in the bank, if he decides upon one project rather than another, he does so because of the future profit that he can visualise, with more or less vividness and sense of realism, as a possible consequence of such investment. These imagined consequences or expectations may indeed spring from his contemplation of past profits gained by others or by himself, in enterprises which had some features in common with the one he now proposes. But that is not to treat the expected and the past profit as the same thing, which conceptually they cannot be. Past profit is known, a recorded fact; expected profit is a creation of the mind, in essence no more than a conjecture, however subtle and exhaustive the comparisons which the enterpriser has made between the circumstances of past success or failure and his apparent situation at the moment of deciding. Thus profit, in some meaning of the word, may be a reward for what the enterpriser has done; and profit, in some sense of this word, may be what induces him to take some course of action; but these two meanings of the word are essentially and radically different. Recognition of this difference need not stop us from believing that realised profit, in, for example, an industry whose product is rapidly conquering new markets, may create in the minds of men with capital at their command vivid hopes of making similar gains for themselves by founding fresh firms in that industry. In such a case profit facts and profit expectations, one springing from the other, are working together to perform just such a function as the Marshallian theory visualises.

When we go on to ask what it is in the nature or character of a real economy, which gives scope and possibility for profit expectations and for the occurrence of recorded profit, the main answer cannot be in doubt. In a world where everybody knew for certain, before he committed himself to any productive expenses, at what price he would be able to sell any given quantity of any product he chose to name; and also knew for certain what quantities of what factors, applied according to what time-schedule, with a given and known system of interest-rates, would enable him to produce that quantity of that product most cheaply, there would be no room for hope or fear, or for guesswork of any kind, about the financial outcome of productive operations. Everyone would know exactly what income he would gain by doing this or that; all incomes would, in effect, have the status of contractual incomes; and no one could be induced to embark on any venture by the pictures he could conjure up of what 'might' be its outcome. There would be no uncertainty, and therefore no freedom of imagination. It is in a world which contrasts utterly with the picture which we have just drawn, that profit in both senses can exist. In the real world there is in the inescapable nature of things a time-gap between the moment when an enterpriser decides to put some good upon the market in some specified quantities, and the moment when those quantities of that good actually appear before the eyes of potential buyers. During that time-gap things will happen that no man can foresee, altering the market conditions, changing the environment of taste, fashion and technique in which those goods will have to be used. They may thus be rendered less desirable than seemed likely when resources were committed to their production, or they may become even more urgently in demand. This unavoidable time-gap thus brings in an unavoidable uncertainty, and it is that uncertainty which gives room for profit expectations, and which also inhibits some of those businessmen, who are in some degree tempted by the recorded profits of others to launch themselves in a particular industry, from doing so; by thus restricting the number of firms in particular industries, the uncertainty which is felt to inhere in those industries tends to make their products specially scarce and valuable, and thus may tend to generate in those industries *recorded* profits which go some way to justify the hopes of those enterprisers who were bold enough to venture in them.

Economic theory has a strong and natural preference for dealing in what the mathematicians call 'scalar' quantities, plain numbers of tons, litres, kilowatts, dollars and so on. So ingrained and seductive is this practice, that economists have usually treated in this same way *expected profit*. They have indeed recognised that profit expectations are entertained in bundles, one bundle for each enterprise or course of action, and some of them have even gone so far as to acknowledge that the members within any one of these bundles are mutually exclusive hypotheses only one of which, at most, can be true. But how can one make sense of a bundle of mutually exclusive hypotheses? Some selective principle seems necessary, by which one or a few members of such a bundle can be allowed to shoulder aside all the others and claim exclusive influence on the individual's assessment of the particular enterprise or course of action in question, as a step in his comparison of this course with others which are open to him, and his ultimate decision amongst them. Such a selective principle must, in effect, consist in assigning to each hypothesis in the bundle some number stating, not the content or 'face-value' of the hypothesis, not, that is to say, the tale it tells, but its claim to be taken seriously, its respectability or plausibility. Thus each hypothesis concerning, say, the future profit which some defined enterprise will earn ceases to be representable as a scalar number and becomes a 'vector' or a 'point', like a geographical 'fix' stated by means of a pair of numbers, latitude and longitude. When several such vectors are involved we have departed still further from the simple notion of a scalar number representing 'expected profit'. The truth is that the concept of uncertain expectations is quite alien to the static economic model with which our first four Books are mainly concerned. We have had, in this chapter, to depart from that model in order to give some degree of completeness to our account of the distribution of income. In Books v (*Employment*) and vi (*Finance*) we shall turn to a different model where the concept of expectation is central.

Chapter 21. *Distribution*

H o w it is that, out of the whole income of an economic system in particular circumstances, the workers all taken together get just so much; the landowners just so much; the owners of equipment, or lenders of the money to buy it with, just so much; and the enterprisers, those who assemble and direct the other factors of production in pursuit of profit, so much: this is what the theory of distribution seeks to explain. We have seen how, in a freely competitive economy, the pricing of the various factors of production will be a part of the process by which all the 'variables' of the system will tend to achieve a general, comprehensive balance or equilibrium. These variables include the prices and the outputs of all products, the prices and the quantities supplied per time-unit of all productive services, and the rates of interest on loans of money. A firm which both sells its product and buys its productive services in perfectly competitive markets will find it profitable to employ each factor of production in just such quantity as will make the wage or other rate of pay per unit of factor equal to the market value of the marginal physical product of that factor. That is to say, just so many units of the factor will be employed that, if one were withdrawn, the difference so made to the physical quantity of weekly output would have a value equal to the weekly pay of one unit of the factor. Factors are thus said to be paid at a rate equal to the value of their marginal product. Now we saw that general equilibrium of the whole economic system implies amongst many other things that every unit of any one factor of production is paid at the same rate no matter which firm in which industry employs it. If so, then we can take this universal rate of pay of the factor of production, multiply it by the number of units employed in the economic system as a whole, and thus obtain the income going to those who supply that factor of production. At first glance we might be inclined to say that the problem of the distribution of income is solved, at least in main principle. But there is a vital question still to be answered.

The output of any firm selling in perfect competition will have a certain market value. That value, in equilibrium, is the sole source of pay for all the factors employed by the firm. If every factor is paid at a rate equal to the value of its marginal product, will there be enough to go round? Or will the market value of output fall short of the total costs of all the factors, so that it is impossible to pay each unit of every factor the value of the marginal product of that factor? Or will there be something left over, some income undisposed of, after all the factors have been paid at a rate equal to the value of their marginal products? This is the famous 'adding-up' problem, still lacking a tidy and complete solution after nearly seventy years. None the less, the marginal-productivity principle does account for the distribution of the whole of the income available, and only what is available, in an important and central class of cases, and so provides us with a fixed base from which to explore other cases and their difficulties.

Let us remind ourselves that we are assuming perfect competition in both the product market and the factor markets of our firm. By this assumption we eliminate all difficulties which might arise from a change of price being associated with a change of quantity. We are free, indifferently, to measure output, and also the quantity employed of each factor of production, in physical or in value terms. With this assumption, everything turns upon the relation between the physical quantities of factors employed, on the one hand, and the physical quantity of output produced, on the other; the relationship which we call the firm's *production function*. If this production function has a certain character, the adding-up problem is solved.

We shall not be able, within the boundary of the purely verbal arguments we are allowing ourselves, to offer a convincing proof of the proposition we now put forward, namely, that if when the employed quantity of *every* factor of production is doubled, trebled, etc., the output too is thus respectively doubled, trebled, etc.; and if when any one factor *alone* is increased in quantity, against a background of fixed quantities of other factors, its marginal product diminishes; then when every employed unit of each factor is paid at the rate of the marginal product of that factor, the whole output will be just and only just exhausted. The proposition can be technically expressed by saying that, if the firm's production function shows *constant returns to scale* and *diminishing returns to each separate factor*, the product will be precisely exhausted when each factor is paid at the rate of its marginal product. Leaving this statement without proof, we turn to the question whether or when it is possible for the firm to have such a production function.

If, amongst the factors of production employed by the firm, we really include every kind of circumstance or influence that can conceivably affect the size of the firm's output, then it seems plain that if a given set of quantities of these factors can produce so-and-so much of the product per unit of time, a second precisely similar set will produce just the same quantity of product; so that by doubling the 'scale' of production we shall have doubled the output; and similarly if we treble the scale we shall treble the output, and so on. Thus the real question is, can we reasonably suppose a firm to be able to 'double the quantity applied' of every conceivable thing which might govern the size of output? Does the idea of doubling or trebling, etc., always in this context have a clear meaning?

In the real world, one of the things which affects the firm's output is the work of the businessman who directs and manages the firm. Will he be able to employ each man and machine as effectively when there are a thousand of each as when there are only a hundred? Can he make his own efforts match the increase in size of operations by working longer hours, or has he perhaps at the small size a large reserve of nervous energy which can come into play when needed? Or will the increase in scale reduce the attention, time and care he can give to each question so that large operations will be conducted with less grasp and skill than small ones, and decreasing efficiency will accompany increase of size? These questions suggest that the idea of *quantity* is inappropriate or insufficient when we are dealing with some of the circumstances affecting production. If there are 'factors of production' whose quantity we cannot measure or even assign any precise meaning to, the argument by which we sought to show that production is always inevitably carried on under 'constant returns to scale' loses its cogency. We are driven to confine the notion of 'production function' to those factors, influences or circumstances which can be looked upon as quantitative. But, of course, when we consciously leave some factors outside the production function, there is no reason why those which are still included in it should be subject to 'constant returns to scale'. If I have a recipe for a cake, which requires a pound of butter for every six eggs, and I use only a pound of sugar no matter whether I am putting in six eggs and one pound of butter or thirty eggs and five pounds of butter, the large cake will not taste the same as the small one.

The businessman who directs the firm can, then, perhaps best be regarded as part of the fixed background of the firm's operations. During a period of years he remains the same person with the same tastes and capacities. These will be drawn upon in different ways and to a greater or less extent according to the scale of the rest of the firm, the quantities employed of the various factors of production other than himself; but his influence on the firm's output will be rather like the influence exerted by the shape of a river channel upon the quantity of water carried into the sea per minute. Heavy rain (large quantities of other factors) will swell the current, but it will be constricted by the shape of the river bed and even if it flows faster its volume per minute may not increase in the same proportion as the rainfall. On the other hand, as the stream rises it may find release in flooding the surrounding valley and thus the rate of flow into the sea may be greatly increased. We cannot say *a priori* whether the businessman will act as a 'bottleneck' or whether his powers will be economised and given greater leverage and scope as the scale of operations increases; but at any rate it is easy, with these considerations in mind, to understand why we may find departures from the position envisaged by general equilibrium, where every factor is being paid at a rate clearly representing the value of its marginal product.

Other things besides the businessman's own character and capacity help to compose the environment within which the other factors collaborate and which determines whether the firm will experience 'economies of large scale' or 'diseconomies of large scale'. An even more important matter is the character of its durable equipment. If, like a railway, the firm cannot operate at all without a very costly and elaborate system of equipment with a large capacity, a small output or traffic, having to bear the whole cost of maintaining and operating this great system, will have a high cost per unit, and as the throughput of the firm increases, the wider spreading of overhead costs will make production far more economical. In strictness we ought not to call the more intensive use of a factor of production temporarily fixed in size an increase of *scale*, for that term really means the increase of *all* factors in equal proportions. But the 'indivisibility' of some items of equipment, the fact that, in the short period (and here we depart from the strict study of general equilibrium, which is a long-period concept) their size is ideal only for one particular output and cannot readily be changed, plainly provides yet another explanation of departures from the perfect matching of total revenue and total factor costs.

In this chapter we have been concerned in the main with a proposition belonging properly to long-period general equilibrium, the state of ultimate perfect mutual adjustment of all economic pressures in a supposedly unchanging environment. So long as we confine ourselves to this abstract conception, we need not be troubled by the fact that the 'businessman', the director and manager of the firm, is not a factor of production amenable, like the others, to quantitative measurement, and that therefore he does not fit into the idea of a production function giving constant returns to scale and diminishing returns to each separate factor, such as provides just enough and only just enough output to pay each factor at the rate equivalent to its marginal productivity. We need not be troubled, because in an unchanging environment where perfect adjustment has been already achieved by assumption, there will be nothing for a businessman to do, and the firm can be looked upon as simply a set of quantities of the other factors ideally adjusted to each other in the general circumstances of the economic system as a whole.

Indeed, if it were not for one thing, we could claim that in long-period general static equilibrium with perfect competition in all product and factor markets the problem of distribution is solved by the notion of a so-called 'linear and homogeneous' production function, that is, a production function of the kind we have been discussing. The unfortunate difficulty is that the two parts of this condition, under which the solution would be attained, are incompatible with each other. For if we had both a linear homogeneous production function, and perfect competition in all product and factor markets, there would be nothing to limit the size of firms. A firm's output would be saleable at a given price no matter how large it became. But it could become indefinitely large without any increase in cost per unit, because the physical size of output could be doubled, trebled, etc., by simply doubling, trebling, etc., the quantities of all factors, and these factors of production could all be obtained in unlimited quantities without increase in price per unit, because we have assumed perfectly competitive factor markets. Marginal and average cost of any product would thus each be uniform for all outputs and equal to each other, while the market price of the product would also be uniform for all outputs. If this market price of the product were equal to or greater than its cost per unit, there would be no limit to the net revenue which the firm would secure by an indefinitely great expansion of its scale.

The difficulty has been resolved by a beautiful and incisive stroke of analysis. We said that the production function must have a character such as gives constant returns to scale. But it need only do so at that particular output which the firm actually adopts. Provided that a small percentage increase or decrease of scale in the neighbourhood of this actually chosen output would increase or decrease output by the same percentage, the fact that larger changes would have a different effect is of no consequence from our point of view. This, as we shall see in a moment, frees us from our dilemma. But is there any reason at all why the firm should choose to operate at just that output which satisfies the condition? Is it certain, even, that there will be such an output? There are excellent reasons why we can say 'yes' to both questions. For if there is a particular output which makes the average unit cost of the product less than it would be at slightly smaller or slightly larger outputs, then we can call this a point of minimum average cost. As we pass in review successive possible sizes of output, each a little larger than the last, the average unit cost, we can reasonably suppose, will decline smoothly towards such a minimum, pass through it with a brief interval where the average cost is the same for all of a group of nearly equal outputs, and then rise smoothly from it as we pass on to larger and larger outputs in excess of that which makes average cost a minimum. Now if, when we pass from one to another of a small group of nearly equal outputs around the one which gives minimum average cost, the average cost does not change, this means that with each movement from one of these outputs to another, the *total* cost is increasing in precisely the same percentage as the total output. We are assuming that the upward steps in output are brought about by upward steps in scale, that is, in every factor of production by mutually equal proportions; and we are assuming that these factors of production are bought in perfectly competitive factor markets where their prices remain unchanged no matter what quantity is bought. Thus a given percentage increase in total cost represents the same percentage increase in scale, and this in turn brings about the same percentage increase in output; always provided we remain in the close neighbourhood of the point of minimum average cost. But *why should* the firm, let us now repeat the question, remain in this neighbourhood? Because in long-period general equilibrium, the price of the product will have sunk to a level where each firm can only just cover its costs by producing at that output which makes average unit cost a minimum. In short, the production function *can* be of a character which, at the relevant output, gives constant returns to scale; and yet at the same time it can be true, because of some *essentially* 'indivisible' factor of production, that output can neither be greatly smaller nor greatly larger without a rise of average cost.

It can fairly be claimed that for the abstract model of general long-period equilibrium in a freely competitive economy, the problem of how the economy's total income is shared out amongst those who contribute to its making is solved. It is solved by the theory whose central ideas are, first, payment of each factor at a rate equivalent to its marginal productivity, and secondly, the universal prevalence of production functions which give constant returns to scale and diminishing returns to each separate factor. This model, however, differs greatly from the real world in some vital respects. Corresponding to these differences there are income-shares of kinds which make no appearance in the model, and which we must consider briefly in the remainder of this chapter.

The most fundamental way in which the model departs from the real world is in its neglect of unforeseeable change and of the uncertainty which therefore clouds the businessman's calculations, giving rise to pure 'profit' in the sense discussed in the preceding chapter. A second and also very important difference is that the model assumes perfect competition throughout the economy, whereas in the real world many markets consist of firms whose position has aspects of monopoly or of 'oligopoly', 'fewness of sellers'.

When there are no obstacles at all to the setting-up of new firms in any industry where, for the time being, total revenue is greater than total cost, we must suppose that such firms will be established in sufficient number, and with a sufficient total capacity, to bring down the price of the product to equality with its average cost. When this has happened in every industry in such a way that everywhere marginal revenue, marginal cost, average revenue and average cost are all four of them equal, we shall have the full general-equilibrium situation. Many different things, however, can in practice destroy this freedom of entry for new firms. Existing firms may possess all the known sources of supply of some raw material vital to the industry, or all the suitable land; or they may have the legal right to exclusive use of some invention; or some piece of equipment indispensable to each firm in the industry may be so expensive, that a new firm will find it difficult to borrow enough money to pay for such an item; or, most radical of all reasons, the would-be establisher of such a firm, though seeing already existing firms earning high profits, may feel unsure whether his own new firm would emulate them. In any such case, the situation will be reached where the excess of total revenue over total cost, which prospective firms have some ground for hoping they might earn, is no longer big enough to induce any more firms to overcome the obstacles. Then the existing firms which compose the industry can continue, so long as the barrier to new entrants remains, to earn a net revenue greater than zero.

The word 'profit' has unfortunately been applied in the literature of economics to a great many widely distinct ideas. Some of these meanings we examined in the preceding chapter. Two of these ideas are in especial need of names which they can keep exclusively for their own use, and until special terms are invented for them, they have perhaps the best claim on the word 'profit'. These two ideas are both connected with the uncertainty and the risk which are inevitably present when resources are committed to the making of a specialised product long in advance of the time when that product will be sold or put to use. During that interval, circumstances of all sorts, needs, tastes, knowledge and the prices and available quantities of other goods can change in ways which it was impossible to foresee with certainty and exactness at the beginning. These unforeseeable changes may make the goods, when they are ready for use or sale, more valuable or less valuable than the factors of production which were committed to their manufacture. The hope of gain from this source, supported by the belief that the corresponding fear of loss will have deterred some potential producers and will thus have restricted the total supply of the product, is one meaning of 'profit'. If such a gain is actually realised, that is the second of our two meanings of profit. Profit of this kind is plainly a type of income which static-equilibrium theory cannot cover.

Economics as a systematic study dates from the middle of the eighteenth century. Amongst the problems which engrossed the early economists, distribution of income was pre-eminent. To them it appeared obvious that the nation was composed of unmistakable classes, labourers, landowners and those who owned and directed firms of which the chief tangible sign was a stock of equipment. The question was, how did the whole produce that resulted from bringing together land, labourers and equipment come to be shared out in certain proportions amongst those classes of owners of these means of production? No real answer was given to this question until, in the last third of the nineteenth century, the modern theory of value showed that prices, costs, outputs and incomes are all explained and accounted for together by one and the same unified body of principles, which nowadays we call the theory of 'value and distribution'. Productive services are goods sold on a market just as truly as consumers' goods are, and the principle which explains the pricing of the latter must in logic apply equally well to the former. In so far as we are satisfied with a static analysis, one from which change and uncertainty are excluded by assumption, we do not need a separate theory of distribution: we need only show how the very same fundamental ideas, the ideas of 'making the most' of limited means of satisfaction or production, of equalising the marginal effectiveness of any one means in all its possible distinct uses, and of equalising the marginal effectiveness of expenditure on different means, can be applied equally well to explain the pricing of productive services and their conditions of supply, as to explain the prices and outputs of products. This was the position to which the theory of distribution was carried by Philip Wicksteed and others in the early 1890's. If his account is less satisfying now than then, that is because the assumption of universal perfect competition, on which the full Wicksteedian theory depends, is even less realistic now than in his day; and because in the unsettled and racking years of the twentieth century, it has become impossible to be content with an analysis which assumes away the unforeseeable future.

BOOK V. EMPLOYMENT

Chapter 22. Saving

IN Chapter 13 (*Outlay*) we saw that when all the people in a self-contained economic system, taken together, use up by eating, wearing, burning and so on, a smaller money value of goods in some particular month than the money value of the transformations of things into more useful forms or places, that are effected in that month, the difference between these two money values measures the net amount by which the economy's total store of wealth has been increased in that month. Now those who compile figures about these processes cannot really peer through the windows of people's houses to see what proportion of the ton of coal they bought at the beginning of the month has actually been burnt by the end of the month, or how much of the bag of sugar or the sack of potatoes remains as an addition to the community's wealth (though stored in the domestic larder instead of the warehouse or farm loft). Moreover, the grocer or the farmer is just as pleased when his goods have been sold to the ultimate consumer, no matter whether that consumer eats them at once or puts them into temporary store. The grocer or the farmer, in these circumstances, does not inquire the consumer's intentions but says to himself 'I must replenish the shelves', and proceeds to order more sugar or plant more potatoes. So for practical reasons economists are in the habit of treating purchases of consumable goods by consumers as the measure of the actual consumption of such goods by consumers; and this practice is justified, even from the viewpoint of theoretical analysis, by the fact that the *purchases* are the only things which the tradesman, the organiser of production, can observe and the only fact (on the demand side) on which he can base his judgment about how much to produce.

Employment

On the side of production we have also a small cautionary point to make. We saw in Chapter 12 (*Income*) that in order to be able to claim that a loaf of bread has been produced, we must make sure that the flour which the baker used and the coal he burnt have been replaced in his stores, and that the wheat the miller ground to make this flour, and the crop the farmer harvested to yield that wheat, have all been replaced at their respective 'stages of production'. Not only so, but the wear and tear of the milling machinery and of the farmer's ploughs and harvesters must be made good. So even if we saw in a certain economy that the building of ploughs and machinery of all sorts was going on, we should not in this fact alone have evidence that wealth was being accumulated. All the tools, instruments and machines, or as we can comprehensively say, all the *equipment*, however durable, that is required merely to *replace* or make good the wear and tear of what is concurrently being destroyed in the total process of production of consumable goods, is paid for by the *consumer* and its cost comes out of the money he hands over the counter. It is only when the businessman, the head of the firm, buys *more* of some requirement of production than he is currently using up, that there is a net accumulation of fresh wealth.

Thus, then, we come back to the picture of several concurrent processes fitting together to make the broad pattern of economic life. There are, in the first place, the two 'real' processes: the creation of fresh usefulness by growing, gathering, fashioning, assembling, transporting and storing goods, and the destruction of usefulness in actual use of such goods. These we call briefly production and consumption. Corresponding to each of these there is a monetary process. To production there corresponds the paying out, to the owners of factors of production, of the value of the services of these factors. These payments, looked at from the viewpoint of those who make them, are costs of production, but looked at from the viewpoint of those who receive them, they are incomes. When we add together all these 'factor incomes' in all their various forms—wages, salaries, rents, interest, dividends and undistributed profits—we have the total value of production per unit interval of time (the interval has, of course, to be the same as that in which incomes are measured). Corresponding to consumption there is the spending of money in shops, theatres, buses and so on by private people, and the spending by the central and local governments of some of the money which they have taken from the people in taxes, and which they are using to pay for the services of airmen, policemen, judges, school teachers, doctors and so on. The benefits of being defended from foreign enemies, protected from robbery, educated and medically cared for and so on are a form of consumption.

It is of course the real processes of production and consumption that vitally and directly matter to us, but without the monetary processes, the real ones could never be organised and carried on in the way they are. The monetary processes, by putting a money price on each item of productive service or consumable goods exchanged in the course of the real processes, enable us to measure each process in terms of the total money value of what is produced or of what is consumed in a unit of time, say one year. When we thus compare the sizes of the two flows, it is in general perfectly possible, and in advanced countries in peacetime it is in fact always the case, that production exceeds consumption and leaves in being a third process, arising directly and inevitably from the disparity of the other two, namely the accumulation of real wealth, the continual augmentation of the economy's pile of goods existing at each moment. The questions to which we want to find answers in this Book v are, first, what influences or forces or mechanisms govern the size of this flow of accumulation, and secondly what effects do changes in its size in their turn bring about?

The actions of a government are motivated and shaped in a different way from those of private individuals or firms, and we shall therefore at first suppose that the total amount of money which the central and local governments, all taken together, annually collect is all raised in direct taxes such as income tax and rates (with no government borrowing), is all spent on consumption of the sorts we listed above, and is constant in size from

year to year. By these assumptions we leave the economic activities of governments as a fixed background against which we can
study the undisturbed play of private motives.

That part of the aggregate money-income of all the individuals
in the economy taken together, which is left after they have paid
their (direct) taxes, we shall call the *disposable income* of the economy. It will be arrived at by writing down for each person how
much money he annually gets from the sale of productive services
of some kind or kinds (there is, by our assumptions, no other source
of income than the provision of productive services), subtracting
from this the amount of money he annually pays as taxes, and
adding together all the remainders, one for each person, to get the
grand total of the economy's disposable income, the income which
is at the free disposal of individuals to spend on whatever they like,
or to *save*.

The first question we are specially interested in is: How much,
all taken together, will they save? On the general grounds supplied
by our observation of other people's behaviour and by our examination of our own feelings, it was plausibly suggested by John
Maynard Keynes that there is at least one broad 'qualitative' rule:
the more income you have, the more you save. His basic rule is
not, as so many people have wrongly supposed, the more income
you have, the larger the *proportion* of it you save. Keynes's rule
merely means that if, starting from an income which has for some
time fairly comfortably supplied your needs for consumption and
enabled you to put a little by, you then attain to a somewhat
larger income, you will, even when you have adjusted your mode
of life to your ampler situation, spend on extra consumption less
than the whole of the extra income, and save a little of that just as
you saved a little of your initial income. Put in this way, the
basis, in individual psychology and conduct, of Keynes's rule that
aggregate *saving* and aggregate *disposable income* grow and decline
together, given time for adjustment of one to the other, seems
almost self-evidently true. But we must not jump without thought
from the individual to the economy as a whole, for there is a big
link in the chain to be tested first.

Saving

If any and every increase in the aggregate disposable income of the economy always implied an increase in the disposable income of every individual, or if, at least, it was never accompanied by any actual decreases in any individual disposable incomes; and if everyone whose income had increased always saved some of his extra income; and if those whose income had not changed never increased their own spending on consumption, as a consequence, for example, of the increased spending of others; then we could say definitely that whenever the economy's aggregate disposable income is raised to a higher level, the size of the gap between this income and the aggregate amount of money annually spent on consumption will also increase. In other words, given the assumptions we have just made, we could say that the aggregate saving-flow is an increasing function of the aggregate disposable income.

Why do we need to make these elaborate assumptions? Because the question how much will be saved out of a given aggregate disposable income cannot be answered merely from a knowledge of how much each individual would save out of each possible size of his own disposable income. We need also to know how each given aggregate is distributed amongst the individuals with their diverse saving-and-spending habits. Let us take an example. Suppose the whole economic system consists of only three people, A who saves half of everything he earns, B who saves a tenth of everything he earns, and C who saves none of his earnings whatever their amount. Now let us imagine that in an initial situation, A's disposable income is £2000, B's is £800, C's is £200, and that in a second situation A's disposable income is £2400, B's is £1200 and C's is £400. Then we have:

	Aggregate disposable income (£)	Aggregate saving (£)
First situation	3000	1080
Second situation	4000	1320

But now suppose that in a third situation the aggregate income of £4000 is made up as follows: A, £2000; B, £1500; C, £500.

Then we should have:

	Aggregate disposable income (£)	Aggregate saving (£)
Second situation	4000	1320
Third situation	4000	1150

It is plain that a change in the *sharing* of income can affect the amount saved out of a given aggregate, without there being any change in the amount saved by any individual out of any given level of his own income.

Nevertheless, it is exceedingly likely that any large growth of aggregate disposable income would make many people better off, and few worse off, in money terms. Even if this rise of money-income were accompanied by a general rise of prices, it is not likely that those whose money-incomes had not increased would be able to spend very much more than before on consumption in order to maintain their 'standard of living' in face of its higher money cost. Thus Keynes's rule, that a growth of the economy's aggregate disposable income will be accompanied by a growth of its aggregate saving-flow, that is, a growth of the *gap* between production and consumption as measured in money, seems to be acceptable. Let us at this point remind ourselves of what this gap is, from a different viewpoint. It is a gap between the total value of goods for whose production firms have paid out incomes, and the total value of goods which they have been able to sell to *consumers*. But firms only make goods if they expect to be able to sell them to *somebody*. To whom, then, are the goods representing the gap between production and consumption to be sold? We shall answer this question in the next chapter. Meanwhile we must consider briefly what consequences will flow from a relaxation of our assumptions about the government and its financial actions.

For it is evident that the central government itself, and even to some extent the local governments, can save or dissave, or rather, can cause the gap between the whole value of goods and services annually produced by the economic system as a whole, and the value of goods and services consumed within it, to be larger or smaller. Hitherto in this chapter we have been taking it for granted that the government's actions will be economically neutral provided their revenue, taken entirely in direct taxation, and their expenditure on immediately consumable goods and services, exactly match each other. In the light of our discussion of the effects upon the aggregate saving-flow, which might be produced by changes in the distribution of income, we must qualify this. For if the annual revenue levied by the government became extremely large in proportion to the value of the economy's annual production, everybody's *disposable* income might be so reduced that, whatever their propensity to save out of large disposable incomes, they would, in fact, out of their small disposable incomes, save little or nothing. Since we are assuming that the whole of the government's large revenue would be spent upon things which count as consumption, it follows that in such a situation, the aggregate saving-flow, that is, the gap between production and consumption, would be very small. Even a *balanced* budget, in the sense of our assumptions, is not necessarily 'neutral' in the matter of how much the economy saves.

But wait: need the government spend on immediate consumption all that it takes away in taxes from individuals? Is it bound, by any law of nature or even of our constitution, to balance its budget? Certainly not. It could indeed (were such a thing politically conceivable) actually take money away from those whose natural inclination and straitened circumstances induce them to spend on consumption all they earn, and could then omit to spend this revenue on consumption. It could do some saving on its own. Equally well it could do the reverse, taking money by taxation away from those who would otherwise have saved it, and then proceeding itself to spend this money on consumption.

A great many people, when the government taxes them, probably forgo some of the consumption they would otherwise have indulged in, even if at the same time they save somewhat less than, with no tax to pay, they would have done. Suppose it turns out that three-quarters of what the people in our simplified economic system, all taken together, pay to the government by way of taxation comes out of forgone consumption and one-quarter out of forgone saving. And suppose that out of this revenue the government spends one-half on consumption. Then plainly the net result of the government's total action is that the flow of spending is less than it would otherwise have been.

Let us recapitulate the argument of this chapter in the terminology which Keynes gave to economics in his *General Theory of Employment, Interest and Money*.

When a person's or a nation's income stands for some time at a particular level, and during some other time-interval at a different level, we can observe, perhaps, the size of that person's or that nation's expenditure per unit of time on consumption when income is at the first level, and when it is at the second level. The ratio of the difference between the two levels of consumption-expenditure, to the difference between the two levels of income, Keynes called the person's or the nation's *marginal propensity to consume*. This ratio might conceivably be unity: the whole of any extra income might be exactly matched by equal extra consumption-expenditure. Or it might conceivably be zero: consumption-expenditure might remain unchanged despite a growth or decline of income. Keynes thought that neither of these things would in fact be true, but that, at any rate for a nation as a whole, the marginal propensity to consume would be a proper fraction, some number between zero and one. If so, it follows that whenever the aggregate income of some economic system gets bigger, the aggregate flow of the saving performed by the people in that economy also gets bigger, though by a lesser amount than that by which their income has increased. Now aggregate saving is the excess of the total value of what is produced in a given time-interval over the total value of what is consumed in that interval. Thus the larger the economy's income, the larger the value of goods which, in any time-interval, must be bought by someone other than consumers. Who can this someone be? And what happens if *nobody* is willing to buy these goods, or to buy enough of them?

We have seen that the argument thus presented in broad outline needs certain refinements before we can accept it as wholly satisfactory. First, the amount saved by all the people in an economy out of a given aggregate of their incomes will depend not only on the size of that aggregate but also on how it is distributed amongst them. If the majority of people have so little income each that they must spend all of it to live, while a large remainder of the aggregate income is in the hands of people so well off that they only spend a little of their incomes and save the rest, it may be that the saving-flow in total will be larger than if the same aggregate income were more evenly shared. Secondly, in a modern economy an important proportion of the economy's aggregate income will not be left at the free disposal of the individuals but will be taken from them in taxation by the government and spent by the government on their behalf. Thus if the government spends on goods or services of some sort all of its tax revenue, and if any growth of the economy's aggregate income is accompanied by a sufficient growth of the government's tax revenue, the problem of what is to be done with goods produced but not bought by individuals for their own consumption may not cause any difficulty.

Despite these qualifying notions, however, we are left face-to-face with two questions: First, who buys the goods which are produced but not sold to consumers? And secondly, what happens if *nobody* is willing to buy these goods, or to buy enough of them? These questions are the subject-matter of the rest of this Book v.

Chapter 23. Equipping

Who, then, in a self-contained economy, buys the goods that are produced but not sold to consumers? Who, that is to say, other than the government? For it may well be that even after the government's economic activities are allowed for, there is still a big gap between aggregate disposable income and the aggregate spending-flow on consumption. Part of the answer might be that merchants and manufacturers sometimes pile up extra goods in their warehouses or storerooms, perhaps because they expect to be able in the near future to sell larger quantities or to ask higher prices. Such net additions to the firms' 'inventories' or stockpiles of materials or partly finished goods are evidently examples of 'goods that have been produced but not sold to consumers' and they meet this description in a special sense. We have seen in Chapter 6 (*Production*) that so long as the miller, for example, is only buying enough wheat to replace what he is at the same time grinding into flour and selling in that form to the baker, and so long as the baker in his turn is only buying enough flour to replace what he is at the same time baking into bread and selling in that form to consumers, the miller and the baker are merely producing the *equivalent* of the goods that are being sold to consumers, and their operations do not constitute a gap between the quantities of goods produced and the quantities currently consumed. It is only if the miller *increases* his stock of wheat, or the baker his stock of flour, that they have done something that can help to fill a gap between consumers' off-take of goods and producers' output of goods.

There is in one sense no radical difference between the motive that induces the miller and the baker to buy wheat and flour, and the motive that induces them to buy milling machinery or bread-making machinery and buildings in which to house these machines. All these things are bought in order that the firms may be able to carry on their business and make an income for their owners and their workpeople. The motive is the same, but the considerations that guide the businessman in deciding whether and when to increase his equipment of buildings and machines are quite special. What is special about machines and buildings is that they are long-lasting; that they are so costly that unless they were long-lasting, and able to yield productive services day after day and year after year, no businessman could afford them; that the question how much their productive services will be worth, in three or six or twelve years' time, is one which the businessman can only answer by conjecture and not by certain knowledge; and that even if he assumes that a particular building or machine will earn just so much in each of the years during which he will use it, he needs to know something else beyond this before he can reckon precisely how much it will be just worth his while to pay for this new piece of equipment, so as to decide whether, at the price being charged for it by its makers, it is, for him, worth having or not. This last thing is the rate of interest, the price of future money in terms of present money or of present money in terms of future money.

If complex machines such as looms, lathes or printing-presses could only be used once like the flour that makes a particular loaf of bread, the construction and use of these instruments would simply constitute a wasteful detour in the process of manufacturing other things. It is only because any such machine, having helped to make cloth or newspapers today, will be almost as good as ever for rendering a similar service tomorrow and for many months and years, that we can get back from the machine, ultimately, an amount of productive service comparable with what we must put into its construction. There may be a few cases where elaborate and expensive preparations do yield a great quantity of product in one moment, and so pay for themselves immediately. Such may be the case with the driving of a tunnel into a rock-face and the blasting of the rock for building material. But the great majority of machines are durable: to exhaust their potentialities of service we have to go on using them for a long time. This means that when it is a question whether or not to install such a machine, the businessman who is taking this decision must look down a long vista of future years and try to imagine what the machine's services will be worth in times when fashion or new invention may have altered the market for the product or brought in rival means of making it.

The dominant inescapable fact about durable equipment, from the viewpoint of the heads of firms, the 'enterprisers', who provide a market for it, is that it is impossible in the nature of things for anyone to know for certain, even within wide limits, how much clear gain will accrue to the firm from buying some particular machine or setting up some plant or other building, or even whether the result of this act of *investment* may not be an actual loss. The equipment must be paid for at once, but its use will mostly occur months or years hence, in a future about which men can entertain only conjectures or fictions. The *expectations* which men construct about the future are not day-dreams lacking any ground, constraint or reasonable basis; neither, however, are they knowledge. These expectations can be based only on the present (in which the past, so far as it can influence us, is of course wrapped up) and although there is no guarantee or even any fair presumption that the conditions of demand, the fashions and tastes, the techniques and political arrangements will remain as they are or continue to evolve in the same directions and at the same pace as they have been doing, yet this sort of assumption is very ready to impose itself. Any abrupt change in the existing state of affairs can cause an even more violent change in expectations, for they are a top-heavy superstructure on a perpetually inadequate basis of current fact. This inadequacy inheres in the nature of things, and will remain no matter how full and how up-to-date our knowledge of what *is* may become. This can never provide us with knowledge of what *will be*. Each different individual will formulate, with greater or less precision and with a nearer or further 'horizon', his own expectations about what consequences would follow for himself if he adopted this plan or that. In the light of these he will choose his plan, and that plan will count, for its success, on the performance by other people of certain actions or their following out of certain policies. If the plans of each person do not envisage for him just those actions and policies which the plans of other people assume that he will execute, somebody's plans must inevitably go wrong.

We shall see in the next chapter what are those special classes of events which bear with peculiar directness on the expectations of businessmen who are approaching a decision whether or when to order some additional equipment for their firms. The point at which those events take effect is in the businessmen's estimation of the profits which a particular machine, building, or other instrument would yield, that is, the excess of what they suppose it would add to their annual incomings from the sale of their products, over what they suppose it would add to their annual outlay on wages of labour and on materials, power, hire of land and so on. Between the size of such expected profits, crudely taken together as a whole, and the reaching of an answer to the question whether, as a whole, they make it worthwhile to pay the price which the constructor of a machine or building will ask, there is a type of calculation, of some complexity, which it is important to understand.

Suppose, then, that our miller thinks a motor-truck of a certain design would cost him £1000 a year in wages for its driver and in fuel, lubricant, tyres, repairs, insurance, and licensing, and that its use would save him £2000 a year in the wages of four draymen and the food and other upkeep of four horses and carts, which he would thus be enabled to dispense with; and suppose that he thinks the truck could be used for three years and then have a second-hand value of £500. How will he use these estimates to answer the question what is the highest price at which it will just seem worth his while to buy this truck?

In each of the next three years the truck will yield to the miller, he believes, a net gain of £1000, for the expense of delivering his flour and collecting his wheat will be £1000 a year less than it would otherwise have been; and at the end of the three years he will recover another £500 by selling the truck. Does this mean that the truck is worth to the miller the total amount of £3500 which all these gains and the second-hand value add up to? Not quite. For let us ask how much money the miller would have to have in his pocket now in order to be able to look forward to having £1000 in one year's time, another £1000 in two years' time, a third £1000 in three years' time, and the final £500 also in three years' time. If he can *lend* the cash in his pocket at ten per cent per annum, he can look forward to being repaid £1000 in a year's time by lending £909 today. He can have the prospect of receiving £1000 in two years' time by lending about £826. For if he lends £826 for one year the borrower will owe him, at the end of that year, £826 plus one-tenth (ten per cent) of £826, that is, altogether, £909; and if, instead of requiring the borrower to repay him then, he allows the debt of £909 to run on for a further year at ten per cent per annum, the debt at the end of the second year will be £909 plus one-tenth of £909, that is, approximately £1000. By an argument precisely the same in principle, he can have the prospect of £1000 in three years' time by lending today £751 8s., and of a further £500 in three years' time by lending £375 9s. So by lending altogether some £2862 today, the miller can look forward to exactly the same series of instalments that he assumes he would get by buying and using the truck. This, then, supposing the market rate of interest at which he can lend out the money in his pocket is ten per cent per annum, is the price it will seem just worth his while to pay for the truck.

The principle underlying the sort of calculation we have just outlined is a simple one. Because 'ready money' in one's possession is convenient in several ways and makes its possessor 'feel better', a price is required by the possessor of ready money to induce him to part with it in exchange for an IOU, a piece of paper acknowledging debt and promising repayment. This price consists simply in the promise by the borrower to repay, after a stated term, a larger sum than the one he borrowed. Thus when money down is exchanged for money deferred, the ratio of exchange is not £1 for £1, but, say, nineteen shillings in spot cash for £1 deferred one year. That ratio would be a rate of interest of a little over five per cent per annum. If the ratio were eighteen shillings in spot cash for £1 deferred one year, we could alternatively call this a rate of interest of a little more than eleven per cent per annum, and a rate of interest of twenty-five per cent per annum would reduce the spot-cash value or, as actuaries call it, the 'present value' of £1 deferred one year to sixteen shillings.

These examples bring out an important fact. The higher the interest-rate, the *lower* the 'present value' of the promise of any stated sum of money to be paid after a stated lapse of time. Now the gains which the miller hopes or expects to get from his proposed purchase of a motor-truck are simply a series of deferred repayments. Truly, they are not sums of money promised him by someone else, they are neither guaranteed in any way by some other person nor, and this is the most essential point of all, are their amounts known for certain. But once the miller has arrived in his own mind at some figure for each of these instalments of future gain, he must then ask himself what is the 'present value' of that series of assumed deferred instalments, and the higher the interest-rate which would-be borrowers are offering him for the loan of his spot cash, the lower will be the present value to him of what he imagines his truck will earn in future years. 'The present value to him of what he assumes that a truck, which he could buy now, would bring him back in future years': this means nothing else than 'What the truck is worth to him', and so we conclude that, if the interest-rate were in the habit of fluctuating rather widely around a level such as we have been assuming, of, say, ten per cent per annum, his decision whether or not to buy the truck at a particular price might depend on whether the interest-rate was at the top or bottom of its swing.

Having seen the logic of the matter, we must ask ourselves at once in what circumstances the principle, that decisions about buying or not buying machines and buildings will be influenced by the prevailing interest-rate, is likely to have practical effect. We assumed an interest-rate of ten per cent per annum, and we found that the 'present' or 'discounted' value of a series of three annual instalments of £1000 each, beginning one year hence, was about £2486. If the interest-rate had instead been five per cent per annum, the present value would have been about £2723. So this enormous change in the prevailing rate of interest, from ten per cent per annum to five per cent per annum, would make a difference of only £237 in a total of several thousands. Can we suppose that the relatively minute changes due to any ordinary alteration of the interest-rate such as could occur within a few months, say of one percentage point or less, would appreciably influence a decision based (and this is what we have above all things to bear in mind) on a series of future instalments of gain that are themselves mere conjectures?

Employment

To avoid arithmetical tedium we have taken, as our example
to illustrate the discounting notion and its effects, a series of only
three annual instalments. We have just seen that when the defer-
ments are so short, any ordinary change in the interest-rate will
have only a negligible effect on present values and consequently
on their sum, which is the demand-price of the asset in question.
Yet this result is itself of first-rate importance, because it is the
realistic one where machines and plant of complex design are
concerned. Some instruments are liable at all times to have their
profit-earning capacity destroyed by the invention of a more
economical technique or a more efficient product. A new discovery
or invention would, of course, take some time to be widely
adopted or applied, and so the makers of existing products by
machines of existing design would have some warning. Today's
situation, today's events and news, do throw some light on the
near future, perhaps as far in some respects as a year, or two or
three years, ahead. But beyond that who can make any worthwhile guess? Thus the businessman, in effect, brushes aside all the
possible profit-making power of a piece of equipment in which
he contemplates investing, beyond the first two or three years of
its life. Everything he counts on from it must arise from these
first few prospective years of its operation. But this means, of
course, that even a machine which, *physically*, is likely to remain
in perfect working order for thirty years will *economically* present
itself as an asset offering only a very short series of annual profits,
and so the leverage which ordinary interest-rate changes can exert
on the demand-price of such machines is negligible.

But machines and industrial plant are only one kind of investment goods. Buildings of all kinds, roads, harbours, pipelines and
forests are also part of the economy's durable productive apparatus, and many of these types of equipment are by no means subject
to uncertainty about their more distant usefulness and earning
power in the same degree as machines. Now if, instead of taking
as our illustration a machine which may become technically obsolete within a very few years of its purchase, we had taken a dwelling
house which can be reasonably counted on to yield valuable

services for sixty or eighty years, the story would have been different. Then we should have found that a change in the interest-rate from four per cent per annum to two per cent per annum would have altered the discounted value of a series of eighty annual instalments of £100 each from about £2400 to about £4000. When tens of thousands of people are asking themselves whether, at a given cost of construction, it is worth their while to buy a house, such a great difference in the discounted value of its future services must evidently affect their decision in a large proportion of cases, and thus make a very important difference to the quantity of goods which can be sold for purposes other than immediate consumption.

Two related questions may now arise in the reader's mind. First, how is it that a change in the interest-rate at which money can be lent or borrowed affects so much more strongly the discounted value of a series of instalments extending far into the future than that of a series concentrated near the present? And secondly, what happens to the discounted value of any one instalment when we suppose its due date to become more and more remote?

To find out how much must be repaid in a year's time, if 100 units are borrowed now at five per cent, that is, one-twentieth, per annum, we add to the original loan one-twentieth of itself, or, what comes to the same thing, we multiply it by $\frac{105}{100}$. To find out how much 105 units, deferred one year, are worth in spot cash, we multiply the 105 units by $\frac{100}{105}$, which gives us back, of course, our original 100 units. If the loan is for two years instead of one, the operation of multiplying by $\frac{105}{100}$, in order to reckon the ultimate amount of the debt, must be done twice over, first, in order to transform the original loan into a sum deferred one year, and secondly, in order to transform that sum deferred one year into a sum deferred two years. And correspondingly, in order to find the spot-cash equivalent of a sum due in two years, we multiply by $\frac{100}{105}$ twice over, once to reduce the sum due in two years to an equivalent due in one year, and a second time to reduce that sum-deferred-one-year to spot cash. If the term of the deferment were three years we should multiply three times over, and if it were so-and-so many years we should multiply so-and-so many times over.

Employment

Now every time we multiply, we bring the particular interest-rate to bear afresh, and give it an extra bit of leverage. Thus the more distant the date on which a stated debt is due, the larger will be the *proportionate* change in the spot-cash equivalent of that debt, brought about by a given change of the interest-rate.

However, it is not the proportionate but the *absolute* change in the discounted value of each individual future instalment that matters, for the demand-price of the asset is the sum of these individual discounted values or spot-cash equivalents, and the change in this demand-price, which occurs when the interest-rate changes, is simply the sum of the *absolute* amounts by which the spot-cash equivalents change. Now while the discounted value of a given deferred sum changes in a larger *ratio*, the longer the deferment, this is by no means uniformly true of the *absolute* size of its change. For the discounted value of a sum due at a very remote date will be so small, relatively to that sum, that even a large proportionate change may be of little account. As we look at nearer and nearer dates, the proportionate change gets smaller, but the thing which is changed gets bigger. Where, then, will the absolute net effect be greatest? It will be at that length of deferment which, in number of years, is the reciprocal or inverse of the rate of annual interest expressed as a proper fraction, so that if, for example, the annual interest-rate is one-twentieth (five per cent) and if it alters to, say, four-and-threequarters per cent, the greatest absolute effect, in changing the discounted value of a given sum deferred so-and-so many years, will occur when so-and-so is about twenty years.

In this chapter we have noticed the two dominant facts about the *demand-price* of long-lasting equipment. First, the value of such equipment depends on conjecture about the conditions which will prevail in future years; whether the product will have enlarged its market or lost it; whether or not more efficient equipment will have been invented for making the product. Secondly, its value depends on the rival possibilities existing 'now' of using the money which would have to pay for the equipment; whether money can be lent now at a relatively low or high interest-rate. We have seen that these two influences bear on each other in a complex way. If the conditions and events of times more than three or four years ahead seem to the businessman too uncertain, he will ignore any profit that the equipment might earn in those more distant years, and count only upon what it may do in the next three or four years. Thus the 'leverage' of interest-rates will perhaps be so much reduced that changes in them have no effect on his decision whether to invest in the equipment or not. But again, a high interest-rate would itself so greatly reduce the 'present values' of the expected profits of fairly distant future years, that those years would drop out of the businessman's calculations. These two ideas can be drawn together if we suppose the business-man to express his distrust of more distant future years by adding to the market rate of interest a 'risk allowance' of the same arith-metical form as the interest-rate itself, so that he discounts hoped-for profits by, say, thirty-three per cent instead of five or seven per cent. Let us call this combined rate of interest and rate of risk allowance the total discounting rate. Then, amongst all the ex-pected profit-instalments, the one whose present value will be changed to the largest absolute (not proportional) extent by a given moderate change in the total discounting rate per annum will be the one whose futurity in years is the reciprocal of the total dis-counting rate per annum. If the total discounting rate, combining interest-rate and risk-allowance rate, is thirty-three per cent per annum, the greatest effect of a change to, say, thirty-two per cent will be on the present value of instalments three years deferred; for thirty-three per cent is about $\frac{1}{3}$, and when we turn $\frac{1}{3}$ upside down the result is 3. To assume that the businessman will apply a high risk-allowance rate, of, say twenty-five or thirty per cent per annum, is very closely equivalent to saying that he will ignore entirely all the years beyond the next three or four or five. We can easily see, too, that a quite large change in the *interest-rate* from, say, five per cent per annum to four per cent per annum will make a relatively small proportionate change in the total discounting rate from, say, thirty-three per cent per annum to thirty-two per cent per annum, and we can see that this latter change is unlikely to affect noticeably the demand-price of the equipment: for 'notice-ableness' will surely depend on the *proportionate* change in the discounted value of expected profits.

Chapter 24. Output

THE *output* of a commodity is the number of physical units of it produced in a unit of time. In order to increase such an output quickly by a large percentage, it will usually be necessary to work the existing machines harder and give them less frequent attention by way of maintenance, and thus to make their wear and tear more rapid; possibly also to bring back into use inefficient machines which had been discarded; to work overtime or double shifts, with the extra pay these entail; and to take on extra labour which, while having to be paid the same money wage-rates as workers already employed, is less skilful and less highly trained than they. At the same time high prices may have to be paid for scarce materials. Thus as output is increased by equal steps the total cost of the output will increase by larger and larger steps: marginal cost is an increasing function of output. But no unit will be added to output unless it is expected to increase total revenue by at least as much as it increases total cost. In perfect competition, the amount by which an extra unit of output increases total revenue is simply the price per unit of the commodity, and so we can say that the supply-price of the commodity, that is, the price per unit just sufficient to elicit a given output, is equal to the marginal cost of that output and will be higher, the higher the output required.

In Chapter 23 we saw what considerations influence the price which a particular businessman will think it just worthwhile to pay for a specified machine or other piece of equipment. Regarding machines of any one type, different businessmen will arrive at different figures for this *personal demand-price*. A given *supply-price* for machines of a particular type will elicit orders for these machines from all those businessmen who, for the time being, have in mind personal demand-prices higher than, or as high as, this supply-price. It is reasonable to say that the machines will be ordered and produced in such a number per unit of time as to carry the supply-price up to just that level where only this number of orders is elicited.

This description of the mechanism, whereby we can suppose the output and the price of any given type of investment-goods to be determined, is exactly analogous to that of the determination of the output and price of any consumer's good. The higher the price the larger the supply and the smaller the demand that will be forthcoming. Thus there will be some price which presses demand down to equality with supply, or lifts supply up to equality with demand, or more probably does both these things at once.

Machines or other pieces of equipment of any one type will be required, not only when a net augmentation of the quantity of them in use is contemplated, but also to replace machines serving a similar purpose which are worn out or have become so relatively inefficient compared with newer designs that they are obsolete. But demand for these machines under both these heads is covered by the same set of considerations we studied in Chapter 23. If our miller perceived that his mill machinery was wearing out, the difference made to his prospective profit by a new set of machinery will be the whole difference arising from being able to carry on his business and not being able to carry it on. If, instead, he learns that more efficient machinery has been invented, whose cost of operation is very much lower than that of his present machinery, there may again appear to him to be a sufficient prospect of gain to induce him to scrap his present machinery and buy the new. Or yet again the price of flour may be tending to rise because of an expanding market, and he may see the possibility of profitably employing extra machinery which will enable him to increase his output. All these kinds of circumstances are alike in that they afford a motive for buying equipment, a motive which appears in the guise of an expectation of profit.

Let us call a personal demand-price high enough to result in an order for the kind of machines in question, an *effective* personal demand-price. We can imagine our businessmen to be arranged in descending order of their personal demand-prices. There will be a *lowest effective demand-price*, and the lower this is, the larger will be the corresponding flow of orders, that is, the number of machines ordered per unit of time. The larger the flow of orders, the higher will be the supply-price, and we have inferred that the output will always tend to be such as to equalise the supply-price and the lowest effective personal demand-price. There is another way of viewing and of expressing this equality, a way which is often used in the literature of economics and which we ought to examine. In order to arrive at any one businessman's personal demand-price, we supposed him to use 'the' interest-rate, prevailing on the loan market, to find the spot-cash equivalents of expected future instalments of profit. Now if the supply-price of a machine of a given type is equal to the lowest effective personal demand-price, it is plain that this same market interest-rate, used in discounting expected future profits, will bring the present value of this series of deferred instalments of profit to equality with the *supply-price*. But suppose that at some moment the supply-price and the demand-price are not equal. Then the prevailing market rate of interest, since it brings the discounted value of expected profits to equality with the demand-price, will not bring it to equality with the supply-price. Nevertheless we can say what the interest-rate would have to be, what percentage per annum would be required, in order that the equality with *supply-price* might be achieved. This imaginary or suppositious interest-rate is called the *marginal efficiency of capital*. To say that the supply-price and the demand-price are equal is to say that the marginal efficiency of capital is equal to the prevailing market rate of interest on loans of money.

Now hitherto in this chapter our argument has been concerned with some one kind of machine. But evidently, if the marginal efficiency of capital invested in one kind of machine or equipment promised to be much higher than in other kinds, there would be a move on the part of enterprisers to invest their money-capital in equipment of this specially promising kind rather than in others, and so the supply-price of this kind of equipment would be driven up in comparison with the supply-prices of the others. As its supply-price rose, however, the marginal efficiency of capital invested in it would fall, for the higher the supply-price, the smaller the rate of discount needed to bring the 'present value' of any given series of expected profits down to equality with this supply-price. So there will always be at work a tendency for the marginal efficiency of capital to be equal in all forms of equipment, used for no matter which technical process and in no matter what industry, except in so far (and it is a very important reservation) as the *uncertainty* about the expected profits is greater in some lines than others. Thus we are justified in speaking of *the* marginal efficiency of capital, without qualifying this expression by referring to some particular kind of equipment. There will always be, amongst businessmen, a range of diverse personal demand-prices for any one kind of equipment. But there will also be a tendency for the lowest effective personal demand-price for each distinct kind of equipment to be such that the corresponding marginal efficiency of capital is the same in all of the different kinds.

What general statements can we make, then, about *the* marginal efficiency of capital? With any one kind of equipment, the larger the output of this kind, the lower the marginal efficiency of capital invested in it, partly because its supply-price will be higher, partly because the prospective rapid augmentation of the stock of mutually competing units of this kind of equipment will weaken the expectation of high profits for each unit. How far does a similar statement hold true of a simultaneous general increase in the outputs of most kinds of equipment?

Such a general simultaneous increase in the quantities produced per time-unit of most kinds of equipment will have an even stronger effect on the supply-price of each separate kind, than

Employment

would occur if the output of this kind alone increased by itself. For the competition for scarce supplies of labour, materials and facilities of all kinds, all wanted at the same time by the firms and industries producing various kinds of equipment, will drive up the money prices of these means of production and so drive up the supply-prices of the equipment which they produce. But there is a countervailing effect to be taken into account, which plays little or no part if only one kind of machine is being produced in larger numbers. This countervailing effect arises from the increase in aggregate disposable income corresponding to the marked increase, which we are supposing to occur, in outputs of all sorts of equipment. We saw in Chapter 22 (*Saving*) that when the economy's aggregate disposable income is augmented, there will be an increase in both the saving-flow and the flow of spending on consumption-goods. But this latter change alters the whole market situation, enables industries to sell the same outputs of consumers' goods as before at higher prices and larger outputs at the same prices, and thus gives the firms composing them a strong inducement to order more equipment. Thus if, for whatever reason, the output of equipment in general (measured by the value of this output at constant prices) is lifted to a higher level, the new situation thus produced will have some inherent power to maintain itself in being, or even to generate a further change in the same direction. The degree of this power will depend partly on how individuals react to increases of their disposable incomes and partly on how businessmen respond to a strengthening of demand for their products, and this latter response in turn will depend on the degree to which their existing equipment of machines, plant and factories is already loaded when the demand for extra output of consumers' goods arises.

We cannot simply say, then, that the marginal efficiency of capital is a decreasing function of the output of investment-goods in general. When larger quantities of all sorts of machines and buildings are produced per unit of time, their supply-prices may rise as a consequence, but so also, as another consequence, may their demand-prices. We may be tempted to ask 'Will there not

156

be an equilibrium level at which the output of equipment in general can settle and continue?' but it is difficult to treat this matter as a straightforward search for a balance of steady opposing forces. The demand-prices of equipment, of investment-goods, depend very much on events, and amongst these relevant events is the very process of augmenting the existing stock of such goods.

There are, however, two types of events quite distinct from the growth of the stock of equipment, which have an especial importance as stimulators of an increase in the output of equipment. These are, first, advances of technical knowledge which suggest the replacement of existing machines and processes by more efficient ones, or the installation of plant for making entirely new kinds of product; and secondly, increases of population which need to be matched by extra provision of houses, schools, hospitals, shops, theatres, power stations, buses and so on.

The concept of the *marginal efficiency of capital* is an instance of a tendency characteristic of economics in all its branches, to produce a sort of atomic nucleus in which a complex of various ideas is compressed into a single powerful but dangerous phrase. It is not difficult to explain the formal meaning of the marginal efficiency of capital, which one can speak of as a sort of phantom interest-rate which becomes indistinguishable from the market rate of money interest when the supply-price of equipment becomes equal to the demand-price. But a host of questions and complexities spring to mind as soon as we look closely at this conception. First, there are countless different kinds of equipment, and we must consider one kind at a time in order to make the argument rigorous. For any one kind of equipment it is reasonable to speak of 'the' supply-price, but what of the demand-price? Whose demand-price? Goods whose valuation depends so essentially on the shape of a conjectural future must mean different things to different people, and there will be a wide range of different demand-prices. In explaining the concept of the marginal efficiency of capital it is necessary at this point, therefore, to explain that the effective demand-price is the one which equates itself to the supply-price at a given output. Yet even for each individual enterpriser his own demand-price for a given kind of equipment will not be independent of the total current output of this kind of equipment: the larger the total output, the larger will be the quantity of this kind of equipment which will be built up in a given time-interval, and the stronger, therefore, the prospective rivalry of competing factories and machines that will be encountered by the machines that he himself is going to own. Thus the effective demand-price for any given kind of equipment must be regarded as a schedule, a function of the output; and the marginal efficiency of capital in general, that is, of money-capital available for investment in any kind of equipment, must be looked on as a function of the output of equipment as a whole, measured, as well as may be, by its *value at constant prices*. When we have our schedule or list of the outputs corresponding to each of a range of different hypothetical marginal efficiencies, we can pick out that level of the marginal efficiency which is equal to the supposed current money rate of interest, and thus determine the output of equipment, that is, the aggregate pace at which the economy's stock of equipment is being replenished. Deducting from this gross investment-flow the part needed to make good current depreciation, we arrive at the net investment-flow, which is the pace of growth or improvement of the economy's store of equipment of all sorts.

This mechanism is sufficiently complicated, but we have said nothing so far of something that is concealed within the individual demand-prices of the various kinds of equipment, namely, the individual enterpriser's judgment of, and reaction to, the uncertainty of his estimates of the future profit-earning power of the equipment. When we say that the output of equipment in general will tend to that level where the marginal efficiency of capital is equal to the rate of interest, it makes all the difference in the world, to the meaningfulness and the validity of this proposition, what kind of allowance for or treatment of uncertainty is implicit in the marginal efficiency of capital.

Nevertheless, the apparatus of thought provided by the idea of the marginal efficiency of capital and its equalisation with the market rate of interest on loans of money is a compact and powerful means, for those able to hold in the back of their minds all the necessary *caveats* and qualifications, of analysing the determination of investment and employment in various circumstances and under various governmental policies.

Chapter 25. Demand

IN the three preceding chapters we have seen that the process of augmenting and improving the economy's stock of equipment is composed of two processes, one carried on by all the people in their capacity as income-receivers and disposers, the other carried on by some of the people in their capacity as businessmen deciding the policy of firms. If, between the beginning and end of any time-interval, the stock is to grow, it is necessary that in that interval the value of goods produced should exceed the value consumed. This requires two things: on the one hand the individual suppliers of productive services must be willing to earn some income in excess of what they need for consumption-spending, and on the other hand businessmen must be willing to produce some goods in excess of what they hope to sell to consumers. Moreover, it is obvious that although these two processes are distinct in the sense that they are performed by different groups of people, they are in another sense one and the same process seen from two different sides. Aggregate income of all income-earners is simply the total value per time-unit of goods and services produced. Aggregate consumption-spending is simply the total value per time-unit of goods and services consumed. The difference between income and consumption-spending, and the difference between production and consumption each measured in value, are two names for the same thing and are inevitably equal when reckoned from an internally consistent body of recorded data. Why, then, distinguish between them? Because they cannot be reckoned from one self-consistent body of recorded facts until the time-interval to which they refer is already in the past, yet to understand how they come, in any interval, to have a particular size we have to look at the state of affairs which exists at the beginning of that interval, *before* the actions, events and processes, which compose the total process of augmentation of wealth, have actually taken place. At that *threshold* of the interval in question these actions and their outcomes are nothing other than expectations in the minds of a multitude of different individuals. If we add together all the various amounts by which income-disposers intend to let their incomes exceed their consumption-spending during this impending interval, and likewise add together the values of the goods which businessmen expect to produce in this interval in excess of the equivalent of those they will sell to consumers, is there any reason why these two totals should agree? There is none. So we make a vitally important distinction between the two kinds of viewpoint from which the actions of any time-interval can be described, the viewpoint at the threshold of this interval, from which what is going to happen in this interval can be imagined variously by various people, and the viewpoint from the close of that interval, from which its events can, in principle at least, be found out for sure from the ledgers and the records in such a way that one self-consistent picture and one only emerges. Quantities reckoned from the forward-looking viewpoint are labelled *ex ante* and those reckoned from the backward-looking viewpoint are labelled *ex post*. These terms and the simple but fundamentally important distinction which they express were introduced into economics by the Swedish economist Gunnar Myrdal, who thus crystallised the great Swedish contribution to economic thinking, the assignment of a central explanatory role to the idea of expectation. Knut Wicksell at the end of the nineteenth century, Erik Lindahl and Gunnar Myrdal in the nineteen-thirties, were the founders of the Swedish expectational school.

Demand

There is one more preliminary matter which we must bring back into focus (we have already looked at it in Chapters 6 (*Production*) and 12 (*Income*)) before we turn to the main business of this chapter, which is to analyse the relations between growth of wealth and size of output as a whole. We have just now been subtracting the value of goods consumed in a year from the value of goods produced in a year, and likewise subtracting a year's consumption-spending from a year's income, and saying that when all these four things are looked at from the end of the year in question, the two resulting differences, of which we call the former *net investment* and the latter *saving*, will be equal. But what do we mean by the value of goods *produced* in a year? Let us recall the ultra-simple model economy we used in Chapter 6, composed only of the baker, the miller, the farmer and their workpeople. Here the farmer harvests in each year (over and above what he sets aside as seed) wheat worth, let us say, £1000; the miller grinds this into flour worth, let us say, £1500; and the baker bakes this into bread worth, let us say, £2500. What is the aggregate income of this economy, or what, to ask the same question in different words, is the value of the goods that its three firms have, in the relevant sense, produced in this year? We well know that we must avoid the too-obvious temptation to add the three amounts together; for does not the bread which emerges from the bakery embody the whole value which came from the mill in the form of flour, and did not that flour in turn embody the whole value which came from the farm in the form of wheat? Thus the measure of what this economy has produced in the year is simply the value of the bread. Even from that we may have to subtract something, if the farmer's implements or the machinery of the mill or the equipment of the bakery have suffered wear and tear which has not been made good.

In these words, 'the making good of wear and tear', we have the clue to avoiding possible confusion. For in every process of production some things are changed into other things, and in reckoning the value of the production which is thus performed, we must not take simply the value of these 'other things', without asking ourselves whether or not the things which have been changed into them have been replaced. If they have not, the value of the things the process started with must be deducted from the value of those it ended with to get the value *which has been added* to those initial things: value of production is value *added* by the process of production to its initially existing materials. In our model, some value is added by the farmer to his seed corn; he prepares the ground and sows the corn, cultivates it and harvests its fruit. Some more value is added to the harvested grain by the miller who grinds it, and yet more value is added by the baker who bakes it. When we add together the amounts of value *added* at all three stages, we get the total income, and also the total value of production, of the whole economy.

By the *net investment* performed in an economic system in a year we mean, then, the value by which production, in the sense of total value added, exceeds consumption. We cannot tell whether, or how much, net investment has been performed merely by seeing what *kind* of goods have been produced, for the very same kinds of goods are needed both to make good the wear and tear of production and to increase the economy's power to produce.

In what follows we shall at first consider a self-contained economic system with no government. All the people who play an active part in its economic life will be receivers and disposers of income and some of them will also be businessmen controlling the policy and conduct of firms. On the threshold of some named calendar interval, say the first quarter of 1961, each businessman, we suppose, decides how much of its own product his firm shall produce in that impending quarter. When he has allowed for the materials that will be used up, the electric power that will be consumed and the wear and tear that his machines will suffer as a consequence of this production, there will correspond to this intended output of his firm some particular amount of *value added*. The total of all these intended amounts of value added, one such amount for each firm, will be the total value of production, according to the intentions of businessmen or firms, in the impending quarter. And since, as we have seen, the total value of production is another name for the total income of all the people in the economy taken together, we can say that the result of adding together all the amounts of intended 'value added' for all the firms is equal to the *total expected income* of the economy according to the expectations of the businessmen.

When each businessman looks at his own firm's contribution to this total in its income aspect, we can divide it into two portions. On the one hand there are the wages, salaries, rents and interest-instalments he has contracted to pay to those who will supply him with productive services, and on the other hand there is his own expected profit. Thus if the businessmen's expectations are all put together, they give between them a figure for the total *ex ante* income of the impending calendar interval, made up of contractual incomes and profit.

When each income-receiver in the economy, in his capacity as a private individual, looks at this impending interval from its threshold, he too, no matter whether he is a receiver of wages, salaries, rent or interest, or whether he is himself a businessman relying on profit, has his own personal expectations of income. If the income-expectations of all the individuals in their private capacity are put together, we shall therefore again get a total representing the total *ex ante* income of the economy in the impending calendar interval, and this total also will be made up of the two components, contractual incomes and expected profits. Now a contractual income is one and the same amount whether it is paid or received, so the contractual component is the same in each of the two totals. And expected profits are one and the same in total amount no matter whether the people expecting them do so in their capacity as private persons or as heads of firms. Thus the 'expected profit' component is one and the same in each of the two totals. It follows that the two totals are equal, and that 'the aggregate income of the economy' means the same thing whichever way it is arrived at.

So much for the plans to produce goods. Now let us turn to their disposal. Some parts of the whole collection of quantities of goods which businessmen intend to produce during the impending quarter are planned in the expectation that they will be sold to consumers, or will take the place of other goods which will be so disposed of. This part of the *ex ante* output-as-a-whole of the impending quarter is thus expected to be matched by consumption-demand. This part includes, we remember, everything that is required to make good the materials which will be used up or the wear and tear which will be suffered in process of matching consumers' off-take with an equivalent set of quantities of goods. The rest of the *ex ante* output-as-a-whole, in our self-contained economy, is planned in the expectation that it will be sold to firms for the *augmentation of their equipment*. This part of *ex ante* output is thus expected to be matched by net investment demand from businessmen themselves. Now it is clear that if the total number of millions of pounds that consumers intend to spend on consumption-goods, plus the total number of millions of pounds that businessmen intend to spend on net investment, is equal to the value of *ex ante* output-as-a-whole, one necessary condition is satisfied for the whole of this planned output to be successfully disposed of. We cannot claim this as a *sufficient* condition, for consumers or net investors confronted with the actuality of the interval may change the plans they made in the light of mere expectations; moreover the individual consumer may intend, for example, to spend his money on something which no businessman is planning to produce to the exact specification the consumer desires; or again, consumers may want more books and less bread than the businessmen have allowed for. None the less, for the practical purposes of statesmanship, it is better to be aware of a necessary condition than to have no understanding of the problem at all. Now let us consider what this necessary condition implies and what will happen if it is not satisfied.

The condition itself can be expressed as equality of *intended effective demand* with the value of intended production or output. Here we mean by 'intended effective demand' the total of all the amounts which income-receivers as such intend to spend in the impending interval on consumption and of all the amounts which businessmen as such intend to spend during that interval on net investment, that is, on augmentation or improvement of their equipment. Now we have seen that the value of intended production is the same as the total expected income of all income-receivers, and we have defined intended *saving* as the difference between total expected income and total intended consumption-spending, so that intended saving is the same thing as the difference between the value of intended production and the total of intended consumption-spending. But intended effective demand is made up of total intended consumption-spending and total intended net investment. It follows that equality between intended effective demand and the value of intended production implies equality between total intended saving and total intended net investment. We can get a bird's-eye view of the argument as follows:

(i) Expected income ≡ value of intended output.

(ii) Expected income ≡ intended consumption-spending plus intended saving.

(iii) Value of intended output ≡ intended consumption-spending plus intended saving.

(iv) Effective demand ≡ intended consumption-spending plus intended expenditure on net investment.

These four equations are all written, very expressly, with the special sign ≡ for identical equality. This sign means that the two things on either side of it are equal, not by 'accident', or on one particular occasion, or subject to some special *condition*, but inescapably by their meaning. In equation (i) we are looking at things from the point of view of the question: where will income come from? In equation (ii) we are thinking: where will the income go to, what will be done with it? We get equation (iii) by putting equation (i) and equation (ii) together. If both these latter are true, it follows that (iii) is true. With equation (iv) we turn to the demand side, to the question: where can effective demand come from? Now the right-hand side of (iii) and the right-hand side of (iv) have an item in common, namely consumption-spending. It follows that *unless* intended net investment is equal to intended saving, we cannot have equality between the value of intended output and effective demand. So we get equation (v) which expresses a necessary *condition* for effective demand for output to be equal to the value of the output needing to be disposed of. Here, in contrast to the four previous equations, we have the sign = for *conditional equality* instead of the sign for identity:

(v) Intended net investment = intended saving.

Let us remind ourselves of what lies behind the wording of this conclusion. We have two totals of intended or *ex ante* amounts, representing on the one hand the intentions of income-receivers and on the other hand the intentions of businessmen as such. The groups, although one includes the other, are distinct, and there is no mechanism other than luck which can make these two totals equal. Even if they are equal, we have no guarantee that all goods produced according to plan in the impending interval will be matched by an exactly corresponding demand in that interval, even if all intentions to spend money on consumption in that interval are executed according to plan. Nevertheless, if all the three sets of intentions, to produce, to spend on consumption, to spend on net investment, are in fact carried out, and if the condition, equality *ex ante* between saving and investment, is not satisfied, it does follow that either some goods which were expected by their producers to be sold will be left unsold, or else some goods will have to be withdrawn from the pre-existing stock to satisfy a consumption-demand greater than the producers have allowed for.

Now we cannot suppose that the businessmen will continue, at the threshold of one quarter after another, to plan an output which proves, at the end of each successive quarter, to have had a greater total value than the effective demand forthcoming to buy it. If output is to *persist* on any given level, it is a necessary condition, within a reasonable interpretation of 'necessary', that effective demand should equal intended production or, in other words, that saving *ex ante* should be matched by net investment *ex ante*. So long as this condition is satisfied, it is possible for a given output to be maintained indefinitely, so far as its successful disposal is concerned.

We have already come across the distinction between the 'short period', the period too short for the buildings and equipment of a firm or an industry to be effectively enlarged, and the long period which permits all sorts of adjustments to be carried through. In the short period a shift from one level of output to another can only be effected by changing the intensity with which the already-existing equipment is used. It may be possible to employ more men in connection with the same outfit of machines, either by overtime working or by double or treble shifts; or machines hitherto idle may be drawn into use again. In either case the change of output will be brought about by, and will be associated with, a change in the number of workers employed or in their hours of labour, or both, and we can say that *employment* is, in the short period, an increasing function of output. Thus we have reached a point where, in the next chapter, we can finally attack the problem of how the level of employment comes at any time to be what it is.

In this chapter we have seen that employment depends on output, that output depends on effective demand, and that effective demand is made up, in a self-contained, governmentless economy, of the two components, consumption-expenditure by all income-receivers and net investment expenditure by businessmen as such. In earlier chapters of this Book v we saw what is the inducement for businessmen to augment and improve their equipment, that is, what circumstances and considerations give rise to a net investment demand for goods. We have still to answer the question what determines the level of consumption-demand. We might be inclined to put a slightly different question and ask whether there is not some connection between the level of net investment and the level of consumption-demand. And we have still to see what follows when we relax our assumptions that the economy is self-contained, having no dealings with any 'outside world', and that it has no government. All these matters we shall broach in the next chapter.

Chapter 26. Employment

STILL using our model of a self-contained no-government economy, let us suppose that for many successive quarters *ex ante* net investment has been equal to *ex ante* saving and that output as a whole has remained constant. Let us also suppose, however, that this output is a much smaller one than the economy could produce if all its means of production were fully employed. We shall assume that there are large numbers of people who would be glad to take employment at the current money wage-rates for their kind of work, and that it would be possible to employ them by working the existing equipment more intensively or drawing some idle equipment into production.

Now suppose that at the threshold of one particular quarter the businessmen's plans imply a noticeably larger flow of net investment for this quarter than has been done in the preceding quarters. Since individual businessmen may be supposed not to know of each other's plans, there will be nothing to suggest an increase in that part of output as a whole which is expected to be matched by consumer demand, but since complex machines and equipment are often ordered before they are built, we can suppose that the firms who will produce these machines receive such orders at the beginning of the quarter in question.

At the threshold of this quarter, then, income-receivers' total income *ex ante* will be larger than in previous quarters by an amount equal to the value of the *extra* net investment which is planned for this quarter: the wages which have been promised to the extra workers who have been taken on to make the extra quantities of equipment, and the extra profits which the firms who have contracted to make these extra quantities of equipment expect to get from them, together amounting to the expected sale proceeds of this additional output, will be an addition to the previous level of total *ex ante* income. What will those who have this incremental income in prospect decide to do with it? We saw reason in Chapter 22 (*Saving*) to suppose that they will plan to save part of it and to spend the rest on consumption. Thus some part of the extra *ex ante* total income is going to become an extra flow of effective demand for consumption-goods. Where are the consumption-goods to satisfy this extra demand going to come from?

We can assume that retailers and merchants have enough goods on their shelves to satisfy the extra demand during this particular quarter. But when at the end of the quarter businessmen look back and see that they have sold more consumption-goods than they have produced, it is reasonable to suppose that their plans for the ensuing quarter will provide for a larger output of consumption-goods. Let us assume that it will be larger by just that amount, measured in value at constant prices, by which the output of consumption-goods in the previous quarter fell short of the demand for them. How can this extra output of consumption-goods be arranged for? Again it will be necessary to engage extra workers and to contract to pay them a stream of income which, with the extra expected profits from the new output, will be a further addition to total income *ex ante*. Thus if we suppose that net investment continues, during this second quarter, at the new higher level it attained in the previous quarter, we now have, at the threshold of this second quarter, a total *ex ante* income augmented by two extra streams. Suppose that the first of these streams, consisting simply of the extra flow of net investment, was £1 million per quarter, and let us call a flow at the rate of £1 million per quarter a *unit* of income. And now let us make some particular assumption about the proportion which income-receivers all taken together will spend on consumption out of any given extra (incremental) income-stream. Suppose this proportion, which we shall call the income-receivers' *marginal propensity to consume*, is $\frac{3}{4}$. Then the second of the additional output streams will have a value equal to $\frac{3}{4}$ of one of our 'units' of £1 million per quarter, and so in the second quarter the extra income *ex ante* will amount to £1$\frac{3}{4}$ million. Before we take any further steps along our line of argument, let us glance briefly at the ones which have led us to this intermediate result.

Employment

Three assumptions in especial deserve attention. One is that the stream of *intended* net investment, having jumped up, at the threshold of one particular quarter, to a new higher level, continues indefinitely quarter after quarter on that level and no other. We must notice here, and we shall explain in detail later, that this assumption does *not* imply that net investment *ex post* reaches and remains at this same single new level. A second assumption deserving particular notice is that the body of income-receivers as a whole spend some particular fraction, between zero and one, of any incremental income stream on consumption. If this fraction were actually zero, our argument would come to a stop as soon as we had said that the extra stream of net investment will mean an equal extra stream of output and of income. And thirdly (and this is an assumption the need for which is often overlooked, or which is treated, without the smallest justification, as something self-evidently true) we assumed that the businessmen, at the threshold of each quarter, would plan to increase output by just that amount (measured, of course, in value) by which output in the previous quarter had fallen short of demand. With these three assumptions we get our result that, if the marginal propensity to consume is, say, ¾, the second additional stream of output and income will be ¾ the size of the first.

But now we have to ask, what will be done with this second extra stream of income? Will it not, in its turn, partly (indeed, to the extent of ¾) be spent on extra consumption? And will not this lead, at the threshold of the third quarter, to a fresh revision of the businessmen's production plans to provide for yet another extra stream of output of consumption-goods, amounting in value, this time, to ¾ × ¾ of the original extra stream of net investment? By the same argument, there will have to be a fourth stream, equal to ¾ × ¾ × ¾ of the original extra stream of net investment, and a fifth stream equal to ¾ × ¾ × ¾ × ¾ of that original stream, and so on. There will, indeed, if we follow our argument to its logical conclusion, have to be an infinity of such streams, each, however, only three-quarters of the size of its predecessor in the series.

Employment

It will be impossible, within the limitations that this book has set itself, to satisfy the reader by a rigorous demonstration that in spite of there being in principle an infinity of extra output streams to cope with, the total of all these will not exceed a definite limit. Readily as this is proved in algebra, we shall not resort to that method. Let us appeal instead to intuition.

Hercules and the Tortoise agreed to engage in a race of one hundred yards. The Tortoise, being admittedly the slower runner, was given a start of fifty yards. In the first five seconds Hercules covered the fifty yards which separated his starting line from that of the Tortoise, but in that five seconds the Tortoise had advanced a yard. In the next tenth of a second Hercules covered this yard, but meantime the Tortoise had advanced a further fiftieth of a yard. In the next five-hundredth of a second—and so on, and so on. This tale, like our own, could go on for ever. The number of 'terms' or items in the series is infinite. But will anybody claim that Hercules never overtook the Tortoise?

The famous Paradox of Zeno depends for its solution, like our own problem, on the mathematical idea of *convergence*. Imagine, if you like, a wall being built of stone slabs each half as thick as the one previously put in place. The first slab, three feet thick, leaves a three-foot gap to be filled to complete the six-foot wall. The second slab, eighteen inches thick, leaves an eighteen-inch gap. The third slab, nine inches thick, leaves a nine-inch space. Plainly there will always be a gap so long as the number of slabs is *finite*. In other words, there is room for infinitely many slabs, and still the wall will never exceed the limit of six feet in height, provided only that the thickness of each slab is some proper fraction of the thickness of its predecessor.

Now in our problem this proper fraction is the *marginal propensity to consume*. Provided it is less than unity, provided the income-receivers do not spend on extra consumption an amount equal to the *whole* of their extra income, the equality between total effective demand and value of total output, even when the latter is measured at constant prices, can be satisfied by a finite, limited increase in output. How great will that increase have to be?

Employment

It will have to be great enough for the extra consumption-spending, which arises from the extra output and income, to be fully matched by such portion of the extra output as businessmen are willing to see sold for consumption. They are not, by hypothesis, willing to see the whole of the extra output so disposed of, for they wish their own net investment to attain a new and higher level, and any part of the extra output which, *ex post*, has been matched by extra consumption has, *pro tanto*, failed to contribute at all to the realisation of the intended extra flow of net investment. In what circumstances, then, will income-receivers be content to leave unconsumed a portion of the extra output equal to the extra net investment-flow that businessmen desire? The answer plainly is, when the ratio of their extra consumption to the extra output is equal to their marginal propensity to consume, and when the difference between the two, namely the extra saving-flow, is equal to the desired *ex ante* size of the extra net investment-flow.

Let us restate this conclusion. A new equilibrium will have been reached when output ($\equiv$ income) has grown by such an amount that the saving which the income-receivers are willing to do out of this extra output is equal to the businessmen's extra intended flow of net investment. The size of this extra saving-flow will bear a determinate ratio to the value of the extra output and income-flow, a ratio which we can call the marginal propensity to save. This is of course merely another way of expressing the notion of a marginal propensity to consume. If the marginal propensity to consume is, say, $\frac{3}{4}$, then the marginal propensity to save, being (one *minus* the marginal propensity to consume) is $\frac{1}{4}$; if the marginal propensity to consume is $\frac{2}{3}$, then the marginal propensity to save is $\frac{1}{3}$, and so on.

Very well, then: turn upside down the marginal propensity to save, and we get a ratio which, *in equilibrium*, will be equal to the ratio of the extra output to the extra *ex ante* net investment-flow. This latter ratio has a special name, and we call it the MULTIPLIER. The theory of it that we have stated differs in one respect from the account of the multiplier given by its inventors, Professor Lord Kahn and Lord Keynes. They have made no mention of the need to distinguish between the *ex ante* and the *ex post* meanings of such terms as income, net investment and saving. For them there was, in consequence, no conceptual or numerical difference between the ratio of extra output to extra saving, and the ratio of extra output to extra desired, planned, *ex ante* net investment. But we have seen that there is no mechanism to ensure that intended or realised saving should *at all times* be equal to intended net investment. If we define the multiplier as the ratio of extra output to *intended* net investment, its numerical value will not be always equal to the reciprocal (the upside down) of the marginal propensity to save, but it will have a higher relevance to understanding and to policy-making.

Where there is a multiplier there must be a multiplicand, and hitherto in this chapter, through our assumption that our economy is self-contained and has no government, we have taken the multiplicand to be simply the net investment-flow aimed at by businessmen. What is there about net investment that enables or compels it to perform this role? simply that net investment involves the production of goods which are not available to be sold to consumers. Now in a *non*-self-contained economy there is another category of production which results in the generation of income without supplying goods upon which this income can be spent-for-consumption. This other category is the production of goods for export to other countries outside the 'open' economy. But is it true that the production and sale of exports results in no flow of goods available to be consumed? What of imports? Exports only contribute to the multiplicand in so far as they are not linked with an *equal* value of imports. It is the 'export surplus' which properly comes in as another component of the multiplicand. This fact has been the source of much heart-searching and of much international dispute. For it is quite literally true that any one country can 'export its unemployment' to other countries, so long as it can persuade them to accept its exports while refusing admittance to imports from them. If country *A* has an export surplus in its trade with country *B*, it follows that country *B* must have an import surplus in its trade with country *A*. And an import surplus is a *negative* item for country B's multiplicand. In years like the early 1930's, when much of the world was suffering from heavy unemployment, there is likely to arise a desperate competition to export and a mounting refusal to import. Economics is turned upside down. In all countries, many men are in dire want, yet the one object of the external economic policies of these countries is to give goods away to other countries without accepting anything, except gold or acknowledgments of debt, in return. Yet unemployment can be cured at home, provided all countries simultaneously take action to this end.

For there is yet a third component of the multiplicand. All those objects of expenditure which only governments can be expected to pay for, external defence and internal order, the education of the great majority of the people, to some extent the welfare of the sick and aged, are again things whose provision generates incomes but does nothing in itself to soak up those incomes by sale of goods or services to voluntary buyers of them. The government is free to take by taxation as much or as little revenue as it likes, out of the incomes of income-receivers, to offset part or the whole, or to more than offset, its expenditure on these services. What effect will such taxation have on the conduct of income-receivers? Some would have spent on consumption-goods what they are compelled, instead, to hand over to the government, some would have saved this money, and some pay their taxes partly out of what they would otherwise have consumed and partly out of what they would otherwise have saved. In so far as taxes are paid out of what would have been consumption-spending, the government is compelling the taxpayer to 'buy' the services of soldiers and policemen and schoolteachers instead of those of airline pilots and actors and automobile engineers. If, instead of compelling people to cut down their consumption-spending, the government taxed away only income which would otherwise have been saved, or did not tax away any income at all, then the government's own expenditure on non-saleable services would be wholly an addition to the multiplicand. This argument, too, is often wrongly put.

Employment

It is not simply the 'budget deficit', the excess of the expenditure of 'government' (in the widest sense, including central and local governments) over tax revenue, which constitutes a third component of the multiplicand; it is the excess of government expenditure over that tax revenue which is paid out of potential consumption-expenditure. If all taxes were paid out of what would otherwise have been spent for other goods, then, indeed, there is no addition to the multiplicand except the budget deficit.

Now if, by spending-without-taxing, the government can add to the multiplicand, and if it can rely on a fairly constant multiplier, it can at will increase the total effective demand for goods and services. It can change total effective demand in other ways; for example, by influencing the conduct of income-receivers so that the multiplier has a different numerical value; or by encouraging businessmen to increase their net investment; and it can do such things by other means besides taxation. But discussion of these policies and methods belongs to other chapters. In this chapter we have been concerned with the basic mechanism of effective demand for output as a whole, for it is this effective demand which gives rise to a 'derived demand' for productive services and which, in particular, provides human employment.

The central concept of this chapter has been the *multiplier*, first given clear and precise formulation by Professor Lord Kahn and later built into Lord Keynes's *General Theory of Employment, Interest and Money*, albeit without that complete freedom from ambiguity which might have been conferred upon it by attention to the Swedish idea of the *ex ante* and *ex post* viewpoints.

The formula we have given in section (*a*) of this chapter often appears in the literature in a slightly different guise. Our formula says that the multiplier in equilibrium, that is, when an attempt to increase the 'multiplicand' has had time to become fully effective, is the ratio of the extra output as a whole, measured in value at constant prices, to the extra amount of multiplicand items in total, the multiplicand being net investment plus export surplus plus excess of government spending over consumption-destroying or net-investment-destroying revenue. This multiplier in equilibrium, we have said, is the reciprocal or inverse of the marginal propensity to save. Now if we add together the marginal propensity to save and the marginal propensity to consume we get *unity*, simply the *whole* of the extra income; for this extra income is wholly disposed of either by the spending or by the non-spending of it.

It follows that the marginal propensity to save is equal to: (one *minus* the marginal propensity to consume), and that the multiplier's equilibrium value is equal to: [one *divided by* (one *minus* the marginal propensity to consume)].

Chapter 27. *Growth*

PLANT and equipment under construction employs labour and other productive services to advance it towards completion; the activity of building it is production, and this activity is measured and registered by the payment of money incomes. The emergence of this plant and equipment into a state of completeness and readiness for use is an addition to productive capacity, an addition to potential supply. Thus *investment*, the activity of improving and enlarging the nation's stock of tools, has *two* effects: it adds to demand for means of production, and it adds to their supply. Is there not a need to keep these effects in balance? What is the test of balance, how do we know that it is being kept? And how is balance to be achieved? Sir Roy Harrod was the first to write upon this problem and to offer a solution. It is his *dynamic theory* that we shall describe in this chapter.

In a society willing to consume, that is, to destroy, in each year the whole of what it could produce in that year at full employment, Harrod's problem would not arise. In that society, under free institutions of government, there would be neither need nor possibility of net investment. For there would be no voluntary saving (and thus, in freedom, no saving) to leave a gap between production and consumption. An excess of production over consumption, in an economy which has no foreign trade, implies the growth of the economy's stock of goods. This is a mere matter of arithmetic. Goods which are produced but not consumed add themselves automatically and inescapably to the general stockpile. But this process is not likely to continue for long unless the additions to the stockpile are desired by business men on the ground of their profitability. What is added to the stockpile, if this process of growth of the stock is to be a self-justifying and self-perpetuating one, must be equipment which promises to be useful and thus profitable. But in the last analysis, such usefulness must arise from a demand for a growing, or an improving, general output. Unless general output is to become bigger, better, or cheaper, there is no need for any change in the quantity or quality of the stock of equipment. Harrod's discussions of the matter[1] take account of advances in technology, but his basic argument is expressed, and best understood, in terms of quantity. Growth of the general stock of equipment will seem worthwhile only to the extent that it is matched by growth of general output. But what does 'matched' mean in this connection? Evidently the proper sense is equality of a month's growth of *production* with a month's growth of *capacity to produce*. Now the tools in an inclusive sense, the plant, equipment and buildings, which make possible one thousand pounds' worth of yearly production may themselves be worth, for example, three thousand pounds. The capital-to-output ratio, that is to say, may be three to one. Whatever this ratio is, the balance between desired or intended saving and desired or intended net investment, when investment depends for its incentive on growth of general output, will consist in the equality of two things: on one hand, desired saving as a proportion of general output, and on the other hand, the desired or designed

[1] 'An Essay in Dynamic Theory', *Economic Journal*, March 1939. *Towards a Dynamic Economics*, Macmillan, 1948; et cetera.

proportion of itself by which general output is to be increased, multiplied by the quantity of tools or 'capital' required per unit of such extra output. *Warranted growth*, as Harrod called it, will consist in fulfilment of the following test: a month's difference in level of output times the 'capital' or tools required per unit of output, equals a month's saving. This test in practical and historical fact may or may not be fulfilled.

One formal point needs explanation. When output is growing in a given way, its increment *per year* will of course be larger than its increment *per month*. But we are free to choose our time-interval of measurement quite arbitrarily. How then does Harrod's theorem hold? It does so because the capital-output ratio will become *smaller* as the measurement-interval becomes longer. If doubling the measurement interval roughly doubles the increment of output, but halves the capital-output ratio, the result of multiplying them together remains invariant against changes of the interval.

Harrod's theorem marries the notion of the Multiplier to an older principle called the Accelerator. When general output (measured by aggregate income) rises by a given increment, the people as a whole will want to consume part and to save the rest of that given increment. But only the saved part is available for providing an addition to the existing stock of equipment. Yet if, when the decisions are taken that result in an increment of general output, all the existing equipment is being used to the full, this increment of general output will require an addition, of appropriate size, to the stock of equipment. Then the quantity of extra equipment *wanted* in a unit interval of time will depend on the size of the *increment* of general output wanted in that time-interval, and on the equipment-to-output ratio; but the quantity of extra equipment *able to be supplied* in that time-interval will depend on the *level* of general output (the amount of production, of all sorts, performed in the interval) and on the proportion of it that people, all taken together, are willing to leave unconsumed. Now when we are engaged in the abstract intellectual process of designing an economic 'model', we are free to choose, *independently of each other*, the *level* of output and its *percentage growth per time unit*. Thus we can so adjust these to each other that what is willingly saved is sufficient to meet the needs for extra equipment arising from the growth which occurs. If, for a *real* economy at some historical moment, we are *given* the propensity to save, the ratio of equipment ('capital') to output, and the level of output, and are told that the existing equipment only just suffices for that level of output, we can then say what pace of growth of output will equalise the demand for, and the supply of, extra equipment. Harrod's theorem can be summarised thus, taking some one stated interval of time for all measurements:

increment of output divided by output is the percentage growth of output;
saving divided by output is the propensity to save;
equipment divided by output is the capital–output ratio (the equipment–output ratio).

Then for *warranted growth* we require:

percentage growth multiplied by capital–output ratio *equals* propensity to save.

Warranted growth means, simply, growth at such a percentage per unit of time as will precisely absorb in net investment the flow of voluntary saving. This percentage per time unit will be *determinate* (i.e. there will be only one numerical percentage which will do the trick) provided the capital–output ratio and the propensity to save are both *given*. Since the propensity to save and the capital–output ratio seem likely to change slowly in comparison with what may occur in the pace of growth of output, the statistician may be justified in practice, as well as in theoretical argument, in treating them as stable characteristics of the economy from which he can calculate the growth-rate which would satisfy people's desire to save while giving them full employment. What is more, the growth-rate is the outcome of business men's decisions, and these can be influenced by government action or directly supplemented by it, while saving policy may be more resistant and the capital-output ratio, resting on technology, may prove intractable in the short period. Harrod's theorem thus gives practical footing to the applied economist.

What Harrod chiefly sought to infer from his scheme of thought is the *instability* of the actual growth-performance of the economy and the consequences of this. For it is strangely true that if the pace of growth which is implied by business men's decisions exceeds the pace for which extra equipment can be provided by voluntary saving, then when existing equipment is fully employed, the order books of those firms which build equipment will be lengthening, and they in consequence will be trying to increase their own productive capacity by adding to their own equipment, and they will thus be increasing the pressure of demand upon themselves considered as a body. It will appear, paradoxically, that the *level* of general output is *too low* to meet demand. And if the pace of growth which business men's decisions imply is *less* than the warranted pace, the demand for extra equipment will be less in a month than what could be supplied in a month, the order-books for equipment will be shortening, and there will appear to be *over*-production. Attempted growth in excess of the warranted pace will lead to inflation, while failure of growth to reach the warranted pace will lead to depression and unemployment. The maintenance of full employment without inflation thus seems to involve the walking of a tight-rope. Harrod's theory may need some qualification and modification on theoretical grounds, but practical experience has done nothing to disprove it.

BOOK VI. FINANCE

Chapter 28. Liquidity

AT any instant there exists in a modern economy a stock of money consisting of some particular number of money units. Neglecting transactions with the outside world, which are not essential to our present problem, we can say that it is beyond the power of any individual or any firm outside the banking system to alter by his own actions the size of this stock. For if he buys something, the seller afterwards holds more money than before by precisely that amount by which the buyer holds less; and this is true even if the seller was in debt to his bank while the buyer was not. For we define the total stock of money in the economy as the result of adding together the cash in everybody's pocket or till, the money owed by the banks to their customers, and the additional money that the banks are willing to lend to their customers, further to what they have lent them already. Now if our supposed seller initially owes his bank £1000, the reduction of his actual debt to his bank to £700 by the sale of something is no reason in general why his bank should thereupon reduce his 'line of credit' and not be willing to let him increase his debt again to £1000. Thus the £300 he has received from the buyer remains available to him; after the sale it still enters into the computation of the total amount which the people and firms of the economy could *simultaneously* pay away at some one instant; and it thus remains part of the economy's total stock of money. Since corresponding statements will evidently be true of loans and gifts of money, our conclusion stands that the size of the economy's stock of money is independent of the money transactions of non-bank firms and of individuals.

Now, money which exists at all must, by our definition of money, be in somebody's possession. The economy's stock of money must at all times be held by individuals, firms and the government between them. Any one of these who at any instant holds some money can exchange it for productive equipment (or shares in the ownership of productive equipment) or can lend it, provided there is someone who is willing to perform the inverse operation, to accept money and give productive equipment or an acknowledgment of debt in exchange. Plainly, then, it cannot be true that at any instant the advantages, for every holder of wealth, lie altogether upon the side of holding productive equipment or acknowledgments of debt, for if they did, no one would be willing to hold money, and those who found themselves in possession of money would offer it so eagerly in exchange for the other kinds of asset that the price of these would be driven up indefinitely, until money units became virtually valueless in comparison. Since we do not observe this to happen, it follows that the possession of a stock of money must have some positive advantages of its own, and also that these advantages on the one hand, and those of holding other kinds of asset on the other, can attain a balance at the margin such that the price of other assets in terms of money is for the time being at rest.

We have now to examine the nature of the advantages conferred by possession of a stock of ready money, advantages usually collected under the name of *liquidity*; to show how the market value of these advantages, and therefore of those which must be sacrificed to gain them, is measured by a *rate of interest*; and to explain how this rate of interest comes to stand at a particular level at any one time.

To make a loan is to part with a given sum of ready money in exchange for the borrower's promise to pay a series of equal or unequal instalments each of stated size and due at some stated date. The interest-rate involved in this transaction is a percentage such that, if the sum initially lent is cut up into suitable slices and each of these is allowed to grow by that percentage per unit of time until the due date of one or other of the borrower's promised instalments, each of these instalments will find itself exactly matched in size by one of the grown-up slices. Suppose, for example, that the sum initially lent, the 'principal', is £500 and the borrower's instalments consist of £110 to be paid after the lapse of one year and £484 to be paid after the lapse of two years. Then the rate of interest here involved is ten per cent per annum. For if we cut up the £500 principal into two slices, one of £100 which is to be allowed to grow for one year, and the other of £400 which is to be allowed to grow for two years, the first slice will at the end of its year have increased by ten per cent of its initial size, that is, by £10, and so will have become £110, while the second slice at the end of its *first* year of growth will have increased by ten per cent of its initial size to £440 and will then during its second year increase by ten per cent of the size it had at the beginning of this second year, that is, by ten per cent of £440, and will thus in the end become £484. Thus the two slices of the initial principal, growing at ten per cent per annum for the appropriate periods, will come to match the borrower's two promised instalments. When the rate of interest is established on a market it expresses the *price* at which ready money can be exchanged for promised money due at future dates, and so in our example, if ten per cent per annum were the market rate of interest, £500 of ready money would have the same market value as two instalments, one of £110 deferred one year and the other of £484 deferred two years. There are, of course, infinitely many other schedules of future payments which would also, at ten per cent per annum, be worth £500 in ready cash. Turning our statement round we can say that if a schedule of promised payments consisting of £110 due in one year and £484 due in two years can be bought today for £500 in spot cash, the market rate of interest is ten per cent per annum.

If that same schedule of promised payments could be bought for £428 in cash down instead of £500, what would have happened to the rate of interest? This £428 could be cut into a £92 slice and a £336 slice. If the £92 slice grew for one year at twenty per cent per annum it would become £110. 8s. and if the £336 slice grew for two years at twenty per cent per annum it would become £483. 16s. 10d. So we can say that the rate of interest represented by a price of £428 for our schedule of promised payments is approximately twenty per cent per annum. A *lower* price in spot cash for a given schedule of future payments means a *higher* interest-rate.

If lending is the exchange of a stated sum of money for the promise of other stated sums which, evidently, when their number is finite, can be added together to give a definite total, are we to take it that lending consists in giving up one known sum of money in exchange for another known sum? No; for the lender can expect to be able, should the need arise at some later date, to find a third party willing to buy from him the right to receive the still-outstanding instalments promised in the borrower's schedule; but when he is deciding whether to make the loan or not he cannot tell whether or when he may need or wish to make such a sale nor *at what price* the sale will be possible. To make a loan, we must conclude, is to exchange a known for an unknown sum of money.

For most people such a state of uncertainty, of ignorance, will be disagreeable. The experience of this, as of any other feeling, is in its quantitative aspect an intensity at a moment of time. Like the speed of a moving object, it is not essentially dependent on the length of the time-interval over which we measure it: the *degree* of the disagreeable feeling can be the same no matter whether we think of it as experienced during a second or an hour. Now if the holder of a stock of money is to be induced to lend instead of retaining it, he must be able, at the moment of decision, to anticipate some other feeling, arising from some circumstance in the situation of a lender, such as to make lending seem worthwhile in spite of the uncertainty. Where can we find such a circumstance? The borrower's acknowledgment of his debt can hardly give the lender pleasure by its mere existence, by his mere possession of it: it is not a work of art. Yet the borrower's debt is in fact in every moment doing something, the formal quantitative aspect of which can only be specified as an intensity at a moment of time: it is growing. The necessary inducement to the lender is provided by the interest-rate which is involved, as we have seen, when a borrower promises a lender a schedule of future payments amounting, in total, to more than the principal of the loan. For an interest-rate is in essence a *proportionate time-rate of growth* of the borrower's debt.

If it is the interest-rate which overcomes the lender's reluctance to lend, arising from his fear lest in the outcome he may be a loser by lending, how do changes in the strength of this reluctance, amongst the body of potential lenders as a whole, bring themselves to bear on the interest-rate and find themselves reflected in it?

In the foregoing we have spoken of interest-rates as being determined on a market. What kind of thing is bought and sold on this market? The objects dealt in are borrowers' acknowledgments of debt, their promises to make payments according to specific schedules. To lend is to buy the right to receive the series of payments stated in such a schedule, or to receive those of them whose due dates are still in the future. As we saw, to say that the price of any particular schedule has fallen is arithmetically equivalent to saying that the interest-rate relating to this schedule has risen. Thus reluctance to lend expresses itself in a low price for these schedules, which are usually called 'fixed-interest securities' (the 'fixity' is that of the absolute amounts of the promised payments, not of their ratio to the market price, at any time, of the right to receive them), and thus expresses itself in a high interest-rate. A general readiness to lend will result in many competing bids for those 'schedules' or securities which are on offer in the market, their price will tend to be driven up, and the readiness to lend, to part with ready money in exchange for securities, will have expressed itself in a low interest-rate.

Lenders may often think of themselves not primarily as lenders but as speculators in securities. When they buy 'fixed-interest securities', they may be concerned principally with the possibility that the price of these securities will rise appreciably in the near future, rather than with the interest that will accrue if they hold the securities for some time. If many such speculators come to believe that the prices of fixed-interest securities are about to rise, they will 'buy for the rise' and thus tend to bring the rise about. We can express this notion alternatively by saying that if the opinion becomes widespread that the interest-rate is about to fall, action will be taken of a kind which will tend to make it fall.

In these considerations we get a hint of our problem's real subtlety and elusiveness. For, first, it is plain that the interest-rate cannot stay wherever, at any moment, it is so long as there is a consensus of market opinion about its next movement. If everybody or nearly everybody believes it is going to fall, they will all decide to buy fixed-interest securities, and the prices of these will, in fact, immediately rise: the interest-rate will fall. Nobody who feels confident that the prices of fixed-interest securities are going to continue rising will be willing (except for reasons quite independent of the prices of securities) to hold money, for it appears to him that by buying securities now and selling them a little later he can have more money. Thus so long as everyone believes in a further price rise, everyone will be anxious to part with money in exchange for securities, and no one will be willing to part with securities in exchange for money, or to remain in possession of money. This situation can only alter when the prices of securities have gone so high as to destroy, in the minds of some of the people in the market, the confident belief that they will go higher still. People who have *doubts* about a further rise will be willing to hold some money. There must be enough of such people, or of people convinced that the next movement will be a fall of security prices, to hold the economy's entire stock of money, or such of it as is not held for a quite different reason which we shall consider below.

The market in which 'fixed-interest' and other securities are dealt in is, of course, the Stock Exchange, and when, in his *Treatise on Money*, Lord Keynes first adumbrated the theory of interest as the price of liquidity, he employed the terms current in Stock Exchange jargon for those of the whole body of buyers and sellers of securities who believe in an imminent rise of prices, and those who believe in an imminent fall. The former are the 'Bulls', the latter the 'Bears'. In this terminology we can say that the interest-rate must move to such a level as will put enough people in the 'Bear' camp to hold the economy's entire stock of money, other than what is needed, as we shall see below, for 'real' transactions. If at any moment there are too few Bears, this situation will cure itself by a general movement on the part of the too-numerous Bulls to buy securities. The resulting rise in security prices will eventually transfer some of the former Bulls to the Bear camp, and the rise will not cease until there is a sufficiency of Bears to hold all the money that needs to be held; for, as we saw at the beginning of this chapter, the size of the stock of money is not altered when the money is passed from hand to hand, and all of it must be held by someone.

The 'liquidity' conferred by possession of a stock of money consists, however, in other things besides the guarantee it offers against loss through a fall in the prices of promises of future specified payments. We have been discussing the 'speculative' motive for holding ready money. Now we turn to the 'transactions' motive.

If a person or a firm could arrange for his incomings and out-goings of money to coincide precisely in date and amount, he would never need to hold any ready money for the purpose of making his day-to-day payments. But in fact of course such a perfect fit is never approached. Money must be held from the moment when it is received to the moment when it is paid away, and every income-receiver and firm will therefore at nearly all times have some stock of money in his or its possession, even if that money consists in 'unused permission to overdraw' at the bank. Why not avoid holding these stocks of money by lending them? It would not in general pay to do so. The cost and trouble of finding a borrower and making a legally binding contract with him, and of recovering the money when needed, do not decrease in fixed proportion with the size of the sum available to be lent, nor with the shortness of the time during which the money could be spared by the lender. The interest, however, that would be earned by such loans would decrease in proportion to the amount lent and the time for which it was lent. Some money, therefore, will always be held, in pockets, tills or the bank, ready to be paid away by the income-earners to the shopkeepers or by the firm to its employees or to other firms. This money will be performing the primary task of money, to serve as a medium of exchange in the 'real' business of producing and distributing goods and services. It is said to be held for the 'transactions motive'. We must realise that even money held for this purpose is providing *liquidity* at a sacrifice of *interest*: for if this money could be spared altogether for long periods, it too could be lent and could earn a worthwhile amount of interest. Interest is the price of liquidity.

In Chapters 15 (*Price-levels*) and 16 (*Money*) we hinted that although money's primary purpose is to provide a common measure of the economic significance of goods and services of all sorts, so that the total value of a mixed collection of such items can be reckoned and compared with the total value of a differently composed collection, yet money cannot perform this service without also possessing other powers and qualities. These other characteristics arise from the fact that money, having been received in exchange for some 'real' good or service, need not be exchanged back *immediately* for some other real goods but can be held, and thus can enable its possessors to put off deciding what to exchange it for. The motive for such putting-off can be the ordinary human incapacity for thinking of everything at once: the mental strain and inconvenience of composing a shopping-list for a whole month ahead, and executing it at the moment when a month's salary is received, would be intolerable. But there is another motive which works on a larger scale. While money is held, prices may change in favour of the holder. If the recipient of money believes that prices of some goods are about to fall, he will defer his purchases.

There are also, however, at all times some other people who would like to buy something now, to complete or improve some collection of real goods (for example, some outfit of productive equipment) on which they have already spent all their ready money; or who simply believe that prices of goods are going to rise and who wish to take even fuller advantage of this supposed impending rise than they can do by parting with all their own money in exchange for goods. All this class of people who want ready money are potential borrowers and will try to persuade those who have a stock of ready money to part with it in exchange for a promise of repayment at a specified date or dates. By agreeing to this, the possessors of money will be imperilling their advantageous position, for they cannot be sure that they will not need their money at some earlier date than the one specified for repayment. So they will require a promise of a larger sum than the one they now part with.

The relation between a list of sums due at stated future dates, and the present sum for which the right to receive those deferred sums can be purchased on the Stock Exchange, is called the 'yield' of the 'fixed-interest' securities which record and acknowledge the debt. This yield is expressed as such-and-such a percentage per annum by which suitable sums lent today would have to grow, in order to become equal, each at its own specified future date, to the particular sum due from the borrower at that date.

The arithmetic of the growth of a 'principal sum' lent today at compound interest, and the arithmetic of the inverse calculation of the 'present value' of a stated sum due after some stated lapse of time, were illustrated in Chapter 23 (*Equipping*), and the reader is strongly recommended to consult that chapter again if he has not in mind a perfectly clear picture of those computations.

The numerical level of the interest-rate at which loans for a shorter or longer term can be made or obtained, is determined on a market where these rates are pushed up or down so as to balance the desire of people and firms all taken together to hold money, with the quantity of money available for them to hold. This market consists, in Britain, partly of the London 'money-market' where very short-term loans, called bills of exchange and Treasury Bills, are dealt in, and partly of that section of the Stock Exchange where British Government and other 'fixed-interest' securities are bought and sold.

Chapter 29. Securities

WE saw in Chapter 28 that what we there called 'the interest-rate' is at any moment pushed to or held at a particular level by forces whose interplay takes place on the Stock Exchange. We must now elaborate in several ways the picture we presented in that chapter. We need to look closer at the psychological and arithmetical mechanism of that market; to take into account that other kinds of securities are dealt in on the Stock Exchange, besides fixed-interest securities; and to recognise that in speaking of 'the' rate of interest we are abstracting from some of the complexities of the real world.

We said that the interest-rate cannot be at rest even for the shortest time unless holders (both potential and actual) of fixed-interest securities are divided into two camps with opposite views about the interest-rate's next movement. Whenever there is a consensus of opinion, that is, whenever the bulk of those concerned with the market are all in one or other camp, the rate will move until it has transferred sufficient former Bulls into the Bear camp or vice versa to equalise the quantity of money which the people and firms in the economy, all taken together, wish to hold with the quantity that actually exists. So long as there are not enough Bears, that is, enough people willing to *sell* securities, the action of the Bulls in trying to secure for themselves a profit, which they believe an impending rise of prices of securities offers them, will drive up these prices and lower the interest-rate. But is there anything to ensure that the rise of prices and the necessarily concomitant fall in the interest-rate will, indeed, have the effect of turning Bulls into Bears? If security prices have risen, is not this a hint that they may well rise further? May it not happen that a rise of security prices will turn Bears into Bulls rather than the opposite?

We have not at all asserted that *any and every* rise in security prices will increase the number of Bears, but only that ultimately a level will be reached where this effect appears. Now if people have in mind some 'normal range' within which, in their experience and knowledge of the past, the interest-rate is wont to vary, and if, consciously or not, they assume that there is some inherent feature of the market which pushes the interest-rate back inside this range if ever it escapes, they will become more and more sceptical of a further fall of the rate, that is, a further rise of security prices, the further the rate goes below the lower limit of this range; and conversely, they will find it harder and harder to be confident of yet another rise of the interest-rate, the further it has already risen above the upper limit of its 'proper' variation. Such a belief in a normal range will continually gain strength the longer it operates: whether or not there are any 'objective' forces tending to keep the interest-rate within certain bounds, however vague these bounds are, the mere belief in them will create a mechanism having just the effect attributed to them. If an interest-rate of two-and-a-half per cent per annum is widely regarded as exceptionally low, then when the prices of fixed-interest securities approach the level corresponding to two-and-a-half per cent per annum, many holders and potential holders will refrain from buying more of them or begin to sell those they have, for it will now seem to them that a fall is 'just as likely' as a rise, or even more likely: it is not worthwhile to risk a loss for the sake of such a problematical further gain. Moreover, those of them at least who are professional operators in the market will realise its extreme sensitiveness in a situation where the interest-rate has departed far from its normal level. They know that there will in such a situation be many doubting and hesitant holders of securities, waiting for any sign that the time has come to sell. The mere slowing-down of the speed of the price rise may be enough to alarm them; its total cessation, at what seems to them already a 'very high' level, will be extremely likely to start a wave of selling.

Besides the mechanism we have just outlined, there is a more positive reason for believing that it might prove very difficult to press down below, say, two per cent per annum the rate of interest on those loans which allow the borrower many years in which to complete his schedule of payments. For at two per cent the security-holder is being asked, for the sake of this modest reward in interest, to run a very insistent risk of losing part of the price he could get if he sold his securities at once. The loss of capital value which could occur in a given time (say a month) could easily be many times as great as the interest which would accrue in that time; if a high rate of income tax has to be paid on this interest, the argument is more powerful still. In historical fact, the year 1947 provided a dramatic instance of such events. Why not, then, avoid this risk by holding money instead of fixed-interest securities yielding so little, and spend this money as required? If it is spent at a rate of only two per cent per annum of the initial sum, it will still last fifty years, and how many of those who own wealth can look forward to a longer remainder of life than this?

The Stock Exchange is a market not only for fixed-interest securities but also for shares in companies formed for industrial and commercial enterprise. A fixed-interest security is a borrower's promise to pay stated sums at stated dates; an 'ordinary share' or 'equity share' is a title to the part-ownership of a firm and thereby of the firm's equipment, goodwill and other assets. A shareholder is not a creditor of the firm, but one of the owners of it. He has a right to share in that part of its profit which the Board of Directors decides to distribute as a dividend. The striking difference between fixed-interest securities and equity shares is that the payments due to be received by the holder of the former are known in advance, and the due receipt of them depends only on the debtor's being honest and solvent; but no one can know in advance what profit a company will make and what dividend it will distribute. By far the greater part of all fixed-interest securities dealt in on the London Stock Exchange are the debts of the British Government; but local governments also borrow from the public, and commercial firms do so by issuing 'debentures'. The yield (the effective interest-rate) of a debenture will usually be rather higher than that of a British Government debt offering a similar time-schedule of payments, because it is regarded as conceivable that the company might go bankrupt, while it is not regarded as conceivable that the British Government might default. This difference of yield will express itself in the fact that if the government and a firm have each promised one and the same schedule of payments, the right to receive these payments from the government will command a higher market price, and therefore offer a lower yield, than the right to receive them from the firm. We must keep clearly in mind, however, that danger of default by the borrower is something entirely distinct from the lender's uncertainty about his own future needs and about the future behaviour of the market in fixed-interest securities.

Despite their differences, fixed-interest securities and company shares both offer a means of holding wealth with a prospect of possible gain. As such they are in some degree substitutes for each other. If a widespread belief that companies are going to make high profits makes shares in them seem to be worth more than before in money, holders of fixed-interest securities will be tempted to sell these securities and buy company shares instead. There will always be people or firms (banks and insurance companies, in especial) willing to hold fixed-interest securities, but only at a price which makes them attractive in competition with other assets. A widespread desire to sell fixed-interest securities and a corresponding reluctance to buy them will make their prices fall. This is arithmetically the same thing as making their *yield* rise: when the market price of such a security is lower, the interest-rate which will equalise the 'discounted' or 'present' value of the deferred payments that it promises with the market price will be higher. This higher yield or effective interest-rate then expresses the influence which the company-share market has exerted on the market for fixed-interest securities. It is perfectly legitimate and correct to say that the interest-rate is determined on the market for fixed-interest securities; for we define it as the yield of these securities. But this does not mean that what happens in the rest of the Stock Exchange leaves it unaffected.

There is another channel of influence of commercial and industrial prosperity or depression on the interest-rate. When output and employment are high, the number of money-units that the productive part of the economic system needs to have at hand, ready mobilised for making payments, is also relatively high: the sum which each firm will need to have at hand to pay its weekly wage bill will be larger, the payments it must make to other firms for materials are likely to be larger on the average and a larger average bank balance must be maintained to meet them, and so on. This extra demand for stocks of money on the part of those engaged in production and trade will leave less money, out of a given total stock, to satisfy the needs of those who wish to hold money as an *asset*, as a means of holding wealth. Competition for this smaller quantity of money, expressing itself in a greater readiness to sell fixed-interest securities and other property in order to get money, will drive down the prices of fixed-interest securities and raise their yield, that is to say, it will raise the interest-rate. Here we have a hint of an idea which our next chapter will be largely concerned with. For suppose that instead of being 'given', the size of the economy's stock of money expands to meet the extra requirements of people and firms for money to hold and to use? Then the pressure to sell fixed-interest securities will be relieved, their prices need not fall, and the interest-rate need not rise. So it seems that the size of the economy's stock of money has a dominant influence on the interest-rate, and indeed we could infer from what was said in Chapter 28 that this is so.

We have shown that fixed-interest securities can be of many kinds. Some may specify a short and some a long series of annual, or more frequent, payments by the borrower. When the due dates of the borrower's payments are stretched out far into future years, there will plainly be 'more room' for occurrences, quite unforeseeable when the loan is made, of such kinds as will make the lender want to sell his security; moreover the price he can expect to get will escape more and more completely from any possibility of reasonable guesswork, the further into the future the supposed date of sale is pushed. Thus for a double reason the uncertainty to which the lender is asked to subject himself becomes more onerous the longer the 'term' of the loan, that is, the more remote the date of the last of the borrower's promised payments. Shall we not expect these differences to be reflected in the interest-rate which, as we have seen, is the lender's inducement to submit himself to the mental discomfort of having parted with his known sum of ready money in exchange for an uncertain prospect?

We do indeed find that in ordinary times 'short-term' securities offer lower yields than 'long-term' securities, but the numerical relation is an inconstant one. The very shortest securities are called 'bills', and are promises by the borrower to make just one payment deferred three months or sometimes six months from the date when the bill comes into existence. The rate of interest on bills has varied in the 1950's between one-half of one per cent per annum and five-and-a-half per cent per annum. The very longest securi-ties are called 'irredeemables', the best-known examples of which are promises by the British Government to make an *unending* series of equal payments. The arithmetic of the matter turns out to be that the ratio of one of these equal annual instalments, promised to be paid in perpetuity, to the market price of the security, is equal to the yield of the security reckoned in the way we have shown above. This makes it specially simple to calculate the effect upon the yield exerted by any given change in the market price of an irredeemable security of this type. If, for example, the market price doubles, the yield is thereby halved, and so on.

Between 'Treasury Bills', which are the bills issued by the British Government, and 'Consols', which is the name for two kinds of irredeemables, there is at any moment, even amongst British Government securities alone, a fairly evenly spaced chain of different maturities, that is, securities whose final promised payment (often much larger than the other payments and thought of as 'repayment of the principal') is due in one, three, five, ...up to as much as forty years. When the yield of Treasury Bills is very low it is possible to observe a very interesting pattern connecting the yield of securities with the length of term they have still to run. We find that as we turn from Treasury Bills, through securities with only a year or two to run, towards those with up to five years to go before they mature, the yield rises steeply. From five years' maturity up to ten years' it rises less steeply, while beyond ten years' maturity it scarcely rises at all. What is the explanation? Surely it is that ten years is long enough for 'anything to happen'. If a man has to wait as much as ten years for the final payment due to him, his uncertainty will be nearly as great as if he has to wait fifty years. However much we may think we know about today's situation, this knowledge throws very little light on what will be the situation more than ten years hence.

There are times when this pattern, showing yields increasing steeply at first and afterwards more and more gently as we pass in review successively the very short, short, medium and long maturities, disappears entirely because the very short-term interest-rates have equalled or exceeded the long-term rates. This situation may come about because it is rather easier for the monetary authority (in Britain, the Treasury acting through the Bank of England) to create the kind of shortage which forces up the short-term rates than one which acts directly on the long-term rates. But it still seems likely that the pattern we have described reflects an underlying reality.

Throughout this Book vi the continuing theme is interest-rates. We have discussed in Chapter 28 what it is about economic life, or life even under its most general aspect, which gives rise to the phenomenon of interest; in Chapter 29 we have examined the market where interest-rates are 'determined', that is, pushed to or held at a particular level at a particular moment; in the next chapter we shall see the source and mechanism of the chief forces which operate in that market; in Chapter 31 we shall recur to the effects of an increase in the net investment-flow on employment and output, already analysed in Book v (*Employment*), and bring the argument round full-circle until it bears upon the question of price-levels at which we had a preliminary glance in Book iii (*Income*); and in Chapter 32 (*Capital*) we shall study the influence of the interest-rate upon the composition or 'structure' of the economy's stock of equipment as a whole.

It might be thought that in thus devoting a whole Book to what, when we look behind the diverse chapter headings of Liquidity, Securities, and so on, turns out to be a single phenomenon, we were making this phenomenon the hub of the economic wheel or the focal point of the whole body of economic theory. There have been times when economists seemed deliberately to be giving the notion of interest this central importance, and this tendency is best illustrated by the title of Lord Keynes's *General Theory of Employment, Interest and Money*. But this is to do the interest-rate too much honour. Having looked behind liquidity, securities and money to find the interest-rate, we have now to look behind the interest-rate to find something far more universal in its presence and effect: uncertainty.

Chapter 30. Banks

MONEY is created by the banking system. With the definitions we have used in previous chapters, it will be no trouble at all to us to justify this assertion. For in our definition of money we have included 'unused permission to overdraw', the permission given by a bank to a customer who wishes the bank to lend him money, to act as though the bank owed him money, up to some stated amount. Sometimes the bank says to such a customer 'Very well; we will open two accounts in your name. Under the first of these you will owe us £1000. Under the other, we shall at first owe you £1000. You will then be free to draw on this £1000 that we are placing at your disposal.' Quite plainly, by doing this the bank has added £1000 to the economy's total stock of money. All else in connection with the creation of money is merely an elaboration of this simple theme: banks create money by lending.

To consider what happens when a bank customer exercises the permission given him by his bank to overdraw, and pays away the money to another customer of this or another bank, is merely to fill in a trifling detail of the picture. If that other customer's account is 'in credit', that is to say, if his bank owes money to him and not vice versa, then plainly the exhaustion of the first customer's permission to overdraw will be precisely offset by the increase in the second customer's credit balance. If the second customer is overdrawn, then his actual overdraft will be reduced by the amount which he receives from the first customer; to this extent his unused permission to overdraw will be restored, and unless there is deliberate action on the part of *his* bank to cut down this permission, the result of the first bank's action in lending will again have been to increase the economy's stock of money.

Banks pay no interest on the money which their customers lend to them on 'current account', that is, on condition that the customer may withdraw his money without notice. It is a great convenience to an individual, and indispensable to a firm, to have a bank account, for the money deposited with a bank in Britain is as safe as anything can ever be in this world, and the owner of this money can make payments to anybody by simply writing a cheque telling the bank how much money to pay and to whom, signing it, and handing it to the person to whom the payment is to be made. In order to render this valuable service the bank has to maintain suitable premises and staff, and sometimes charges its customers a fee towards the expense of these. But the bank's chief remuneration comes from its own lending, which, as we have seen, is simply the 'other side of the coin' without which there would be no money for people to lend to the bank. It may seem more natural to think of the banking process as consisting, first, of the public's act of 'depositing' money with the banks, and, secondly, of the banks' action of lending this money to some members of the public. We have seen, however, that the truth is rather the other way round: the banks create money by lending to some members of the public, these members pay away this money to other people and these other people deposit it in, or lend it back to, the banks. But the question is of slight importance. The essential idea is that money arises through the *mutual* indebtedness of the ordinary individuals and firms, on the one hand, and the banking system on the other.

If the banks make a profit by lending, why do they not lend unlimited amounts, so as to make as large a profit as possible? Plainly, it would do their profits no good to lend to borrowers who turned out in the end to be unable to pay back the loan and the interest on it. To give themselves ground to feel reasonably sure that they will get their money back, banks require would-be borrowers to provide 'collateral security', consisting of property which, in the event of default by the borrower, would by due process of law be sold in order to reimburse the bank. But this requirement is not the only thing which limits the amount the banks can lend.

In Britain weekly wages are largely paid in legal tender money, that is, in Band of England notes and in minted coin of the Realm, and even people who have bank accounts use cash and not cheques for their train and bus fares and their casual purchases in shops where they are not personally known. Thus when the total stock of money and the total income of the economy have increased together, as they usually do, it is likely that the total annual value of payments made in cash will also have increased, and that therefore the total value of Bank of England notes 'in circulation with the public', that is, outside the banks, at any moment will be higher as well. So if the banks, by increasing the outstanding amount owed to them by their borrowing customers, increase the total stock of money, they will cause all their customers to want extra amounts of notes and coin in their pockets and safes. These customers will come into the banks and cash larger cheques, and the banks will have to part with some of the notes and coins in their tills. It is, of course, their legal obligation to pay out notes and coin to any customer who demands them, up to the full amount of money that they owe him, and they must, therefore, at all costs avoid any danger of exhaustion of their stock of legal tender money. In fact, however, they are subject to a much more stringent limitation than this, for it is a custom having the force of law for each bank in Britain that it shall not allow its total deposits, that is, the total amount that it owes to its depositors, to exceed a ratio of 100 to 8 to its total available quantity of cash. What, then, does this cash consist in, what governs its amount, and how and by whom can this amount be changed?

On the 'assets' side of the balance-sheet of each commercial bank there stands amongst other items 'cash in hand and at the Bank of England'. Part of this item, as its name suggests, is at any moment in the commercial bank's own vaults and tills, the rest is owed to it by the Bank of England. Just as the commercial banks owe to their depositors far more money than they could pay, all at once, in notes and coin, so the Bank of England owes to *its* customers, the commercial banks, more money than it could pay all at once in existing notes and coin. Nevertheless, the principle is recognised by everybody concerned that the commercial banks can properly regard their deposits with the Bank of England as the equivalent, in every way, of notes in their own safes; and if we can conceive of the need ever arising, they would have the right to draw out the whole of these deposits in tangible cash, in legal tender notes and coin; and in such circumstances the Treasury, empowered by Parliament, would no doubt increase to the necessary extent the Fiduciary Issue, that is, the total value of Bank of England notes that, at any moment, may exist over and above the quantity, very small nowadays, which the Bank of England can match by gold in its vaults.

The economic system's total stock of cash can be thought of, then, as the sum of three component parts: first, the total value of notes and coin 'in circulation with the public', that is, lying in the pockets and safes of people and firms *other than banks*; secondly, the total value of notes and coin lying in the tills and safes of the commercial banks; and thirdly, the deposits of the commercial banks with the Bank of England, that is, the money owed by the Bank of England to the commercial banks. The second and third of these parts together make up the commercial banks' cash reserve, and it is this cash reserve which they must not allow to fall below a ratio of $\frac{8}{100}$ to their total deposits. How does it come about, then, that this cash reserve stands at this level or that at different dates? The most important function of the Bank of England, the function which marks it out as a 'central bank', is to regulate the size of the economy's money stock in accordance with the policy and decisions of the government by setting at an appropriate level and altering from time to time the total cash reserve of the commercial banks. How can it do this?

The Bank of England is free to buy and sell British Government securities on the 'open market', that is, the Stock Exchange, without knowing or minding who is the seller of the securities it buys or the buyer of those it sells. What happens when, for example, it sells securities? The buyer will be a customer of one of the commercial banks, let us call it the Westmidland Bank, and will pay for the securities by giving the Bank of England a cheque drawn on his account with the Westmidland. The Bank of England will 'present' this cheque to the Westmidland, which must then pay to the Bank of England the amount stated on the cheque. How can it do this? By allowing the Bank of England to reduce the amount standing in the Bank of England's ledger as owed to the Westmidland by the Bank of England. Now money owed by the Bank of England to the commercial banks counts as *cash*, as legal tender money, for any one of the commercial banks can draw out legal tender money from the Bank of England at any time, up to the full amount standing to its credit there: the 'cash reserve' of each commercial bank appears in its balance sheet as 'cash in hand and at the Bank of England'. It is this cash reserve which the Westmidland is obliged to maintain at not less than eight per cent of its total deposits. When the cash reserve goes down, through a purchase of securities from the Bank of England by one of the Westmidland's customers, the Westmidland must take steps to reduce its deposits by an amount $\frac{100}{8}$ times as great as the reduction of its cash reserve: in short, it must reduce the economy's stock of money.

If the Bank of England *bought* securities in the open market, that is, from the anonymous customer of the Westmidland Bank, the whole process would work in reverse: the Westmidland customer would receive from the Bank of England a cheque which he would pay into his account; the Westmidland, in turn, would pay this cheque into its account at the Bank of England; and the Bank of England would add the amount of the cheque on to the amount which its ledger said it owed to the Westmidland. Thus the Westmidland's cash reserve would be increased by, say, £1000, and it would be free to increase its deposits by £12,500. When, by extra lending, it had done so, the economy's stock of money would have been increased by £12,500.

We saw in Chapter 28 (*Liquidity*) that all the money that exists in the economy at any moment must be held by people who at that moment are either willing holders of the money or are actively exchanging it for other assets and thus tending to drive the price of those other assets up; or if there is not enough money in existence to satisfy all the willing holders of it, they will be selling other assets for money and thus tending to drive the prices of these other assets down. Amongst these other assets will be fixed-interest securities, and when the price of such a security, giving the holder the right, say, to receive £3 a year in perpetuity, falls from £100 to £75, the *yield* of this security, expressed 'per annum', rises from $\frac{3}{100}$ or three per cent to $\frac{3}{75}$ or four per cent. Now if by 'open-market operations' the Bank of England increases the size of the economy's stock of money, it is likely that some people or firms into whose hands the extra money has come will feel that they have now more ready cash than they need and will use some of it to buy fixed-interest securities. The consequent rise in the prices of these securities will, by definition, mean a lowering of their yield, that is, of the interest-rate. Thus it is by open-market buying or selling of fixed-interest securities that the Bank of England, carrying out the purposes of the government, can lower or raise the interest-rates at which loans of money can be obtained or made.

It can also act on certain interest-rates by a more direct but less widely and profoundly effective means. The Bank of England is often referred to as the 'lender of last resort'. It is contrary to custom and convention for the ordinary commercial banks to borrow directly from the Bank of England, but they can at need do so indirectly, in case of a temporary pressure by their own customers to borrow more than the commercial banks can conveniently lend, by *refusing* loans to a very special class of their own customers. These special customers are the Discount Houses, who act as a sort of cushion or buffer between the commercial banks and the Bank of England. The business of these Discount Houses consists in buying bills of exchange, Treasury Bills and short-dated government bonds (all of these three things being promises by a borrower to pay a stated sum at a stated date only a few months or even weeks in the future) for a price somewhat less than the face-value, the promised payment itself. The difference between what the Discount House pays and what it later receives in these operations provides it with its income. The Discount Houses buy the great bulk of their assets (bills of exchange, etc.) with money borrowed from day to day from the commercial banks. When the latter find the demands of other would-be borrowers pressing upon the $\frac{100}{8}$ ratio of their permissible total deposits to their cash, they can simply refuse to renew part of their loans to the Discount Houses, who are then driven to borrow from the Bank of England at what is called 'Bank Rate'.

Now the level of Bank Rate is set by the Governor and Court of the Bank of England in consultation with the Treasury, and is announced each Thursday morning. By reducing the commercial banks' 'cash in hand and at the Bank of England' by means of open-market selling of securities, the Bank of England can force the commercial banks to cut down their loans to the Discount Houses, can thus force the latter to borrow from itself, and can prescribe the rate, Bank Rate, at which this borrowing shall take place. Thus the Bank of England can, whenever the British Government and the Bank's own Governor and Court so decide, set the interest-rate for short-term borrowing at a level chosen by itself. Moreover, the commercial banks keep the interest-rates which they charge on loans to their own customers closely in step (one or two percentage points above) Bank Rate, and thus Bank Rate has a very widespread and rapid influence on most other short-term interest-rates.

By open-market operations and by its Bank Rate, the Bank of England, we can say in sum, has a positive control over the size of the stock of money and a strong influence on the level of interest-rates both short and long, though this influence is more calculable and more rapid in its effect upon short-term rates than upon long.

The underlying simplicity of the banking mechanism, which can look superficially so complicated, appears most vividly if we invent a model of it such as to exhibit only the essentials. Let us imagine a self-contained country where a single bank constitutes the entire banking system and takes the place both of the central bank and of the commercial banks; and let us suppose that in this country all payments of every kind are made by cheque. Such a system is perfectly conceivable, and even feasible in practice, though perhaps not very convenient. Then the single bank, acting in its capacity as regulator of the size of the country's stock of money, would have to exercise moral restraint upon its own commercial banking activities. For in the conditions we have supposed, there would be nothing (except for a consciousness of doing social evil) to prevent the bank from making unlimited loans to any customer who desired them, and by that very act creating money in identical quantity with the loans. Since no cash is used in this imaginary economy, no one would ever demand to cash a cheque, and the only response the bank would ever have to make to any customer's act of writing a cheque in favour of someone else (who could not help being another customer of the bank) would be to deduct the sum in question from what its books recorded as owed to the drawer of the cheque and place this sum to the credit of the payee of the cheque. To make unlimited loans, which would be the same thing as creating unlimited quantities of money, would of course have disastrous social consequences, soon reducing the currency (the official 'medium of account' for all debts and exchanges) to a mockery which everyone would ignore, and driving people to use instead commodities useful in themselves, such as cigarettes, reels of cotton, bales of cloth, etc., whose value as currency would be anchored to their value as commodities.

The British banking system is in some degree safeguarded against such a debacle by the use of paper and metallic tokens as small change. The quantity of these which may legally exist is regulated by Parliament, and the legal obligation of the banks to repay any deposit on demand (or virtually so) in the form of these tokens compels the banks to keep their creation of money within a total suitably related to the quantity of these tokens that they can, at need, get possession of. This system is all that remains of banking's old aspect, when customers thought of it as a system for the safe-keeping of their gold. It was this gold which they thought of as their money, lying ready for them, and all else, notes or cheques, was a mere superstructure, an 'economising' of the precious metals. Nowadays the 'cash', consisting of tokens worthless in themselves, acts as a mere thermostat or servo-mechanism regulating, by a feed-back of messages, the size of the country's total money stock.

Chapter 31. Living Costs

IMAGINE a river-gorge with its sides sloping gently from the floor at first and getting steeper and steeper as they rise in cliffs towards the lip of the gorge. When the floods come down, the river can spread sideways over the flat floor and gentle lower slopes of its gorge, but as the volume of water which flows down per minute gets greater and greater its depth also must increase, and because of the steepening sides, this increase of depth must proceed by increasing steps as the width of the river increases by equal steps.

In this picture let the gorge itself, with its shape that remains virtually unchanging in the short period but is enlarged by the river's action in the long period, stand for the economy's material and organisational frame of productive apparatus. Within this frame, constant in the short period, a larger output (a larger volume of water per minute) can flow, and at first the increase in the size of the flow from a very low level can take place with little increase in the depth of the stream (in the money prices of goods), because there is still 'elbow-room', there are still reserves of unused capacity which can be drawn into production. But as the increase of volume proceeds, the water must rise up the steepening sides of its channel, the further increase of output will encounter shortages and 'bottlenecks' and the need to draw in inferior resources which, nevertheless, will require as high a money wage as the more efficient resources already in employment. Thus prices will rise, and this rise will more and more outpace the growth in the flow of 'real' output as one difficulty is piled upon another to block the road of expansion of output.

Writers back to Ricardo and beyond were well aware that an increase in the size of the economy's money stock, coming about, for example, through a sudden willingness of the banks to increase their outstanding loans even if this could only be done by reducing the interest-rate, would have the effect of raising the general price-level. But it was not till 1898, in his *Geldzins und Güterpreise*, that the Swedish economist Knut Wicksell explained with precision how this effect could be supposed to come about; and it was not until the 1930's that his ideas, interpreted by Keynes and Hayek, began to displace the conventional Quantity Theory of Money. However, Keynes's *General Theory*, shouldering the burdens of the *Treatise on Money* as well as fresh burdens of its own, provided a chain of ideas by which we can trace in detail, through human judgments and decisions, the connection between an increase in the stock of money and a rise of prices in general. All the necessary materials for this have been assembled in our Books v and vi and we have now only to fit them together.

The links of the chain are as follows:

1. An increase in the economy's stock of money enables the 'Bearishness' of those who wish to hold money, not in preparation

for making payments, but as an asset instead of buying securities, to be more fully satisfied. Willing holders of the extra money will only present themselves in the securities market if the rate of interest falls (in other words, if the prices of securities rise).

2. A fall in interest-rates makes a larger flow of investment, a faster pace of improvement and enlargement of the economy's equipment, seem worthwhile. The discounted value of any given series of assumed future profits is now higher, a higher supply-price of the equipment expected to earn these profits can now be tolerated, and the quantity of such equipment produced per unit of time can accordingly be increased: supply-price and effective demand-price of equipment can now be equalised at a higher level of output.

3. The Multiplier Theory tells us that when the economy's pace of net investment is higher, its output and income will be higher.

4. In the short period, a large increase of output will involve the drawing into use of less efficient resources than those already employed, and both the money cost and the real cost of both the marginal and the average unit of output will be increased.

In this chain there are at least two links of seriously questionable strength. First, when the prices of fixed-interest securities have reached a sufficiently exceptional height, it may prove impossible, by further increases in the economy's stock of money, to maintain any preponderance of Bullish over Bearish sentiment. For each person who becomes persuaded that the prices will go higher still, some one else will come forward who is willing to sell at the current price the securities that the first person wishes to buy. All the extra money which is created will simply find its way into the money stocks of those who are willing, at the current prices of securities, to hold this money. Thus the interest-rate will fail to respond by a further fall to any further increase in the size of the money stock.

Secondly, for the reasons we saw in Chapter 23 (*Equipping*), a fall in interest-rates may have little effect on the pace of investment. If investment is unresponsive to changes in interest-rates, if, as we say, it is 'interest-inelastic', the chain is broken, there is no rise in output and no reason for any rise of prices.

It is far from true, then, that any and every increase in the size of the economy's money stock is bound to result in a rise of the general price-level. Under what conditions will it have this effect, and under what conditions not? In the picture we drew at the beginning of this chapter, of the river-gorge with steepening sides where the depth of water increased slowly at first when the flood water began to come down because there was room for the river to spread sideways, but afterwards increased rapidly as the river climbed up the steepening slopes, it was the initial size of the river, together with the size and shape of its channel, which decided how much difference to the depth would be made by a given increase in the volume of water flowing down per minute. In the economic system with its temporarily rigid framework of productive facilities, it is the initial size of output in relation to these facilities that decides how much prices will be raised by a given increase of output. When there is a great deal of 'unused capacity' or 'reserve capacity', that is, factories, machines and ships standing idle or only employed part of their time, output of goods in general can be largely increased without any extra strain being put upon the economy's equipment, and prices need hardly rise at all. But when all the factories, railways, docks and power stations are working hard all the time, this outfit of equipment will be reduced in efficiency if it tries to produce more still. At some points of the complex network of interweaving processes the bins of raw and partly manufactured materials will be exhausted before fresh supplies can come in from other parts of the system, some processes will be temporarily halted and this in turn will cause other shortages in other industries and firms depending for their supplies of materials on those which have been stopped. The spreading shortages will tempt firms and their customers to offer higher prices in order to outbid their rivals, and the increase of output will have begun to push up the general level of prices.

In the *General Theory of Employment, Interest and Money* the interest-rate occupies a central place, and so it does in the theory of the price-level which emerges from that book. But in the light of those empirical studies, in England and the United States, which have cast doubt on the idea that interest-rates greatly influence investment in industrial capacity, it no longer seems so clear that the interest-rate ought to be so prominent in a theory of *output and prices of goods in general.* In judging the rival merits of the older approach and the Keynesian theory, we shall not give all the marks to the latter. For when the size of the economy's stock of money is increased, this increase does not come about through Father Christmas silently putting extra money in everybody's bank account in the middle of the night. It often comes about because some particular people or firms or the government itself have in mind some specific schemes, for the realisation of which they need to be able to buy certain materials and machines and hire labour of particular kinds, for which purpose, in turn, they borrow extra money from the banks. Thus the question whether anyone will or will not have any inducement to spend the extra money on goods and factors of production, and whether this inducement will be afforded by a fall in interest-rates, is in these cases answered in advance, *before* the extra money is created by the extra bank loans which the promoters of the schemes require. The money is created *in order* to be spent, and if the interest-rate is to claim any important role in the whole business, this role must be performed as an antecedent to the creation of the extra money and not as a consequence of it. It is true, however, as we saw in Chapter 30, that the Bank of England, carrying out the Government's wishes, may sometimes buy fixed-interest securities from all sorts of holders of them, thus making such securities scarcer and money, with the help of the banks' 100 to 8 rule, very much more abundant. The Bank of England may do this with the purpose, clearly understood by the Bank itself and by the public, of stimulating investment by making the borrowing of money easier and cheaper. In such cases it may be that interest-rates are relied on to play a central part.

Our river-gorge analogy was intended to suggest the central notion of that theory of the price-level which was laid down by

Professor Kahn in his famous article about the Multiplier (*Economic Journal*, June 1931) and taken up by Keynes in the *General Theory*; namely that prices will not rise so long as there is general reserve capacity. They will rise as soon as 'bottlenecks' begin to appear. What was not so clear in the 1930's as it is in the 1970's is that when there is virtually no reserve plant capacity and no reserve of labour left anywhere, the strong demand and high profits which accompany this very full employment (in one way as cause and in another way as consequence) will induce such competition amongst firms for the very scarce labour that trade union action finds it easy to push money wages continually upward even if demand is no longer *autonomously* increasing. Thus we get the famous 'vicious spiral' of prices—wages—prices.

What we have said in this chapter may suggest to the reader that an increase in the stock of money is more likely to be something which makes it easy for money prices to rise when other forces are at work increasing effective demand and output and employment, than to be itself as it were a spontaneous cause of this increase of output and employment and of the rise in prices which, when output begins to strain capacity, accompanies the growth of output. This suggestion is nowadays widely judged amongst economists to be the truth. The stock of money has been compared to the cable of a balloon. If the balloon is to be able to rise, the cable must be let out; but merely letting out the cable will not of itself make the balloon ascend.

We have been able to account for this passive role which the money stock plays by pointing to the two weak links in the chain that might be supposed to lead from an increase in the money stock to an increase in the price-level. First, there is the widespread conviction that interest-rates are tied by an elastic string to some level around six or seven per cent per annum, and that a long-term interest rate of two-and-a-half per cent is 'too low to last', so that when security prices rise to a level corresponding to two-and-a-half per cent, Bulls become very nervous and melt into Bears. Secondly, there is the fact that businessmen will not invest in industrial plant except on the strength of profits which can be looked for in two or three years from the date of beginning to use the new plant; for beyond that the future is hardly at all illuminated by knowledge of the situation 'now'. This implies that investment is 'interest-inelastic', that is, unresponsive to changes in interest-rates.

Let us finally notice that this conclusion fully supports the view of those who claim that *if* the government felt able to keep the Fiduciary Issue rigidly constant, there would be, somewhere, a definite step beyond which the general price-level could not rise.

Chapter 32. Capital

THE word 'capital' has been the centre of so much confused thinking and writing that it might be better for us to avoid it. But do we, perhaps, still need some of the ideas that 'capital' has stood for, and do we still need a 'theory of capital'?

It may seem to the reader that the inclusion in this Book VI, on 'Finance', of a chapter headed 'capital' is natural and inevitable, for are not 'finance' and 'capital' very intimately related ideas? However, what really links this chapter with the other chapters of Book VI is the very same skein of ideas that links together those other chapters themselves, namely the ideas about interest-rates. During the 1930's the 'theory of capital' changed its role. Until then it had been the means of explaining the nature of interest-rates, the purpose they served and the mechanism which at any given time pushed them to or held them at a particular level. But in 1930 and 1931 some powerful ideas, introduced a generation earlier by the great Swedish economist Knut Wicksell, were suddenly seized upon by two men of very divergent outlook, and used, paradoxically, to prove apparently opposite theses. In his *Treatise on Money* of 1930 J. M. Keynes began the destruction (completed six years later in his *General Theory*) of the idea that interest is the price of savings. He showed it instead to be the price of liquidity. In his *Prices and Production* of 1931 Professor Hayek showed that, none the less, the *structure* of the economy's stock of equipment is important and that, because of this, plans to extend this stock may be defeated unless they have, in effect, the consent of those from whom savings will be required for this purpose. From that time a theory of capital was needed, not to explain the origin of interest, but to trace some of its effects. What, then, do we mean by the 'structure' of the economy's stock of equipment?

To earlier economists it appeared possible without distortion of essentials to treat labour as a homogeneous factor of production, and to treat land as another such factor. But what was to be done with that immensely various collection of instrumental goods, comprising stacks or bins of materials, tools of every kind, machines, buildings and constructions, all of them evidently associated with the productive process but yet not seeming to possess that active power to forward this process which belongs both to men and to nature? Men plough and sow, nature germinates the seed and ripens the corn, but what do the inert implements contribute of their own accord and out of their own essence?

Two questions present themselves: first, why should the owner of a collection of objects without life or life-giving power be able to claim an income merely in virtue of his possession of such a collection? And secondly, what is the proper measure of the size, in some significant sense, of such a diverse collection of things? Böhm-Bawerk, the Austrian contemporary of Wicksell, may not have put precisely these questions to himself, but he supplied an idea which seemed to answer them both. He gathered 'produced means of production' of every kind under the heading of capital. And capital, he said in effect, is the visible symptom of the part played in the productive process by the *lapse of time* between the putting-in of the services of labour and land, the 'original means of production', and the enjoyment of the fruits of that process at a later date. How can we say that 'time' is productive? Because *given* quantities of human effort and of 'land' can yield a larger quantity or better quality of product if we are willing to wait longer for it. The classic example is the maturing of wine, where, once the fermenting grape-juice is in the cask, time only is required for the securing of a better and better product.

However, it was not so easy to think of many convincing examples having this degree of simplicity. Even the extra growth of a tree when left standing longer could be ascribed to the efforts of nature, at work all the while in the soil and the air and the sunlight, rather than to the effect of the mere passage of time. So a different twist was given to the theory, and it was claimed that time allows of the use of a more 'roundabout' process of production. Now, when we look closely, it is not plain that a greater number of distinct operations or 'stages' of production need necessarily mean that a longer period will elapse between the performance of work and the gathering of its fruits, on the average over all the occasions when work is contributed to the making of some one thing; for each 'stage' in a chain of more numerous stages might occupy less time than those of a shorter chain. But there is one route by which time does unmistakably come into the picture, and that is when one of the 'stages of production' consists in the making of a durable instrument. For the work of making the instrument is evidently part of the work of making the final product in whose manufacture this instrument is to play a part, and the durability of the instrument implies that a long time can elapse between the date when the instrument is made and the date when it helps to make some particular 'packet' of the final product. Ten years may elapse between the building of a fishing-boat and a particular voyage to the fishing grounds. It is worth-while to examine carefully the economic aspects of the matter.

A complex, expensive machine can pay for itself by performing a kind of task which, in each separate instance of its performance, is relatively unimportant and of low value, provided it performs this task often enough. But all these numerous occasions of performing the task must, in the nature of things, take place, as it were, end-to-end, in temporal sequence, and in consequence the machine can only perform enough of them provided it lasts a long time. The machine's power may enable one man to move as many tons of earth at each scoop as a hundred men with shovels, but this high efficiency is only brought within reach provided the machine is durable enough. Durability, then, is not an economic end in itself but a means to higher efficiency in the use of the 'original means of production', and since durability of instruments implies a lapse of time between the making of these instruments and their use in the making of the ultimate product, the conclusion emerges that time itself is productive: by using more time in producing a given commodity we can get more of that commodity with given quantities of work and of the services of nature.

Now a question will certainly have arisen in the reader's mind. The multiplication of the effect of the fisherman's exertions by his possession of a boat will be about as great when he has had the boat ten years as when it was new: yet the lapse of time between the building of the boat and the use of it will be altogether different on the two occasions. How can we reconcile this fact with the claim that it is the lapse of time which achieves the greater efficiency? Evidently it is the *average* lapse of time that we have in mind, but how is this average to be reckoned?

And in the first place, what is to be averaged? If we think of the productive services of human beings and of nature being put into the productive process in 'packets', each packet going in at a particular calendar date, and if we likewise think of the ultimate product emerging in 'packets' each at a particular date, then if we can say of each packet of product: *This* particular packet of product is the result of *that* particular packet of original means of production, and if we make a weighted average of all the lapses of time thus observed, weighting them according to the relative values of the packets of product, we shall have got the kind of answer which the theory evidently seeks. Before we go on to ask whether, in fact, it is possible in principle to link up a 'packet of input' with a 'packet of output' in the way we have suggested, let us see how an increase in the length of this 'average period of production' would manifest itself at any one moment.

Suppose that in a Post Office one customer enters every minute and another customer leaves every minute, and it takes five minutes for each customer to be served. Then at any moment there will be five customers in the office. But if instead it took ten minutes to serve each customer, there would at any moment be ten customers in the office. In just the same way, the longer, on the average, each packet of input remains 'embodied' in the production process before the corresponding output emerges, the larger will be the 'number of packets' of input embodied at any moment. What do we mean by 'packets of input embodied' in the productive process? How will they appear, what form will they take? The only form they can take is that of partly processed goods or, as the exponents of the Austrian theory of capital habitually say, 'intermediate products'. If we interpret the term '*intermediate* products' appropriately, it will include *all* the sorts of things which are made merely in order to help in the ultimate emergence of some final consumable product, and amongst these there will be all the durable instruments and machines. Thus the collection of all the intermediate products as a whole, in the process of manufacture of all kinds of consumable goods taken together, is nothing other than the entire equipment of the economy, and we are led to the result that an increase in the length of the 'average period of production' will be reflected in an increase in the total quantity of equipment existing at any moment.

It will also be true that an increase in the total quantity of equipment possessed by the economy *can* take a technical and organisational form equivalent to a lengthening of the average period of production; and we have seen that this lengthening can in various ways make possible productive techniques of higher efficiency, in the sense that given inputs result in larger outputs. It follows that if people are willing to forgo some of the immediate consumption which their disposable income would allow them to enjoy, and by this abstention build up a larger stock of equipment, they can be rewarded for this sacrifice by the prospect of a larger ultimate quantity of product; not merely a once-for-all bonus, as it were, but a larger *stream* of product able to be maintained in perpetuity by the same stream of inputs of 'original means of production' which formerly only sufficed for a smaller stream of output.

It was to this conception that the Austrian economists appealed in their endeavour to explain the nature, role and manner of determination of the rate of interest. *Saving* was an act involving sacrifice and therefore needing a reward as inducement; lengthening of the average period of production was a means of making such a reward available. There was a supply side and a demand side for saving, and so there must surely be a price which would establish equilibrium on the market for saving. The Austrians saw the price in the rate of interest.

The reason why this theory of interest does not today command acceptance is principally that interest-rates as we observe them are obviously so much more volatile and swiftly and widely variable than could possibly be accounted for by any changes in people's willingness to save or in firms' desire to build up extra or improved equipment. The yield of Consols has in recent years shown itself able to swing up in a few months from two-and-a-half per cent per annum to three per cent and later from four-and-a-half per cent to five-and-a-half per cent. Short-term interest rates have varied since 1945 between one-half of one per cent and eight per cent. This volatility can be accounted for by reference to the swift changes of expectation in the minds of speculative Bears and Bulls, and to government manipulations of the size of the money stock, but not by reference to changes of settled saving habits or even to fluctuations in the number and scale of businessmen's investment-schemes in process of execution.

Nevertheless, the Austrian picture of the 'time-structure of production' has a value of its own. It reminds us, first, that there must be a certain 'balance' amongst the different forms of equipment if the situation is to be tolerable for long. To put a large part of the national effort for many years into building so-called 'heavy industry', iron and steel works, electric power schemes, railways and so on, will during those years entail hardship without visible reward. People will be working hard but enjoying much less of the products of their labour than would be the case if the 'average period of production' were not being so strenuously lengthened. If, before the lengthening is brought to the point where extra streams of consumable output begin to flow, the people's patience breaks down and they refuse to continue consuming so little of what they produce, the lengthening may never be completed and large blocks of equipment which would have been appropriate to a very large total stock of equipment may be rendered useless. Secondly, in explaining that 'capital is time' the Austrians gave us an insight which need not be rejected merely on the ground that less can be built on it than was at one time believed.

Besides the unrealism of its explanation of the nature and determination of interest, the Austrian theory of capital has two 'technical' weaknesses which greatly impair its cogency and usefulness. First, the assumption we made above, that each 'packet of output' can always be linked with its own 'packet of input' is untenable when we admit *durable equipment* into the theoretical scheme. It would be possible to find a place for durable equipment if we could suppose, either that a machine comes into existence instantaneously or else that it is used up instantaneously; but when we admit that in fact a machine takes time to build and time to use up, we can no longer link outputs with inputs in a unique and unequivocal pattern. Secondly, the 'quantity of capital' corresponding to a given 'length of the average period of production' will vary when the interest-rate itself varies: for a 'packet of input' must be conceived of as growing in value at compound interest all the time it is 'embodied' in the capital structure. Thus we lose the simple and direct link between quantity of capital and interest-rate, and are reduced to extremely complicated mathematical analysis for the sake of a result which has little realistic relevance even when it is established.

BOOK VII. GOVERNMENT

Chapter 33. Taxes

ACCORDING to an old-fashioned view, the government of a country differs from a private firm mainly in having the power to compel its 'customers' to buy its products in quantities and at 'prices' fixed by itself. These products used to consist of the services which the government rendered to the citizens as the umpire and watchman of their serious game of making and spending their incomes. The government ensured that the game was played without cheating and without violence amongst the players, and without intrusion and interference from foreigners. In order to maintain this frame of law and order and safety, the government must employ many of the citizens themselves as judges, policemen and members of the armed forces, and must pay them incomes for their work. Where does the money for this purpose come from?

But ought we to frame this question in terms of money, which, in that one of its roles where its flow represents *income*, is, we have often insisted, merely a means of keeping account of what is happening amongst the things that really matter, the production and consumption of goods useful for their own sakes? Let us put a different question: How can the judges, policemen and soldiers be enabled to live when, instead of producing crops, clothes, electricity and so on, things which they could use or sell, they are merely watching over such activities on the part of others? How are they themselves to be fed, clothed, warmed and so on?

Plainly, the farmers and tailors and electricity engineers must go without some part of the goods they produce and hand over that part to the guardians of law and order and safety. 'Fair exchange is no robbery.' The policemen and soldiers will get food and clothes, the farmers and tailors will get protection and peace

Taxes

of mind. All of them will be contributing, in one necessary way or the other, to the total process of the orderly and secure production and consumption of income by the economy as a whole. All that needs to be arranged is the exchange itself.

This exchange is effected, like almost all other exchanges in a modern economy, by means of money, and we can now answer our former question, where does the money come from to pay the policemen and the soldiers? It comes from the farmers, tailors and engineers, who, out of the money they earn in their full week of producing food, clothes and electricity, must hand over, say, one day's earnings to the government, who hand it on to the policemen and soldiers, who pay it over the counter to buy that part of the farmers' food and the tailors' clothes and the engineers' electricity which those types cannot buy for themselves because part of their week's pay has been taken away from them. It all fits together as we showed in our square table on page 83 of Chapter 14 (*Circulation*). To make our picture exact and complete we need only add that the judges, policemen and soldiers exchange their services with each other also, by means of money, each paying a part of his money income to the government to pay for the services he receives from the others.

Now the services of judges, policemen and soldiers are not packaged in unit quantities, so that the farmers, tailors, engineers and other citizens, including the judges, policemen and soldiers themselves, could each buy as much or as little as he liked. In order to keep in being the frame of law and order and safety at a given level of strength, comprehensiveness and effectiveness, a certain minimum yearly expenditure of money (the rates of pay of judges, policemen and soldiers being given) must be maintained. In order to serve its purpose, that of giving to the judges, policemen and soldiers (the State Servants, as we will call them) command over the intakes of real goods which they need, this expenditure must be precisely matched by the *revenue* or total of yearly amounts which the citizens, all taken together, deduct from their yearly earnings and treat as *not spendable* on consumption. For if, out of the total yearly quantities of food, clothes, electricity and so on,

8-2

which are produced by the economy (that is, by all its citizens taken together) certain portions are to be made available to the State Servants, these precise portions must be *forgone* by the farmers, tailors and engineers, and other such non-State Servants, who actually produce them. The farmers, tailors and engineers must therefore be prevented from spending on food, clothes, electricity and so on, the whole of what they earn in producing these things. They have got to take out the real equivalent of part of those 'gross' earnings in the form of the services of State Servants. That particular part of their gross earnings has to be taken away from them by *taxation*.

Taxes fall into two great classes. There are those which exact from the individual a certain fraction of his income or of his fortune; and there are those which exact from him a certain fraction of his outlay on particular goods and services. Taxes of the former kind are called direct taxes, and of the latter, indirect taxes or commodity taxes. Remembering what has so often been insisted on in these pages, the universal interdependence and mutual influence of economic variables, we shall expect the imposition of a new tax or a change in the *rate* of a tax to have a pervasive effect in various degrees on everything in the economic system. In principle, every price, output and income is liable to be changed, much or little and sooner or later, by any change in the character or rates of the economy's taxes. It is this fact which makes almost impossible the task of tracing, let alone forecasting, the ultimate or equilibrium effect of any given tax-change on any given person's income and on his pattern of consumption, so as to be able to say who 'ultimately pays' the tax and how much loss of satisfaction in direct consumption of goods is entailed, with a given set of taxes, in order that the people of the economy as a whole may enjoy the peace of mind, and freedom from interference and coercion, that are provided by the policemen and soldiers. There is, perhaps, a more reasonable hope of getting meaningful results from such tracing for direct than for indirect taxes.

We have supposed that in order that State Servants may be given a livelihood, may be able to acquire the food, clothes, shelter and so on that they need, the government must collect a certain annual sum of money as *revenue*. Some procedures, some tax systems, for collecting this revenue will have more to be said for them than others. What ought we to require of a system of taxes, what tests can be applied to find the best system? We speak here of a system of taxes, rather than of an individual tax, because what matters is the combined effect of all the taxes which are in force together. Taxes of different kinds can supplement and correct each other; it is not necessary for each separate tax to possess by itself every quality desired in the system as a whole.

It can be plausibly maintained that a tax system should not discourage people from *producing*, that is, from working, from engaging in enterprise, from allowing means of production which they control to be used by others who could employ them profitably. In brief, a tax system should not offer a 'disincentive' to effort and enterprise. If it does so, it will make people in general poorer, will reduce their real incomes. Secondly, since any work or trouble that the actual collection of the taxes entails does no good to anybody, and is pure loss, it is plain that if two systems are in other respects equal, that one will be better which leaves the smaller gap between the yearly total collected from the taxpayers and the portion of this which remains available for the government to spend after it has paid the tax collectors (in the broadest sense of the word tax collectors) for their work. Thirdly, a tax system ought to rest as lightly as possible on those of the citizens, even, who suffer most from it. There are, unfortunately, bound to be some citizens upon whom the taxes bear with special harshness, since we cannot suppose that any system will be able, in any clear sense, to claim to inflict 'equal' degrees of hardship on everyone. Thus our third requirement is that the greatest hardship it inflicts anywhere should be the least possible. And fourthly, despite what we have admitted under heading three, a tax system ought to seek to be in some reasonable practical sense 'fair', its real subjective burden ought not to be manifestly and widely unequal for different citizens.

It is, unhappily, far easier to say what would be the character of an ideal tax system than to say what are, in fact, the effects of taxes of particular types. Nevertheless, there is one kind of difference between taxes that has quite clear-cut consequences. This is the presence or absence, or the degree, of *progressiveness*. When, of two men in otherwise similar circumstances, the one who has a larger income has to pay a higher *percentage* of it over to the government, the income tax is said to be progressive. Now there can be little doubt that when a given revenue is got by means of a progressive income tax, the disincentive effect, the discouragement which the tax exerts on work and enterprise, is stronger than when an equal revenue is collected by means of a *proportional* tax; that is, one which exacts one and the same percentage from incomes of all sizes. For when the question faces a man whether he shall take a job where he would have to work six days a week, or another with equal daily pay where he would only have to work five days, what matters to him is not the rate of tax on the whole week's earnings, but the *marginal* rate, the percentage of his *sixth* day's earnings which would go to the tax collector. When an income tax is progressive the marginal rate, the rate on the 'top slice' of income, is higher than the average rate on all the slices taken together, that is, on the income as a whole. For suppose that out of an income of £1000 a year I have to pay one-tenth in tax, but that out of an income of £2000 a year I have to pay two-tenths. Then by increasing my income from £1000 to £2000 I increase my tax liability from £100 to £400, and thus on the second thousand of the larger income the marginal tax rate is three-tenths. It seems evident that a tax which leaves me £900 to dispose of out of my first thousand and only offers me the possibility of keeping £700 out of my second thousand is giving me less inducement to earn that second thousand than a tax which left me only £800 out of my first thousand but allowed me to keep another £800 out of my second. The reason can be summed up, if we are willing to use somewhat old-fashioned language, as residing in the 'diminishing marginal utility of income'. The £900 left me by the progressive tax out of my first thousand will leave me with less acute needs unsatisfied, and consequently a less strong desire to earn more money, than the £800 left me by the proportional tax would do. And then when it is a question of whether or not to earn the second thousand, £800 offered by the proportional tax is plainly a stronger inducement, more especially when my unsatisfied needs are more acute, than the £700 offered by the progressive tax.

But suppose that one man has £1000 a year and another has £2000. May not a marginal £300 out of £2000 mean the same to the latter as a marginal £100 out of £1000 does to the former? Then a progressive tax might be fair. And what of a tax which is the opposite of progressive, which is, as we say, *regressive*? The question almost answers itself. A regressive tax would make a poor man pay to the government a larger percentage of his smaller income than a rich man. We might, for example, have the situation where both the man with £1000 a year and the man with £2000 a year paid the same absolute amount of tax, say £200. Almost instinctively our reaction to that would be that it is 'unfair'. Now if a strongly regressive tax is unfair, may it not be that even a mildly regressive tax is somewhat unfair? Is even a proportional tax fair? Where are we to stop? Might it not be claimed that a man with £2000 a year can better afford to pay £300 than a man with £1000 a year can afford to pay £100?

As economists we shall not be surprised to find two desiderata conflicting with each other. It is the economist's proper business to be able to say *how strongly* a given progressive tax will exert a disincentive effect, compared with another tax which is proportional, or which is regressive in some stated degree. But it is none of his business to say how much 'fairness' should be forgone in order to achieve a strong inducement to hard work or to bold enterprise. That question is for the moralist or the politician, or for you and me in our *private* capacity, as citizens and voters, *not* in our capacity as economists.

In discussing progressiveness and regressiveness of taxes, we have been using an income tax as our example. In western societies today an income tax system regressive in total effect is, however, unheard of in practice. But a very large part of the revenue of some western nations is, nevertheless, collected by means of a kind of tax which can easily be regressive, in the sense that it draws a larger contribution, *relative to income*, from small incomes than from large ones. This is true of commodity taxes as a class. A rich man who smokes ten cigarettes of a particular brand a day pays no more tax on them than a poor man who smokes ten cigarettes a day of the same brand; and however rich a man is, he cannot smoke an unlimited daily number of cigarettes. Unless, therefore, commodity taxes are confined to goods which only the rich consume, they are very likely to have a regressive effect.

In this chapter we have shown how citizens who wish to receive part of the reward for their work in the form of services rendered by the government, instead of receiving the whole of it in the form of goods and services sold to them 'over the counter' to meet their individual and private needs, must be willing to be deprived by taxation of part of the money-income their work earns, so that this part is not available to them to spend in shops. By this means those citizens, the State Servants, who actually perform the tasks needed in order that the government may render its services, are enabled to buy the food, clothes, electricity and so on which they need in order to live. The taxes provide them with money-incomes, and the portions of food, clothes, electricity, etc., which the other citizens have produced but have, because of taxation, not been able to consume, provide the State Servants with real goods on which to spend those money-incomes.

Taxes, we saw, may be 'direct', like income tax, or 'indirect', like the duties which the importers of some commodities have to pay when these commodities cross a national frontier, or like the tax which producers of certain commodities inside a country must pay in proportion to the quantity or to the value of their output. An income tax can, if the legislators so decide, be made 'progressive', so that the recipients of larger incomes pay a larger *percentage* of each such income to the government. Commodity taxes, however, are by their nature likely to have a 'regressive' effect.

We listed the desirable qualities of a tax system as, first, absence of 'disincentive' effect upon work and enterprise; secondly, as not involving great expense in collection relative to the ultimate yield of revenue to the government, or relative to the money taken, in the first place, from the citizens, the gap between revenue *collected* and revenue *available* for the positive purposes of the government being small when the tax system is efficient; thirdly, as avoiding 'excessive' hardship to any citizen; and fourthly, as being, in some broad sense whose interpretation is no concern of economists as such, 'fair'.

Chapter 34. Expenditures

AT the beginning of the preceding chapter we hinted that the view of the government as a firm which purveys certain services in exchange for a revenue just sufficient to cover the cost of providing them was an old-fashioned one. Nowadays in Britain and many other western countries the government's activities differ in three ways from what we were there supposing. In the first place the list of services which the government provides has become very much longer. In Britain in the second half of the twentieth century, besides justice, order and defence, it includes a large part of the country's systems of communications and transport; primary and secondary and, to a large degree, higher education; medical care; and a great part of housing and its ancillary services such as water and electricity. Some of these kinds of services are such as private enterprise can and does still provide, and when the government provides transport or electricity it does so in just the same way as a firm in the 'private' (that is, non-government) sector of the economy would do, by simply selling these things in whatever quantities the customer wishes to buy at the price. We are not really concerned, in this Book VII, with the government as an enterprise trading in the market. When the government provides justice, order and defence it is, of course, not an enterprise trading in the market with willing buyers, but an authority exercising powers which, though democratically conferred upon it, are, so far as the individual is concerned, compulsory and inescapable.

The second way in which a state like modern Britain or Sweden differs from the old-fashioned model is more interesting. For nowadays the government undertakes to relieve or remove 'poverty', variously defined (and not merely, as in earlier times, utter destitution) and it necessarily does so by taxing the richer citizens, not in order to provide services which, like law and order, benefit everybody, but in order to give the poorer citizens things which they otherwise could not or would not afford. In this way taxes are used for a purpose entirely distinct from that of providing a general 'umbrella' of protection under which orderly and civilised life can go on: this other purpose is to *redistribute* income. The extent to which it is proper or desirable that this should be done is again a matter for politicians and not for economists as such. But this use of revenue makes it plain that in studying how the 'burden' of taxation is ultimately distributed over people engaged in various industries and receiving incomes of different sizes, we cannot be content to isolate for study the process of gathering government revenue, but must consider it together with that of making government expenditure. For clearly a family which pays £3 a week in taxes but receives free education and health care and subsidised food to a total value of £5 a week is not a net sufferer, unless in the matter of independence.

So far we have implicitly retained the assumption that whatever the government pays or gives to one set of people it must take by taxation from another (possibly overlapping) set. But there are other possibilities. The government can *borrow* from the citizens as well as taxing them. And even beyond that, the government can distribute money to the citizens which it has neither taxed nor borrowed from them, but has brought into existence, *in addition* to the pre-existing stock of money, by borrowing it from the banking system. But this is the subject of the following chapter.

In origin the word 'fiscal' means 'to do with taxation'. But nowadays it is recognised that all aspects of the gathering and the spending of government revenue, and of the government's borrowing and its use of borrowed funds, need to be studied together as a whole. 'Public finance' is the name of this whole subject. Its three accepted divisions are *fiscal policy*, which is concerned with taxation and with government expenditure of funds obtained in any manner, whether by taxation or by borrowing; *debt management*, which deals with the terms and amounts of the government's borrowings and repayments; and *monetary policy* which discusses the changes in the size of the nation's stock of money, and in the levels of interest-rates, which accompany by design or accident the government's other financial operations. We have briefly considered fiscal policy in this chapter and the preceding one; in the next two chapters we shall look at the government's motives and methods in borrowing and see how monetary policy is bound up with them.

Chapter 35. Deficits

THE government, when it wishes, can overspend or underspend its revenue, it can allow the expenditure it makes within some interval to exceed or to fall short of what it receives, from taxation and from profitable trading taken together, in that interval. In most countries the comparisons of revenue and expenditure are made for the twelve-month period ending on some fixed yearly date. If, in such a 'financial year', the government's expenditure has exceeded its revenue, it is said to have a *deficit*; in the opposite case, a *surplus*.

The ways in which the government can achieve a deficit, or as we may say instead, the concomitants of its achieving a deficit

Government

(besides the obvious one of simply disbursing to individuals and firms money accumulated in some earlier year and now standing to its credit in a bank account) fall into four types. First, it can borrow money from individuals or from non-bank firms; secondly, it can borrow from the banks, other than the central bank, money which they would otherwise have lent, or stood ready to lend, to individuals and firms; or thirdly, it can receive from these banks loans which are *additional* to an unchanged total of actual or available indebtedness of individuals and firms to these banks; or fourthly, it can borrow from the central bank a sum of money created for this purpose. The first two of these ways cause no net change to the size of the nation's stock of money, but the third way adds to that stock an amount equal to the sum borrowed by the government, and the fourth way adds many times as much as that sum; for it increases the 'cash' standing in the books of the central bank to the credit of the other banks (so soon as the government has paid the money away to the customers of these other banks and these banks have lodged with the central bank the claims thus coming into their possession) and enables them to build on this basis a superstructure of extra lending to firms and individuals in some conventional ratio to the extra cash. In the British banking system, for example, this ratio is 25 : 2. The effect which overspending by the government produces on the economy will be enhanced if the overspending is accompanied by a growth of the stock of money. This we shall discuss below.

In earlier times a deficit or surplus happened only by accident, since it was thought to be the government's duty to take enough, but not more than enough, out of the incomes of the citizens to pay for the government's services; except in time of war, when this 'balancing of the Budget' was difficult and the government accumulated debts which, perhaps, it afterwards sought to pay off by slow degrees by having a small annual surplus. It was, according to that former view, as undesirable for the government to get into debt as for a private person to do so, while on the other hand the government should practise every economy and leave in the hands of individuals all of their incomes except what was strictly necessary for the maintenance of the orderly frame of living. Nowadays, even though the list of services which it is thought proper for the government to provide is so much more extensive, their provision is only one aspect of its responsibilities, for it is required also to ensure, as freedom of competition and enterprise cannot by themselves always be relied upon to do, the full but not overstrained employment of all available resources.

We saw in Book VI (*Finance*) that employment can be sustained only at that level where the aggregate supply-price of the resulting output (the minimum weekly or yearly sale-proceeds, the expectation of which would induce firms to produce this output) is matched by its aggregate demand-price, that is, by the aggregate number of money-units offered for it in each week or year. This demand, in a self-contained economy, can come only from three sources: consumption, net investment by businessmen, expenditure by the government. Now let us suppose that in an initial situation the government's Budget is in balance, revenue just equalling expenditure, and that the government then increases its yearly expenditure while collecting an unchanged revenue by taxation. The *direct* effect of this change will surely be to increase the number of people (as well as of machines, farms, etc.) who have employment; for the extra government expenditure will augment demand without anyone having been compelled to spend on consumption, or to invest, less per year than before because of having to pay more in taxes. Indeed, since the extra people who now find employment in meeting the government's extra needs will partly pay their own wages through having themselves to contribute to revenue, and since their own extra demand for consumption-goods (which, being employed, they can now afford) can only be met by extra output, probably requiring still further recruitment of labour, the total extra numbers employed will actually be much larger than the extra government expenditure could itself account for. Will there, however, be any secondary effects which could work against this employment-giving effect? Here we see the relevance of our discussion of the various *monetary* expedients by which a deficit could be achieved. If the government borrows money from citizens and firms, these may be tempted to reduce their consumption or net investment for the purpose of having more to lend to the government. A similar consequence may ensue if the government borrows from the ordinary (non-central) banks money which would otherwise have been lent or made available for lending to the citizens and firms. But if government borrowing *increases* the economy's total stock of money, there will be an additional consequence favourable to employment: for then the extra yearly value of transactions, arising from the extra employment and output, can be mediated by money without there being any need to draw into the active stream of money some of the 'idle' bank balances that had been serving to satisfy the liquidity preference of Bears, which drawing-off would have doubtless required some rise in the rate of interest to effect it.

We can easily see that similar arguments to those of the foregoing paragraph apply to a deficit achieved by reducing tax revenue without reducing government expenditure. Deficit spending, in short, is a means whereby the government can increase employment when the factors of production are less than fully employed.

We must not suppose, however, that an 'unbalanced Budget', an excess of expenditure over revenue, is the only means by which the government can augment the total flow of effective demand. If it can impose a tax which is paid partly out of what would otherwise have been *saved*, then when the government spends the proceeds of this tax, total yearly spending will be larger and total yearly saving smaller than in the absence of the tax. How can a tax discriminate against saving in this way? It may not be easy to devise a tax which falls *explicitly* on saving, but it is easy to find one which falls on the incomes of those who would otherwise save the largest yearly amounts, and one which, by making them poorer, will tend to discourage this saving. If we can assume with Keynes that the larger is a person's disposable income, the larger, in most cases (the prices of goods being given), will be the absolute size of the flow of saving made out of that income, then a *progressive* income tax, which takes larger percentages out of larger incomes, may do what is wanted. For such a tax presses down the disposable portions of large incomes nearer to equality with the disposable portions of medium incomes. The disposable incomes are thus crowded more thickly into the middle brackets (the classes of medium-sized incomes) and less thickly in the higher brackets, than would be the case in the absence of a progressive tax. But we are assuming that a larger absolute yearly amount will be saved by any particular person out of a larger than out of a smaller disposable income, and so this general lowering of the larger disposable incomes will cause less to be saved. It is to be noted that this argument assumes either that the tax change increases the levy on large incomes without relieving small incomes, or else that any relief given to small incomes is confined to those so low that any extra saving out of them, due to the tax relief, will not be sufficient to offset the reduction of saving from large incomes.

To express the matter a little differently, we may say that saving is what an affluent man does with what is left of his disposable income after he has spent all he wants to. (This is true of at any rate some part of the total flow of saving by individuals.) In so far as saving is a residual in this sense, it seems plain that any reduction of the disposable portions of large incomes will, at least, be allowed to cut into saving as well as spending out of these incomes. How far this diminution of saving by the rich will be offset by the possible increased saving of those with smaller incomes, will depend on whether the rate of income tax on these smaller incomes is reduced at the same time as the rate on larger incomes is increased. If the tax change is not a mere steepening of progressiveness, but exacts extra contributions of revenue from large incomes without relieving smaller incomes, there will be no such offsetting. If then we assume that the whole of the extra revenue will either be spent by the government itself on goods and services, or else handed on to pensioners, unemployed or sick persons, mothers of families and others who can be relied on to spend the whole of what they thus receive and not save any of it, it follows that the net result of the government's action is to increase the economy's aggregate spending and reduce its saving.

Government

The government's power to augment the economy's aggregate effective demand without departing from a balanced Budget can perhaps be made more evident if we consider what would happen were the government to take away from everyone so large a part of his income that he and his family could barely survive on what was left. In that case the whole of the disposable income left in the hands of individuals would be spent by them on consumption, provided the government took care to spend the whole of the revenue it had taxed away from them on some object, such as armaments, which would in no way relieve their poverty. Thus the whole income of the economy, no matter how large, would be safely spent on something or other, and everyone would be fully employed. This *reductio ad absurdum* shows also that full employment is not by itself a sufficient test of the economy's well-being.

There is, of course, an opposite possibility to that of insufficient effective demand. The aggregate of demand, from consumers, businessmen seeking to augment their equipment, and the government pursuing its purposes, may be a greater monthly or yearly total of money than the total money value, at the current market prices, of all the goods and services that can be produced in each month or year when all resources are fully engaged. In that case there will be a strong and persisting tendency for prices to rise. One cause of their rising will be their natural inevitable response to market pressure, where the proper function of a price is to rise to such a level that demand, *given the incomes* of the would-be buyers, is confined to what supply, at that price, can match. It is easy to see what goes wrong with this mechanism when not just one price, but *all* prices seek simultaneously to adjust demand as a whole to supply as a whole. When the prices of *all* goods and services rise, the incomes of those who produce these goods rise also, and these incomes constitute the great majority of all incomes. Those whose incomes have risen can face the higher prices of goods without reducing the quantities they demand per month or per year. Thus rising prices fail to check demand and fail to regain an equilibrium for themselves. This mechanism by which excessive aggregate demand generates a persistent rise in the general level of prices depends partly on the willingness, in such circumstances, of employers to concede repeated claims for higher wages; for the employers will be competing strenuously amongst themselves for the too-scarce factors of production.

Now a persistent general rise of prices has many evil consequences. It is in fact the precise modern equivalent of the practice of the kings of former times who gathered in, by taxation, coins each containing a stated weight of gold or silver and produced from them twice the number of superficially similar coins by adulterating the gold or silver with cheap metal. *Debasement of the coinage* was obviously a wrong, but deficit spending by the government in times of already full employment is less readily stigmatised as a wrong, perhaps because it is more subtle and its true nature more difficult to understand. A piece of paper, worthless *in itself*, does not lend itself to the practice of governmental robbery by the substitution of another piece of paper, also worthless in itself. But the worthlessness of the paper material of a banknote, or of the ink of an entry in the ledger of a bank, is of course beside the point. It does not justify a government in so behaving that the quantity of real goods which this banknote or book-entry can purchase is halved or reduced to a fraction of what it was. When that happens, all those people whose incomes do not float on the tide of 'inflation', the pensioners, the people who have lent money to the government itself at fixed interest, the salaried professions, all these are steadily further impoverished as prices rise and their incomes fail to follow. Inflation destroys the basis and meaning of the market mechanism, renders prices delusory, robs some for the profit of others, and enables a few men to live richly on 'capital gains' which are the very fruit of the inflationary process, while the pay of others for hard work sinks ever lower in real terms.

If a *deficit* increases effective demand, plainly a *surplus* will reduce it, as compared with a balanced Budget. If the government taxes away income that consumers would otherwise spend, and refrains from spending this revenue itself, total effective demand in the economy will be by so much the less. To be as effective as possible in reducing demand, however, the taxes must evidently be such as will be paid out of what would have been spent and not out of what would have been saved. In so far as a government Budget surplus is achieved at the expense of potential saving, it does nothing to reduce the pressure of demand on prices. Thus to be effective against inflation, taxes must bear upon incomes out of which little would in any case be saved: inflation cannot be stopped by taxing only large incomes.

If all incomes are to be taxed, however, another consideration enters. A man naturally regards his disposable earnings or profits, what is left after income tax has been deducted, as the measure of his reward for work or enterprise. If the rate of tax on the marginal hour of his weekly earnings is high, he may be discouraged from performing that marginal hour. Then his output, measured in physical units, will be lower, and the aggregate flow of goods and services of all sorts, coming on to the market to meet the monetary demand, will *pro tanto* be smaller. A *lower* rate of tax, leaving him a larger disposable share of his gross earnings for the marginal hour, might have kept him at work for that hour and elicited a corresponding output; the higher tax abolishes the whole hour's output while reducing potential demand by only his gross pay *less tax*: it might have been better, from the viewpoint of curing inflation, to tax him at the lower rate.

The most effective action that the government can take by Budgetary means against inflation is to reduce its own expenditure. This reduces aggregate demand without having any direct effect on the incentives of businessmen and their employees to produce goods to meet that demand.

So long as there are unemployed factors of production of all sorts, suitably located so that they can be readily combined in any desired proportions, an increase of aggregate monetary demand for *goods in general* will effect an increase of employment and of *output as a whole*. When there are no unemployed factors of production, there can plainly be no increase of employment, and if, with a given state of knowledge and given exploitation of it, production is everywhere being carried on with the cheapest combinations of quantities of factors, there can be no increase in productive efficiency; thus there can be no increase of output no matter how great the increase of aggregate monetary demand, and the only effect of the latter will be to raise *prices*. Between these two extremes there will be a band of conditions in which some factors of production, in some places, are fully employed while other factors, or the same factors in other places, are still under-employed. While the economy is within this band, the growth of output under the influence of rising aggregate demand will encounter successive and cumulative obstacles, in the form of shortages of partly processed goods whose output cannot be increased because the necessary factors are not all available in the same place, or because some of these factors are already fully employed everywhere. Then prices of first one good and then another will begin to rise, and the factors of production themselves, especially labour, will find it increasingly easy to obtain higher pay. The practical problem for the government is to manage its own Budget so that aggregate effective demand just maintains full employment, in a reasonable sense of the word 'full', without pressing prices upward. Economic theory alone, however, cannot tell us whether there is even a hair-line between unemployment and inflation, or whether we have to have some degree of inflation to avoid unemployment, or else of unemployment in order to avoid inflation.

Chapter 36. Debts

WE saw reasons in the preceding chapter why it is sometimes proper and desirable for the government to spend more in a given period than it receives in that period by way of taxation and profitable trading; in other words, to have Budget deficits. These deficits build up a debt to banks or to citizens and non-bank firms, and we have to consider how such a debt should be 'managed', that is, what considerations should govern the terms on which the government should seek to borrow and what policies or measures will enable these terms to be secured; what ideas, other than those concerned with deliberate change of aggregate demand for goods, should govern the pace of growth or of reduction of the debt; and what purposes such management can serve and in what way.

In order to borrow, the government must pay interest, and these payments *transfer* income from taxpayers in general to those particular citizens or firms who have lent money to the government. The wide and complex diversity of circumstance which can surround such transfers makes it impossible to urge in any general or abstract way that they should be kept small or allowed to grow large. Taxes, it might be said, are paid largely out of the earnings of effort or enterprise, while lenders have made little sacrifice to deserve their interest. But such an argument, or its opposite, couched in such broad and abstract terms would be meaningless. The taxpayers may be rich, the savers who have forgone consumption to accumulate funds which they have lent, perhaps indirectly through life-insurance companies, to the government may be poor; a thousand such facts bear upon the question, and make broad judgments even more illegitimate, if possible, than the worthlessness of 'inter-personal' comparisons of experience render them in any case. There is nothing to be said in general on this ground.

However, if high rates of interest are obtainable on loans to the government, lenders will require equally high rates on any loans they make to businessmen, who may thus be discouraged from ordering additional equipment and so giving employment to those who would construct that equipment and to others also who, according to the Multiplier principle that we saw in Book VI (*Finance*), would supply the consumption needs of those extra people who had been given employment in constructing equipment. If the economy's factors of production are under-employed, the government will be unwilling to push in the wrong direction by borrowing at high interest and imposing high taxes to pay that interest, since both these things will tend to discourage enterprise and the giving of employment. So if in such circumstances the government needs nevertheless to borrow large sums, it will have to take care that in doing so it does not soak up all the money which 'Bears' require in order to satisfy their liquidity preference at *low* rates of interest. How can it borrow money without depleting the liquid reserves of citizens and firms? By creating the extra money itself, or causing its central bank to do so; and this in Britain simply means that the government borrows from the Bank of England. The Bank of England (with a parliamentary authorisation to meet any cash shortage by increasing the Fiduciary Issue of banknotes issued without gold backing) can write any required amount in its ledger as standing at the government's disposal; or alternatively it can buy already-existing government securities on the 'open market', thus creating extra money to many times the value of the securities bought, in the manner explained in Chapter 30 (*Banks*), and this extra money the government can then borrow by means of a public issue of fixed-interest securities, that is to say, by selling fresh interest-bearing IOU's of its own to citizens, firms and probably to commercial banks. The whole operation we have outlined, by which the government increases the economy's total stock of money, and then borrows some of this money and spends it on schemes of equipment-building such as road construction, nuclear power-station development and so on, is precisely what would be appropriate in time of business 'depression' and serious general unemployment.

How far can the government go in increasing its debt to its own citizens? The fact that, in 1957, the *interest* on the British national debt was roughly equal to the whole *amount* of that debt as it stood in 1913, shows that there is no absolute upper limit. The two things that matter are, first, the relation between the number of millions of pounds or dollars, etc., that must be paid annually as interest on the debt, and the number of millions of pounds or dollars that measure the national income; and secondly, the pattern in which ownership of the debt is distributed. Plainly in so far as large holders of the debt are also large taxpayers, they are merely transferring money from one pocket to the other via the Exchequer. So far as the debt is held in small parcels by people of modest income, to whom (in the absence of inflation) it can mean a safe reserve against unforeseeable emergency or foreseeable old age, or in so far as it is held on behalf of such people by insurance companies and similar institutions, it is doing a useful service. None the less a large national debt has hitherto nearly always represented merely the aftermath of wars in which governments found it easier to secure by borrowing than by taxation a large part of the money they needed in order to wage war. No tangible assets remain after such wars to correspond to the vast outlay that has been made, and in so far as it is true that holders of the government's IOU's are merely paying themselves interest out of their own taxes, the existence of such a debt may seem pointless. But a certain volume of government 'fixed-interest' securities does serve as a useful *masse de manœuvre* for the central bank, enabling it the more conveniently to raise or lower the long-term interest-rate according as there is inflationary pressure or unemployment.

The government of a country can have two kinds of debts, quite different in their implications. It may owe money to the governments or citizens of other countries. These debts are like those owed by one citizen or firm to another, in that they mean that the citizens of the borrowing country, taken all together in their capacity as a nation, have acquired goods whose equivalent they have not themselves produced. To this extent they have, as it were, been able to mortgage their future income and productive powers. On the other hand, the government may owe money to its own citizens. When we regard all these citizens as together forming a nation, the *internal* national debt merely means that the nation owes money to itself. It is sometimes regarded as 'more moral' for a government, which is resolved to build hospitals, schools, roads and so on, to pay for these goods by taxing the citizens rather than by borrowing from them; it is said that borrowing places a 'burden on posterity'. Except in one aspect, this is wholly fallacious. No burden can be placed on posterity by today's citizens merely through the creation, by today's citizens, of buildings and facilities which posterity will later have the use of. For these buildings and facilities are built by the labour, natural forces and machine services which today's citizens could equally well have used to gratify their own immediate and transient needs. Any sacrifice involved is made today by today's citizens out of their own productive powers, and except in so far as they use up minerals or soil qualities which nature will not replace, no 'burden' on posterity can be involved. What is involved is the imposition upon posterity of a pattern of income-transfers between future taxpayers and those who will hold government securities. But there is no ground in general for declaring that such a pattern must be harmful in any specific way, still less, that on balance it will do more harm than good, since we cannot in general know what the pattern will be.

A large internal national debt is like the scar of an old wound: that wound, when it was suffered, may have lost the nation blood and strength; but the scar itself is of little consequence.

Chapter 37. Planning

IN Book VI (*Finance*), we saw how it may become necessary, and in this Book VII we have seen how it is possible, for the government to intervene in the life-process of the economy as a whole, in ways which go beyond the roles of mere umpire and watchman that we referred to in Chapter 33 (*Taxes*). Now it would be easy to argue as follows: There is nothing special about the role of umpire and watchman, which permits it to be spoken of as constituting complete governmental non-intervention. Even in preventing violence and fraud, the government is intervening in the essential business by which individuals and families and larger societies struggle to survive. The very essence of government and its only reason for existence is to intervene. Why then (the argument might go on) should we be specially anxious about the extent of this intervention? Events have shown that a free-enterprise economy can suffer heavy unemployment. If scarcity reigned alone as the dominant economic factor, if the organisation of the economy were so primitive that every man was free to divide his own time between employment and leisure (as Robinson Crusoe was, or as each man would be in a barter economy) then individual freedom could by itself ensure 'full' or at any rate 'optimum' employment of all resources. But (the argument continues) in reality there is another factor, as powerful as scarcity, and that is uncertainty, which at times so inhibits enterprise that great numbers of people and their equipment are unemployed. Governments can prevent this unemployment, and to this extent their intervention is necessary. But why stop there? The government is in the position (so the argument proceeds) of a guardian who knows what is best for everybody, and it should control the economy in detail so as to give everybody what, in its opinion, is best for him.

Now it must be said at once that if the reader accepts such an argument in full, this book is not for him. What we have sought to explain is the working of an economic system where the guiding principle is to give each individual person the greatest scope for his own spontaneous use of life. There is some scope of government action which will *best* ensure this utmost potentiality of the individual human life. We cannot say nowadays, as it used to be said, that this best scope for government is the role of umpire and watchman merely. We can go some way with the argument rather crudely outlined above: we can admit that the government should concern itself with 'the great aggregates', the percentage actually employed of all the people who want to be employed and the movement of the general level of prices; and that it should ensure that everyone has the essentials of decent life and the opportunity to use and develop his or her whole personality. But this is almost the precise opposite of the view that each person should have his job and his consumption prescribed for him under a regime of complete 'centralised planning'.

'Planning' can thus mean widely different things. When it means the detailed prescription of the outputs and prices of all goods and the arbitrary fixing of the rates of pay of all factors of production, the purpose to be served is evidently something quite different from that of giving the utmost scope to the individual free human personality. Advocates of planning in this sense may wish to give him as much meat and as little tobacco, or obtain from him as much work in the production of iron and steel, as possible, and they may believe that detailed central planning, in which the only chooser is the government, is the best way to do this. But they cannot then claim that their system is 'better', 'more efficient', than the free economy; they cannot do so because efficiencies can only be meaningfully compared when they are in some sense ratios of different means to one and the same end; and here the ends are totally different.

It is because of this difference of ends that we must beware of the idea of 'degrees' of planning. It would at first sight perhaps be tempting to speak of an intermediate degree of planning, lying between that of the economy centrally directed in detail and that of the economy merely policed by the government. But to describe thus the policy which accepts for the government the responsibility for keeping aggregate effective demand optimally related to available total quantities of the various means of production would be misleading. Planning in this sense adds, as it were, an extra dimension to the frame of law and order within which people are free to choose their own work, their own consumption and their own risks; it leaves the *ends* to be chosen by individuals for themselves. Planning in one sense is like a palisade built to enclose more of the desert for men's use; planning in the other sense is like a fence built to confine them to till ground they have not chosen and do not own.

Government

With this chapter we complete the study of a self-contained and isolated economic system whose parts are not in any way artificially separated from each other by legal obstructions to the movement of goods or people. Perhaps the example which most nearly illustrates such a system is the United States of America, which could, if necessary, do without any economic connection with the rest of the world, and simply 'live at home', bringing nothing in and sending nothing out. Within the United States there is virtually no legal restriction to the free movement of people and of almost all goods; no one is *taxed* for moving himself or his products about inside the country. At the opposite extreme from the United States there is the United Kingdom of Great Britain and Northern Ireland, which would find it literally impossible to exist without bringing in every year a flow of goods from other countries; the flow actually brought in during peacetime approaching one-quarter of the national income.

BOOK VIII. TRADE

Chapter 38. Imports

SPECIALISATION can be fruitful amongst regions and amongst nations as well as amongst men. In studying the central theory of value in Books I (*Value*) and II (*Production*), we considered the effects of varying, according to circumstances, the proportions in which different factors are combined to produce this good or that. We assumed that in the whole economic system the quantity existing of this factor and that, or the quantities forthcoming when certain prices were offered for these factors, were *given*, and that the ultimate pattern of production would have to adjust itself as best it could, on one side to this set of supplies of means of production, and on the other to the demands of people all taken together, arising from their tastes and constrained by their money-incomes. We showed how, in a freely competitive economy, the inducements to attain the best adjustment, and the signals as to the directions in which movements of factors from one industry to another should take place, were furnished by the system of relative prices which would arise naturally in the free markets of such an economy. We did not ask ourselves what would happen if, instead of there being just one economy with a given endowment of means of production, there were two or several economies with *different* endowments, so that in one economy the number of workers was, for example, one for every four acres of cultivable land, while in the other economy it was one for every twenty acres. If we suppose that there are in the world a number of differently endowed economies, and that it is expensive, difficult or impossible to move factors from one economy to another so as to obtain in that way the best 'mixture' of factors which is possible, given the world endowment as a whole; and if we ask what then can be done to make the best use of the factors where they are, we have the problem of *international trade*, with which this Book VIII is concerned.

One class of problems which arises from trade between different parts of the world concerns the relations between national currencies; but we shall defer consideration of these until Chapter 40 (*Currencies*), and simplify some other aspects of trade between geographical regions by assuming here a single world currency or money-unit, in terms of which the price of every factor and commodity in every country can be expressed.

Suppose, then, that a ton of food (of some homogeneous kind) can be produced in a year by three workers and three acres of land, and that the same quantity can alternatively be produced in a year by one worker and ten acres; and suppose that in Lilliput the yearly wage of a worker is two money-units and the yearly rent of an acre is two money-units, while in Blefuscu the wage is five money-units and the rent one money-unit. Then in Lilliput it will be cheaper to produce a ton of food by means of three workers and three acres at a cost of twelve money-units, while in Blefuscu it will be cheaper to produce a ton of food by means of one worker and ten acres at a cost of fifteen money-units. We can show the alternative possibilities in a small table (Table 1).

LILLIPUT

Method 1	Workers	Acres
	3	3
Pay per unit	2	2
Cost per ton of food	6 +	6=12

Method 2	Workers	Acres
	1	10
Pay per unit	2	2
Cost per ton of food	2 +	20=22

BLEFUSCU

Method 2	Workers	Acres
	1	10
Pay per unit	5	1
Cost per ton of food	5 +	10=15

Method 1	Workers	Acres
	3	3
Pay per unit	5	1
Cost per ton of food	15 +	3=18

TABLE 1: ONE TON OF FOOD

Let us further suppose that ten tons of fuel can be produced in a year either by three workers and four acres or by one worker and seven acres. Then in Lilliput the first method will supply fuel at fourteen money-units for ten tons and the second method will supply it at sixteen money-units for ten tons, while in Blefuscu the respective costs will be twelve for the second method and nineteen for the first (Table 2).

LILLIPUT	Workers	Acres	BLEFUSCU	Workers	Acres
Method 1			*Method 2*		
	3	4		1	7
Pay per unit	2	2	Pay per unit	5	1
Cost per ten tons of fuel	6 +	8=14	Cost per ten tons of fuel	5 +	7=12
Method 2	Workers	Acres	*Method 1*	Workers	Acres
	1	7		3	4
Pay per unit	2	2	Pay per unit	5	1
Cost per ten tons of fuel	2 +	14=16	Cost per ten tons of fuel	15 +	4=19

TABLE 2: TEN TONS OF FUEL

If we assume that the costs of transport of food and fuel between Lilliput and Blefuscu are negligible, it is plain that so long as wages and rent remain at the stated levels in the two countries, Lilliput will be able to obtain fuel more cheaply by importing it from Blefuscu than by producing it herself, provided she can get ten tons of fuel in exchange for anything less than one-and-one-sixth tons of food, while Blefuscu will be able to obtain food more cheaply by importing it from Lilliput than by producing it herself, provided she can get a ton of food in exchange for anything less than twelve-and-a-half tons of fuel. Plainly an exchange will be profitable to *both* countries at any ratio between two limits, namely one ton of food for about eight-and-a-half tons of fuel, and one ton of food for about twelve-and-a-half tons of fuel. The question that remains is: what comparative circumstances in Lilliput and Blefuscu would make it plausible that wages and rent could stand in the two countries at the relative levels we have supposed?

Two features are the basis of the explanation. We may assume, first, that in Blefuscu the number of people is much smaller in relation to the land area than in Lilliput; and secondly, that it is prohibitively difficult and expensive to transfer people from Lilliput to Blefuscu, and even more so, to transfer land from Blefuscu to

Lilliput! We saw in Chapter 6 (*Production*) how, for example, the usefulness of one extra man on a farm of given size will be less when there are already twenty men on the farm than when there are only three. If wages are low enough and farm produce is dear enough, it may still pay to employ a twenty-first man; but at any given prices of farm labour and farm produce, there will be some size of the farm's labour force beyond which it will not pay the farmer to go. If a still larger number of men, all equally capable, wish to find employment on the farm, they will all have to accept a lower wage. In Blefuscu there are few workers on a great area of cultivable land. One man fewer on a farm would reduce that farm's output severely, by a yearly amount of relatively high value. That value will be the *marginal product*, in value terms, of labour on that farm, and the wage in equilibrium will be equal to it. In Lilliput, by contrast, there are very many people crowded on little land, and one man fewer on a farm would make much less difference than in Blefuscu, so the marginal product of labour, and hence the wage, in Lilliput is lower. In short, we have the following situation: in Lilliput, land scarce, rents high; labour plentiful, wages low; in Blefuscu, labour scarce, wages high; land plentiful, rents low. The words scarce and plentiful, high and low, are of course all used here in the sense of *comparison*: labour is scarcer in relation to land in Blefuscu than in Lilliput.

The reader will be well aware that in the foregoing we have done no more than sketch in merest outline the *qualitative* explanation of how specialisation and exchange can be fruitful between countries just as it is between people. Deliberately, for the sake of simplicity, we have left many things unsaid. For example, we named just two pairs of quantities of labour and land which, we assumed, could each produce a ton of food. These must evidently be regarded as selections from a 'production possibility schedule', a long list of different pairs of quantities all able to yield just one annual ton of food. If we had brought this entire schedule into our picture, we should have gone on to assume that in Lilliput the cheaper of the two named pairs of factor-quantities for producing food was the *cheapest* of all possible such pairs for producing one annual ton of food; and similarly in Blefuscu, we would have assumed that the cheaper of the two pairs of quantities for producing fuel was in fact the cheapest of all ways of producing an annual ten tons of fuel. Again, we have said nothing about how the precise exchange-ratio between Lilliputian food and Blefuscan fuel will be settled; we have only shown the limits of a 'contract zone', the range of prices of one good in terms of the other within which any actual exchange-ratio must lie if it is to be acceptable to both parties. In speaking of 'both' parties, however, we are tending to mislead ourselves. Within each country there will be, we may suppose, a great number of mutually competing buyers and sellers of the two goods, and thus there will be a genuine competitive market on which an exact price can be supposed to establish itself. This explanation still leaves us to examine how it comes about that the price of fuel in terms of food, or vice versa, and the quantities of the two goods exchanged, reach levels at which the annual sum of *money* owed by Lilliput to Blefuscu for fuel is equal to the annual sum owed by Blefuscu to Lilliput for food, so that there is a 'balance of payments'; or of how this balance is achieved should the annual exchanged values of the two (or more) commodities traded by the two countries fail to be equal. This is the subject of the next two chapters.

Chapter 39. Payments

LET us retain for the time being the supposition that Lilliput and Blefuscu use a common money-unit, and let us call this unit the crown. In a particular year, Blefuscu buys from Lilliput so-and-so many tons of food at so-and-so many crowns per ton, and Lilliput buys from Blefuscu so-and-so many tons of fuel at so-and-so many crowns per ton. If the number of crowns' worth of this food is greater than the number of crowns' worth of this fuel, the mere interchange of these two quantities of the commodities will leave a loose end in the transaction; a gap, the manner of filling which must be the subject of an agreed and explicit procedure on the part of the two countries or their citizens.

In one such procedure, the citizens of Blefuscu would simply fill up the gap by handing to the citizens of Lilliput the appropriate number of crowns. Thus Blefuscu would receive, say, fifteen thousand crowns' worth of food while Lilliput would receive ten thousand crowns' worth of fuel plus five thousand crowns. These crowns could be received by Lilliput in the form of actual metal coins or in the form of deposits in Blefuscan banks. In the latter case the Blefuscan banks would simply record in their ledgers that they owed a certain number of crowns to this Lilliputian citizen or that. To do so would not involve these banks in any loss, for they would have received from any such Lilliputian citizen a cheque of the appropriate amount drawn in his favour by some Blefuscan citizen who had received food from Lilliput in excess of the value of fuel he had despatched to Lilliput. The Lilliputian owners of these deposits in Blefuscan banks would be free to spend them on Blefuscan fuel whenever they liked, and if, in some later year, they exercised this right, the effect would be to make, in that later year, the value of fuel imported into Lilliput greater than the value of food imported into Blefuscu, if those values would otherwise have been equal.

Instead of deposits standing to the credit of Lilliputian citizens in Blefuscan banks, the acknowledgment of debt could take the form of securities. Blefuscan citizens or firms or institutions of some kind could 'float a loan' in Lilliput. They could offer for sale, that is to say, pieces of paper each acknowledging a debt of so-and-so many crowns and promising to pay interest of so-and-so many crowns per year until the security was redeemed, that is, the principal of the debt paid off. The money which the Blefuscan issuers of these documents received for them from Lilliputian citizens could be spent by the Blefuscans on food for which no equivalent *quid pro quo* in the form of fuel was available.

The essential idea in all of these arrangements is that, within any period, the total value of everything transferred by Lilliputian citizens to Blefuscan citizens must (if our accounting is to make sense) be regarded as exactly equalled by the total value of everything transferred by Blefuscan citizens to Lilliputian citizens: total payments in each direction in every week, month or year must in principle exactly balance. If Blefuscu receives fifteen thousand crowns' worth of food she must pay fifteen thousand crowns; if in the same period Lilliput receives ten thousand crowns' worth of fuel she must pay ten thousand crowns; when the fifteen thousand crowns owed by Blefuscu are confronted with the ten thousand owed by Lilliput, all that need actually happen to balance the accounts is the handing over of five thousand crowns by Blefuscu to Lilliput, or the handing over by Blefuscu to Lilliput of documents acknowledging a debt of five thousand crowns. This is all that is meant by the mysterious assertion that 'the balance of payments must always balance'. What does the slippery word 'must' mean here? Simply that our accounting would be disrupted if we did not regard payments in the two directions in any period as equal to each other.

Now this is all very well, but the formal balancing of payments by means of transfers of money or of acknowledgments of debt does nothing, in itself, to ensure any appropriate relationship between the quantity of food imported, and the quantity of fuel exported, by Blefuscu, given Blefuscu's and Lilliput's respective factor endowments. How is such an appropriate relationship brought about or preserved?

And first, what sort of relationship will be appropriate? Suppose the citizens of Lilliput are rich, having large incomes out of which they find it easy to leave a part unspent on consumption. We have seen that, corresponding to this flow of saving, there will have to be an equal flow of investment, that is, of production of goods over and above those which merely match simultaneous consumption; for only thus will the saved part of income be generated.

But when we are thinking, not of a closed, self-contained economy, but of an 'open' economy such as Lilliput represents within the economic world consisting of Lilliput and Blefuscu, we have to mean by 'investment' the production of goods *not for consumption in Lilliput*. The citizens of Lilliput produce each year goods worth, let us say, fifty thousand crowns. If out of this they only wish to consume forty-five thousand crowns' worth, they must produce five thousand crowns' worth of goods (within their annual total output of fifty thousand crowns' worth) which they will not themselves consume. Now this five thousand crowns' worth of goods annually produced, but not consumed, in Lilliput can either be allowed to pile up inside Lilliput in the form of buildings, machines and stockpiles of materials, or it can be *sent to Blefuscu without the Blefuscans sending anything in return*. In so far as the Blefuscans do send anything in return, the export of goods from Lilliput will not serve the citizens of Lilliput as a process of investment, for though they will not be consuming their own production they *will* be consuming something got in exchange for it.

Now in so far as the citizens of Lilliput wish to accumulate wealth by producing goods over and above what they consume, and in so far as they find that this wealth can most conveniently and profitably be accumulated in the form of goods owned by themselves *but situated in Blefuscu*, the fact that Lilliput sends to Blefuscu in each year a greater value of goods than Blefuscu sends to Lilliput will give rise to no difficulties. Lilliput's 'export surplus' will serve, either directly by consisting of goods suitable for accumulation, or indirectly by being consumed by Blefuscans who give durable goods in exchange, to build up in Blefuscu a stock of wealth belonging to Lilliputians. In this process, Lilliputians will be 'exporting capital' to Blefuscu; that is to say, they will be exercising in Blefuscu rather than in Lilliput the power conferred on them, by their willingness to consume less than the equivalent of what they produce, to create specialised equipment in the form of machines and buildings. Thus a persisting export surplus is tolerable so long as one country is willing to become the owner of a steadily growing pile of assets situated in the other country, and the other country is willing to become increasingly a debtor to the first country or the site of the first country's directly owned equipment.

But now, what would happen if Lilliput had a persisting export surplus but Lilliputian citizens were *not* willing to become owners of 'long term' assets, whether debts due to them or equipment belonging to them, situated in Blefuscu? In this case, Blefuscan citizens would find themselves parting with more and more of their money to Lilliputians. Since we are assuming that the two countries have a common currency, coins themselves could be sent from Blefuscu to Lilliput; and if Blefuscu had no banking system but only a metallic currency, that is what would have to happen. But what would be the consequences of this progressive draining away of coins from Blefuscu, and the flooding in of these coins to Lilliput? Soon it would become tiresomely difficult for Blefuscan employers to arrange to have enough coins in hand on pay-day to pay their workpeople. Shopkeepers would cease to give credit to their customers, and would insist on all goods being paid for in cash. Income-earners would find it desirable to post-pone purchases of things not essential to immediate needs, in order to have coins available in case of emergency. In short, everyone would be trying to accumulate coins by parting with as few as possible of those that came into their possession; and many would seek to borrow coins from lenders who would share everyone's reluctance to let coins go. Thus the interest-rate in Blefuscu would go up at the same time as goods began to be less readily saleable to Blefuscans. The rise in the interest-rate and the decline in the profitability of enterprise in Blefuscu would have a chain of successive consequences. Investment, that is the construction of equipment, would be discouraged in Blefuscu, employment would be reduced and so, therefore, would incomes, and Blefuscans would thus be further discouraged from buying goods, both goods of Blefuscan *and of Lilliputian* origin. Blefuscan businessmen, finding it harder to sell their goods, would be strongly inclined to reduce their price, and this would encourage Lilliputians to buy more of them per month or year than they had been doing.

9-2

Meanwhile, what would have been happening in Lilliput? There the inflow of coins would have caused all the opposite kinds of reactions to those which the drain of coins had caused in Blefuscu. Many exporters of goods to Blefuscu would find more coins in their possession than they needed for convenience and safety. They would be more ready to lend, the interest-rate would go down, construction of buildings would be encouraged, employment would be increased and extra incomes would be paid out, the Kahn-Keynes multiplier would work and the general demand for goods both of Lilliputian *and of Blefuscan* origin would increase. So gradually forces would arise from several sides tending to eliminate the Lilliputian export surplus.

Let us enumerate these forces. The decline of employment in Blefuscu, arising from the difficulty Blefuscan enterprisers would encounter in selling as large an output as before at the old prices, would tend to induce Blefuscan income-earners to accept lower wages. Less employment at lower pay would mean smaller incomes, and if out of these smaller incomes the same *proportion* as before was spent on imports from Lilliput, the absolute amount spent on imports would be lower. Meanwhile the lower prices, by which Blefuscan enterprisers would try to restore demand for Blefuscan products, would tempt Lilliputians, so far as their incomes were still unchanged, to buy larger quantities than heretofore of Blefuscan products, and if the price-elasticity of Lilliputian demand for imports were greater than unity, the absolute amount spent by Lilliputians on Blefuscu's exports would increase. But would Lilliputian incomes in fact be unchanged? Would not the decline in Blefuscan demand for Lilliputian goods perhaps reduce them? This tendency would be countered and perhaps more than offset by the inflow of money into Lilliput, which would lower interest-rates and increase investment, employment and incomes in Lilliput. The relatively high interest-rates offered in Blefuscu would also tempt Lilliputians to lend money to Blefuscan enterprisers, and thus to fill what remained of the export-import gap by an export of capital.

The course of events would be essentially similar if Blefuscu had a banking system. Instead of sending coins to Lilliput, the Blefuscans who were buying goods from Lilliput over and above the value of their own goods concurrently sold to Lilliput would give the Lilliputians cheques drawn on Blefuscan banks. Whether the Lilliputian owners of the resulting deposits in Blefuscan banks elected to retain them, or to cash cheques and carry away coins to Lilliput, the result would still be that Blefuscans would become more and more short of their medium of payment, and would be willing to offer higher interest-rates to borrow it. Lilliputians might be willing to lend their accumulating bank deposits back to Blefuscans, but we are assuming that they are not willing to do this as part of a process of export of long-term capital; we are supposing that they would need some special inducement, and this would have to take the form of the higher interest-rates, which would discourage Blefuscan investment, output and employment, lower Blefuscan incomes, wages and prices, and virtually compel Blefuscans to spend less on Lilliputian goods while inducing Lilliputians to buy in each unit of time larger quantities and possibly a larger total value of Blefuscan goods.

Has not the line of thought we have been pursuing in this chapter a strange air of familiarity? We have been seeking an explanation of how outputs and prices would be pushed towards an equilibrium, and for the purpose of this explanation we have invoked the idea of demand as a function of incomes and of prices, the idea of the size of the flow of lending as a function of interest-rates, and the idea of interest-rates themselves as functions of the size of the stock of money. And this is just the sort of thing we did when we were discussing, in Books I (*Value*) and II (*Production*), the central theory of value in a self-contained economy, and when we were discussing, in Books V (*Employment*) and VI (*Finance*), the theory of employment and the theory of interest in a self-contained economy. Indeed, it is plain that international trade is merely a special case. It stands in the same relation to the proceedings in a self-contained economy as an obstacle race does to an ordinary race. In international trade there are barriers against the movement and free combination of productive factors, barriers which exist to some extent even within one nation's frontiers, but are dramatised when the frontier itself intervenes. The same principles and ideas which give us insight into the working of a self-contained economy are applicable to the case of relations between two or more 'open' economies, the case which is so overwhelmingly important for Britain; the only difference is that these principles have to be seen operating under special constraints.

In the two first chapters of this Book VIII we have greatly simplified our view of international trade by assuming that the two countries use one and the same money-unit. In this way we avoided all problems arising from the existence of a price of one currency in terms of the other. In the next chapter we have to take this added complication into account.

Chapter 40. Currencies

IF each of the two countries has a currency, that is, a named money-unit, of its own, then each of these currencies or money-units can have a price in terms of the other, and this price by its variation sometimes provides an extra means of adjusting to each other the prices and quantities of goods exchanged in each time-unit between the two countries.

Suppose, then, that Lilliput uses crowns while Blefuscu uses florins, and that there is a market on which crowns can be exchanged for florins at a ratio of exchange which emerges freely from the play of supply and demand. The Lilliputian export surplus will now have an additional effect, besides those we considered in the last chapter. For now the Blefuscans who desire to buy goods from Lilliput will have to acquire, on the 'exchange-market' where florins are sold against crowns and crowns bought for florins, enough crowns to pay for the Lilliputian goods which they are buying. Whence will come the *supply* of crowns to this market? From the sale of goods by Blefuscans to Lilliputians. But we are assuming that at the prevailing crown-prices of Lilliputian products, and the prevailing florin-prices of Blefuscan goods, and *at the prevailing florin-price of crowns*, not enough Blefuscan goods are being sold to Lilliput in each time-unit to equal in total value the Lilliputian goods which are being sold in each time-unit to Blefuscu. So on the exchange-market the supply of crowns will be less than the demand. The most central proposition in the whole of economics tells us what will be the consequence: the florin-price of crowns will rise. But what will be the consequence of *that*? It will make the *florin*-prices of Lilliputian goods higher than before. If the elasticity of Blefuscan demand (refresh the memory in Chapter 10, pp. 58–61) for Lilliputian goods is numerically greater than unity, a price rise of one per cent will depress the yearly quantity bought by more than one per cent, and thus will reduce the total value of Lilliputian goods bought per time-unit (e.g. per year) by Blefuscans. Moreover, this weakening (i.e. reduction of quantity demanded at *each* crown-price) of the demand for Lilliputian products may induce the Lilliputians to reduce the *crown*-price of their products, and it will do so to a larger extent, the *smaller* the numerical elasticity of *supply* of Lilliputian exported products. Any such reduction of the *crown*-price of Lilliputian products will, in itself, be a help to Blefuscu in restraining its tendency to spend too much on Lilliputian goods. But there is more. The rise in the florin-price of crowns will mean that each Lilliputian crown will now buy a larger quantity than before of Blefuscan goods, and this will tend to raise the yearly quantity of Blefuscan exports. If the Lilliputian crown-price-elasticity of demand for Blefuscan goods is numerically greater than unity, the flow of crowns into the exchange-market will be increased. And this will be the more likely to happen, the *smaller* the florin-price-elasticity of *supply* of Blefuscan goods. So the exchange-market will introduce into the problem a whole set of reactions of its own, which, according to the size (greater or less than unity) of four elasticities, will ease or aggravate the problem of eliminating the Lilliputian export surplus. And it is reasonable to say that, even if the elasticities are of the wrong size at the point where things are when the problem arises, they will, some of them and enough of them, become of the right size when the exchange-ratio has moved a certain distance. For example, if the florin-price of crowns rises high enough, Blefuscans will simply have to stop buying Lilliputian goods altogether, and so the Lilliputian export surplus will necessarily be abolished.

Reduction of florin-prices of Blefuscan goods, reduction of their outputs and of the corresponding employment will be painful and wasteful. It may be easier and better to let the exchange-market do most of the work in restoring international trade equilibrium and abolishing an export surplus, if this cannot be adjusted to by establishing a flow of capital export.

In the foregoing part of this chapter, we have been assuming that the crown-price of florins can change to any extent under the push and pull of the market, and that there is nothing in the nature of things to restrict its movement, any more than there is when butter is exchanged for tea. Butter and tea, however, are distinct substances which cannot be physically transmuted one into the other. With crowns and florins the case may be different. They may both be made, say, of gold, and it may be their gold content, rather than the stamped inscription announcing them to be coins of the Blefuscan or the Lilliputian realm, which gives them their value. Then a person who possesses a given quantity of gold will not mind whether this is in the form of crowns or of florins, and in fact there will not really be two currencies but only one. The exchange-ratio of crowns for florins will in this case always approximate closely to the ratio of the quantity of gold in a florin to that in a crown, so that if a crown contains five grammes of gold and a florin only two, it will take five florins to buy two crowns.

How can the exchange-ratio of crowns and florins, as *currencies*, be separated from, and made independent of, the exchange-ratio of their substances? By making them of something which is nearly worthless in itself, such as pieces of paper or, better still, mere entries in a bank ledger. Then the substance-value of a crown being nil, and the substance-value of a florin being nil, we can if we like say that the substance-value of a crown can be obtained from any number of florins we care to name, from zero to a number beyond all bounds: if a florin has a substance-value of nothing, an infinity of florins can have their total substance-value squeezed into that of a single florin, or of no florins at all. Substance-value will be meaningless, and the crown and florin will be free to exchange for each other at ratios reflecting the relative economic circumstances of Lilliput and Blefuscu.

We have now discussed international trade under two different assumptions about the currency arrangements which mediate it. At first we assumed that both countries used one and the same currency, so that no variability of the exchange-ratio between Lilliputian and Blefuscan money units could come into the picture at all. This assumption, we have just seen, corresponds very closely to the situation where both currencies consist partly of coins made of one and the same 'precious' metal, no matter whether or not the Lilliputian crown happens to contain the same quantity of this metal as the Blefuscan florin. This situation is not radically altered if either country introduces banknotes, provided these are genuine 'promises to pay' stated numbers of the precious-metal coins, and that the banks issuing the notes are always ready to honour these promises. In the present chapter we exchanged the supposition of a single currency used by both countries for that of two currencies whose prices in terms of each other were perfectly free to vary in response to market forces. Such freedom of variation is impossible if both currencies consist of coins made of the same *precious* metal, i.e. the same metal valued for its own sake as a commodity. It is only if the currency of Lilliput is a given quantity of one substance while that of Blefuscu is a given quantity of another, or if, better still, neither unit is linked in any way to the value of anything desired for its own sake, and each is represented instead by tokens or symbols of worthless paper or ink, that a freely variable 'rate of exchange' is possible.

Trade

However, although such freedom of the exchange-rate between, say, Lilliputian crowns and Blefuscan florins is rendered *possible* by the use of token currency or of book-keeping currency, it does not follow that this freedom is made use of. The Blefuscan government may set up an 'exchange equalisation account', well stocked with Lilliputian currency, and announce its willingness to buy for some stated number of crowns per florin any quantity of Blefuscan currency that may be offered to it, and likewise to sell for the same or some other stated number of crowns per florin any quantity of Blefuscan currency that may be demanded of it. In this way it can set limits, wide or narrow, to the price-range within which the exchange-market for crowns and florins can move. Suppose the Blefuscan exchange equalisation account stands ready to give two crowns for every five florins up to any amount of florins, and to give four florins for every two crowns up to any amount of crowns. Then the crown-price of florins can never rise above a crown for two florins, and can never fall below a crown for two-and-a-half florins.

When a country's currency consists of gold coins, or of paper 'promises to pay' which can in fact be exchanged for gold coins at will, so that the citizens of that country who import goods from other countries are obliged, in effect, to pay for them in gold, that country is said to be 'on the gold standard'. So long as it has an import surplus, a country on the gold standard will be continually losing gold to the countries which have the corresponding export surplus, and thus will suffer the same sort of deflationary process that we described as happening in Blefuscu when, in Chapters 38 and 39, we supposed Blefuscu and Lilliput to use a common currency and to be out of balance in their mutual trade, with Blefuscu exporting a smaller total value of goods to Lilliput than it imported from Lilliput.

In such a situation the role of the central bank, if the country in question has a fully developed banking system, is very important. To say that the country is fully on the gold standard is to say that gold is available to its citizens on demand from its banks in exchange for the cancellation of some of those IOU's which the banks

Currencies

have given to the citizens in the form either of banknotes or of deposits in the banks' ledgers. Should the situation ever arise where the banks still owed the citizens money but had no more gold to give them, the banks would be in default and would have to close their doors. To guard against such a catastrophe, the central bank must so regulate the size of the nation's money stock, consisting largely of indebtedness of the banks to the citizens, that the gold stock is always a sufficient fraction of that total indebtedness to enable the banks to meet the citizens' day-to-day demand for encashment of their cheques in gold. An external drain of gold will mean that the citizens on the whole will be drawing out from the banking system each month more gold than they are paying in (and sending the difference abroad) and the natural reaction of the cental bank to this continual shrinking of the system's gold reserve will be to reduce the size of the stock of money. We saw in Chapter 30 (*Banks*) the measures available to the central bank for this purpose, which it will pursue until, by reducing the prosperity of the citizens sufficiently, it has cut down the total value of the goods they wish annually to import, to equality with the total value of the goods they can annually export.

The government of a country which, while not on the gold standard, has adopted the policy of 'pegging' the exchange-rates between its own currency and the currencies of other countries, will no more be able to contemplate with equanimity a persistent import surplus than if this import surplus were draining away gold. For instead of gold, the import surplus will be draining away the reserves of foreign currency which the exchange equalisation fund needs if it is to be able to buy the home currency, in whatever quantities it is offered, at the prescribed exchange-rate and thus keep the rate pegged. Thus it will have to adopt one means or another of dissuading or preventing its citizens from buying goods from abroad in excess of the value of those they can concurrently sell abroad. It can do this by impoverishing the citizens, by causing unemployment and lowered wage-rates and thus lowered incomes and lowered prices; or it can directly limit, by imposing legal 'quotas', the physical quantities or the values of goods of various kinds that it will allow to be imported; or it can make the prices of foreign goods artificially high to its own citizens by imposing *tariffs*. These we shall consider in the next chapter. Here it remains to be mentioned that, amongst the goods which one country exports to another or imports from another, we include of course intangible services as well as visible material 'wares', and that if Blefuscu has an import surplus from Lilliput, it may balance this by means of an export surplus to Brobdingnag, provided Brobdingnag balances its import surplus from Blefuscu by having an equal export surplus to Lilliput.

A country's currency is said to be 'fully convertible' when anyone can use as much of it as he likes, up to the full amount that he can get command of, to buy the currency of any other country that he chooses. Since no country's reserves of gold or of foreign currencies can be limitless, this freedom is only allowable provided some market mechanism or some administered control adjusts to each other the supplies of foreign currencies earned by the country's exporters and the flows of foreign currencies spent by the country's importers. We have seen that several different sections of the total market mechanism of an international economy can contribute to this adjustment. If internal prices in each of the open economies making up the international economy are flexible, the fall of prices in an import-surplus country and the rise of prices in an export-surplus country will tend to abolish these surpluses, when the prices have moved far enough to bring into play elasticities of demand and supply of a suitable size. Adjustment may be powerfully aided if *incomes* in the import-surplus country fall and those in the export-surplus country rise, but this may be accompanied by unemployment and hardship in the import-surplus country. Lastly the exchange-market, if left free, will carry the exchange-rate of the two currencies to a point where their relative internal purchasing powers will be such that the elasticities of demand and supply of internationally traded goods have, as a team, a favourable effect and tend to eliminate the export–import unbalance.

The exchange-rate between the two currencies can be held constant, provided the level chosen for it is such that, over a term of years, there is no persistent one-way surplus, and provided that each country has a sufficient reserve of the currency of the other country to tide over any temporary import surplus. A fixed exchange-rate has the advantage of removing from the operations of exporters and importers one source of uncertainty, namely the effect of exchange-rate changes on the relation between their costs and their revenue.

Chapter 41. *Tariffs*

IF, when a Blefuscan citizen pays, say, one hundred florins to a Lilliputian citizen for some particular kind of goods imported into Blefuscu from Lilliput, the Blefuscan has to pay some specified number of florins to his own government, we say that this government has imposed a tariff on imports from Lilliput of this particular kind of goods. The payment may, instead, be related to the physical quantity rather than the value of the goods, and we shall not here concern ourselves with a distinction which is of only secondary theoretical importance. In imposing a tariff, a government may wish to gather revenue for itself; or it may wish to increase the price which its own citizens have to pay for certain goods imported from abroad, in comparison with the price of similar goods produced at home; or it may wish to discourage the importation from abroad, or from one particular country, of goods of no matter what kind.

Behind the three kinds of purpose thus stated may lie further thoughts. In so far as the tariff collects revenue, the Blefuscan government's gain is somebody else's loss, and the Blefuscan government may believe that by means of the tariff it is, in effect, taxing Lilliputian rather than Blefuscan citizens. If so, this effect must arise from a change in the *terms of trade*, so that in the new situation each ton of Blefuscan fuel buys a larger quantity than hitherto of Lilliputian food. In so far as it collects revenue, however, the tariff necessarily forgoes its other possible function, of preventing or reducing the importation of goods from abroad: if no goods or little goods are imported, no revenue or little revenue will be collected from them. Behind the wish to raise the price of imported food relative to that of home-produced food may lie the intention to make Blefuscan farmers more prosperous, by enabling them to sell food at higher prices or more food at given prices. Behind the wish to discourage imports in general may lie a belief that this will tend to eliminate a Blefuscan *import surplus*, a tendency for the total annual value of Blefuscan imports to exceed, at some given ratio of exchange of crowns for florins, the total annual value of Blefuscan exports. Behind the wish to reduce an import surplus or to replace it by an export surplus may lie the wish to avoid a fall in the value of the home currency in terms of other currencies, and this again will have behind it such ideas as the insecurity introduced into international trade by exchange-rates which seem liable to sharp fluctuations, and the unwillingness of foreigners to hold balances of the home currency if its value in terms of other currencies seems unreliable. But there may be a yet more important motive for abolishing an import surplus and establishing an export surplus, namely to increase employment in the home country through the operation of the 'foreign trade multiplier'; for we have seen that in an open economy the Keynesian 'multiplicand' can comprise home net investment, government deficit spending, and the export surplus.

We have to consider in what circumstances and how far it is true that these various ulterior purposes can be served by the imposition of a tariff; and whether in serving these national purposes a tariff will be in conflict with the interest of the world economy as a whole.

There are two questions to be answered. First, can a tariff benefit the international economy as a whole; can it, that is to say, have such an effect as would be produced by the discovery of a new

Tariffs

generally applicable method of obtaining power or of improving the fertility of land? Secondly, can a tariff increase the well-being of the country imposing it by reducing the well-being of other countries?

The answer to the first question is quite unambiguous. For the international economy considered as a whole, tariffs obstruct international specialisation and thus reduce the world's income. If, in the absence of a tariff, Blefuscans would buy Lilliputian food, this is because Blefuscans can get more food by given exertions and sacrifices of their own, when those efforts are directed to the production of fuel for export to Lilliput in exchange for Lilliputian food, than when the efforts are directed to the production of food at home. And likewise the Lilliputians who are willing to buy Blefuscan fuel by exporting Lilliputian food do so because they can thus get more fuel from given productive resources of their own than if they used those resources in the direct production of fuel in Lilliput. Anything which stops or reduces this exchange of Blefuscan fuel for Lilliputian food is likely to injure both parties, and certainly must injure one of them. There can be circumstances, however, in which the tariff-imposing country can hold other countries to ransom, and so be a gainer itself in a world which as a whole is a net loser by that country's actions. The answer to the second question, therefore, is not absolute but depends upon circumstances.

If, with a fixed crown-florin exchange-rate, the Blefuscan demand for Lilliputian food at current prices is elastic, while the Lilliputian supply of food at current prices is inelastic, the main effect of a Blefuscan import-duty will be to reduce the crown-prices charged by Lilliputians for the food they sell to Blefuscu, for only thus, perhaps, can they prevent a rise approximately equal to the duty, in the florin-prices which Blefuscan citizens have to pay for the food. Such a rise would, by hypothesis, greatly reduce the quantity of food which the Blefuscan citizens would buy; and such a reduction, again by hypothesis, will not be tolerated by the Lilliputians if a price-reduction will avert it. The large reduction in the crown-price and the slight reduction in the quantity of Lilliputian food sold to Blefuscu will together have greatly reduced the annual number of florins received by Lilliput from Blefuscu. If, therefore, the supply of Blefuscan fuel is elastic, the quantity of it annually supplied in exchange for this reduced annual number of florins earned by Lilliput will be reduced, rather than the price per ton. Thus in the new equilibrium, Blefuscu will be obtaining hardly less Lilliputian food than before in exchange for a greatly reduced quantity of fuel: the terms of trade will have changed in Blefuscu's favour.

Against the idea that tariffs can help a country to 'export its unemployment' there is an overwhelming case both moral and practical. In reducing imports the tariff impoverishes the would-be exporters in other countries and renders those countries less able to buy the home country's exports. It also invites retaliation which can scarcely be delayed long beyond the moment when the home country's tariff begins to have visible effects in reducing the other countries' exports.

What of the tariff intended to 'protect' particular industries? There are perhaps two valid kinds of reason why such protection may sometimes be justifiable. There is first the notorious 'infant industry' argument which claims that in certain industries a firm becomes increasingly efficient as it gets bigger. A large firm, it is said, may enjoy 'economies of large scale', and be able to make its product at a lower average cost per unit than when it was small. But how is it ever to become big if foreign exporters can always undersell it so long as it is small? A tariff may enable it to survive during the stages of early growth when its costs are high; then when the firm is big and has secured the economies of large scale, the tariff can be removed. The question remains: Will the tariff ever be removed? Employers and workers in a protected industry always strongly resist the loss of this protection. There is one other kind of argument, a non-economic one, by which a tariff may be justified. This claims that certain industries, which under free trade would be unable to survive competition from abroad, are necessary for the nation's safety or well-being. The best-known example is that of agriculture, which the mystique of the soil always has, and always will, set apart from other industries. The appeal of this view, that the farmer performs a rite as well as a mere prosaic productive operation, probably affects everyone who has ever smelt the new-turned furrow or seen the sea of golden grain. The economist, as such, is at any rate unqualified to combat it and out of his depth in attempting to do so.

If there were no weapons we should all be better off. The same argument applies to tariffs, which are weapons rather than tools. With a tool a man can benefit others while benefiting himself, but with a weapon he can only benefit himself by damaging others. The theory of international trade studies the principles on which men make the best of a bad job, namely the circumstance that pools of productive resources are isolated from each other by natural barriers and man-made frontiers, and cannot therefore be combined in the ideally best proportions. Tariffs are a means of making the bad job worse. Most existing tariffs are the result of a failure of understanding or an insufficiency of vision, or, at any rate, of a failure of nations to co-operate in a sufficiently daring mood of enlightened self-interest.

Chapter 42. Models

ECONOMIC theory seeks to explain the real economic world by constructing models of it. In any one of these models there are far fewer pieces, and each piece is far simpler, than in the real world; an immense quantity of complication and detail and 'background' is deliberately left out, and a small number of key ideas gather to themselves all that is supposed to be really essential and operative in economic life. The process of selecting those features of the economic world which are believed to make it work, and to make it work in a particular way with particular results, is called *abstraction*. No rules prescribe how it should be done, every theoretician is obliged to take his own initiative and use his own judgment. There is in consequence an endless variety of models and complete freedom to add continually to their number. Yet it is no more possible to invent a model which is not founded on ideas shaped by centuries of human intellectual struggle and groping, than it is to feed oneself without using materials which, ultimately, nature has provided. Thus models fall into distinguishable types according to the character of the simplifying assumptions on which they chiefly rely, or according to the aspects or phenomena which they chiefly seek to explain, and it is helpful to form in one's mind some picture of how these types are related to each other.

One such scheme classifies all models into four quadrants by dividing them first into the two classes of 'situation' and 'process' models and then by dividing each of these into expectational and non-expectational models. The longest tradition and the most subtle and refined development belong to the non-expectational situation models, the 'static equilibrium' models. These in their most honest and efficient form are strictly time-ignoring. The question they seek to answer is: Given the tastes and resources of every person in the economy, what set of outputs and prices of all the various goods, of quantities employed, in this industry and that, of all the various factors of production, and of prices of the services of these factors, together with their resulting incomes, would leave each of these persons with no desire to alter any of these things in any way which was possible to him? But although they speak of outputs, incomes and other economic quantities which in the real world are *flows*, the static equilibrium models really treat all these things as magnitudes existing at an instant, without any time-dimension at all.

From a different assumed set of tastes and resources of individuals, a different equilibrium situation arises, and this can be compared and contrasted, as to its particular prices, outputs and incomes, with the former one, the differences of the two equilibria being traced to the differences in the governing conditions. Such

Models

a study is called 'comparative statics', and its essential feature is its entire and deliberate abstention from considering any *process* by which the transition from one equilibrium to the other might occur. All changes in the values of the variables (the prices, outputs, incomes, etc.) are supposed to take no time at all, and to occur simultaneously and instantaneously in immediate response to shifts of the governing conditions. In this way a great difficulty is evaded. For if the variables were supposed to change gradually, some fast and some slowly, those which arrived first at what could have proved to be their ultimate equilibrium levels would be dragged out of those levels by the other variables, on which they depend, and which had not yet reached positions compatible with the equilibrium levels of the former variables. Theory would then have to study a complex interactive process with gradually diminishing swings around the ultimate equilibrium. Such labour would be lost, for the character of this process would depend on a mass of very precise assumptions no one set of which could have much claim to represent the truth.

Within the class of static equilibrium models there is an important subdivision, between models of general equilibrium embracing all the variables of the whole economy, and models of partial equilibrium, each of which selects a few closely interrelated variables (such as the price of a single good and the quantity of it demanded) and studies the mutual interdependence of these few against a background of fixed values of all the other variables. General equilibrium models serve only one purpose, though an exceedingly important one: to convince us and keep us in mind of the interconnectedness of all economic quantities, that each one is functionally dependent on all the others. Except for presenting the grand synoptic statement of the oneness of the economic organism, general equilibrium models are not usable: like the centipede which, once he became aware of his hundred legs, was quite unable to get anywhere with them, the general equilibrium model is too vaguely endowed with knowledge about too many things to help us much in practice.

In practice, whether to get a feeling of real intellectual contact with the working of an economic system, or whether to be able to advise the statesman about the effect of this tax or that monopoly, we need to cut up the general model into manageable portions where we can assume each variable to be influenced by only one or two others. Alfred Marshall laid down once for all the kind of procedure by which this can be done. It seems likely, however, that Marshall would not have considered the distinction between situation and process a very useful one.

Just as static equilibrium methods treat the economic world as a blind mechanical system seeking a state of rest, so non-expectational process models treat it as a machine whose design causes its parts inevitably, given the character of the initial push, to follow certain paths of movement through time. Such a path may be one of regular growth in compound-interest fashion, or of oscillations like those of a pendulum or the tide, or of successive impacts and departures at fresh angles like a billiard ball in play. Whereas in static equilibrium models time plays no part at all, in non-expectational process models it is present only as that experienced time which is part of the nature of *events*; which gives, as it were, room for an event, a difference between situations existing at distinct instants, to occur. *Imagined* time, the mind's concern with the future, is totally absent. There are no decisions in any sense except a mechanical response to actually experienced circumstances. The only difference between the two kinds of non-expectational model is that in one the interplay of forces results in a tableau and in the other sets the pattern of a dance. In both the result is *calculable*. It is because in real life the result seems so little amenable to calculation that time in a different sense must be brought in.

We saw in Chapter 20 (*Profit*) that the producer's acts are decided on in the light of what he believes and hopes their consequence will be. In Book v (*Employment*) we discussed the similar basis of investment. A great deal of economic life is a hand-to-mouth process, habitual acts of buying and consuming goods for immediate use. But the level of employment and the pace at which the economy is improving its productive outfit depend on a vista of future months or years filled in by the imagination of individual enterprisers or administrators under the constraint of what his personal experience and reading of history has led him to consider feasible or plausible. Expectational models again fall into those of process, like the sequence analysis developed by Swedish economists, from Wicksell at the turn of the twentieth century to Lindahl and Myrdal and their successors, and those of situation like J. M. Keynes's under-employment equilibrium model which, so far from representing stability, shows the economy at the mercy of changes of expectations, themselves resting, in the nature of things, on a flimsy and shifting basis of 'news'.

Economic theory has two central tasks: to explain the use made of a *given* collection of available productive resources when the whole of this collection is being used and is insufficient to satiate all needs; and to explain how it comes about that sometimes not all of such a collection is actually being used. The first task belongs to the theory of Value and Income Distribution, and the second belongs to the theory of Money and Employment. This present volume falls, though not quite tidily, into halves concerned respectively with these two problems. Books I and II were wholly devoted to Value and Distribution: Chapters 12, 13 and 14 of Book III describe the circulatory (rather than the allocatory) aspect of systems both repetitive and developing; but Chapters 15 and 16 are concerned with Money and therefore with expectational models. Book IV, except for Chapters 18 and 20, is again a part of the theory of Value and Distribution; but Chapter 18 looks at Bargaining and Chapter 20 looks at Profit, and these chapters are therefore expectational. In Books V and VI we are wholly engaged with an expectational theory of Employment and Money. Book VII is in a sense an Appendix to that same theory, though partly also it is an Addendum to Book IV. Book VIII, except for this present chapter, deals with aspects both of Value and Distribution and of Employment and Money. This interweaving of the two main strands of our subject is very far from haphazard. Economics is not merely a collection of ideas but a system of ideas. Their intricate relation cannot be indicated except by an arrangement of our subject-matter which somewhat reflects that intricacy.

INDEX

abstraction, meaning of, 266
accelerator
  in Harrod's dynamic theory, 178
account
  medium of, 33
  money a necessity for keeping, 33
  unit of, 33
accounting, system of, by means of money,
    81
activities
  inter-necessary and inter-determined, 50
activity, an
  defined for *activity analysis*, 51
activity analysis
  and maximising or economising, 51
  linear programming a special form of, 51
activity level, 51
adding-up problem
  and sharing of income, 123
  defined, 100
aircraft in flight, economic system com-
    pared to, 62
Austrian theory of capital
  and meaning of increase of average
    period of production, 215
  weaknesses of, 217
average period of production
  and theory of capital, 214
  difficulties of concept of, 217
  lengthening of, 215, 217

baker and farmer and miller, constituting
    whole economy, 24
balance of payments, meaning of, 247
balloon, money stock compared to cable of,
    210
bank(s)
  central, role in international trade, 258
  create money by lending, 98, 197, 198
  obtain revenue by lending, 198
Bank of England
  and short-term interest-rates, 196
  as 'lender of last resort', 202
  as lender to Government, 237
  can control size of money stock, 204, 209
  can influence interest-rates, 202
  is the bankers' bank, 200, 201
  regulates size of nation's money stock,
    201
  role in international trade, 258
Bank Rate, explained, 203

bargaining
  and bilateral monopoly, 106
  and contract zone, 107
  and determination of wages, 104
  and loss of face, 109
  and uncertainty, 109
base-date, of index number, 90, 91
batsman's score, average and marginal, 42
'Bears' on Stock Exchange
  and Budget deficit, 230
  'Bulls' changed into, by fall of interest-
    rates, 187
  changes of expectation of, 216
  and Government borrowing, 237
  and stability of interest-rate, 190
  are willing holders of money, 186, 190,
    206
bilateral monopoly
  and expectations, 109
  and static analysis, 109
  explained, 106
bill of goods for final use, 50
bills of exchange, 195
Bills, Treasury, 195
'bit at a time' method, 53
Blefuscu
  cost of producing food and fuel in, 244,
    245
  wages and rent in, 244, 245
Böhm-Bawerk, E. von, and theory of
    capital, 212
borrowing, and augmentation of equip-
    ment, 74
budget
  and need to choose, 2
  balanced, and size of saving-flow, 139, 232
  deficit, and employment, 175
  deficit, and monetary consequences, 228,
    229, 230
  deficit, and the multiplicand, 175
  deficit, implies debt, 236
  deficit, sometimes desirable, 235
  principle of composition, 13
  subject to double requirement, 17
'Bulls'
  and 'Bears' on Stock Exchange, 186,
    190, 206, 207
  melt into 'Bears', 211

Cambridge
  k, 94, 95, 96

Index

Cambridge (*cont.*)
  school, 53, 93, 94, 97
  version of Quantity Theory of Money,
    94, 95, 96, 97
Canada, need of capital in, 8
canals, circular, as model of economic
  system, 72, 73, 78
capital
  as category of productive resources, 7, 8, 9
  defined, 7
  export of, 250, 252, 256
  how created, 8, 9
  is man-made, 8
  maintenance of, 70
  theory of, formerly explained interest-
    rates, 211
capital-output ratio, 177, 178
cash
  as a servo-mechanism, 205
  banks' need to hold, 98, 199
  banks' reserves of, 200, 201, 202
  ratio, 200
  required for payment of wages, 98, 199
category(-ies)
  distinct from factors of production, 8
  of productive resources, 8
centipede, general equilibrium compared
  to, 267
ceteris paribus, assumption of, explained,
  16, 18
choice
  is the heart of economics, 50
  scarcity calls for, 6
coinage, debasement of, 233
coins, as means of keeping account, 33
comparative statics, meaning of, 267
competition
  and cheapest production, 35
  and firm's control of price, 36, 53, 54, 56
  imperfect, and elasticity of demand, 58
  perfect, and determination of outputs,
    41, 53
  perfect, and determination of wages,
    101, 104, 123
  perfect, and elasticity of demand, 58
  perfect, and rent, 113
  perfect, defined, 36, 43
  perfect, includes mobility of factors of
    production, 54, 65
  perfect, in factor markets, and size of
    firms, 128
complementary goods
  and prices, 18
  explained, 17
condition, of equality between aggregate
  demand and output, 164

Consols, are irredeemable British Government securities, 195
constant returns to scale and income-
  distribution, 124, 125, 127
consumers' goods, relation to resources,
  5, 6
consumption
  defined, 3, 4
  forgoing of, to build up equipment, 73
  means destruction, 74
contract zone
  agreement not ensured by, 108
  explained, 107
  in trade between regions, 247
convergence, mathematical idea of, 171
cost(s)
  average, 42, 43, 128
  average, and general equilibrium, 130
  average, as function of output, 42
  average, at a minimum in general
    equilibrium, 65, 129
  average, equal to price so that net
    revenue is zero, 43, 65
  average, lowest where equal to marginal
    cost, 42, 65
  direct, 42
  lowest possible, and factor proportions,
    39, 65
  marginal, and exchange value, 11
  marginal, and general equilibrium, 130
  marginal, equal to average cost when
    latter is at its lowest, 43
  marginal, equal to price in firm's
    equilibrium, 44, 65
  marginal, equal to price so that net
    revenue is at maximum, 43, 52
  marginal, explained, 10, 11
  marginal, varies with output, 11
  of living, 89
  overhead, 42
  overhead, and economies of large scale,
    126
  prime, 42
  total, 41, 42, 43, 52, 53, 55
  unit overhead, 42
  unit prime, 42
criterion, in activity analysis, 51
currency(-ies)
  convertibility of, 260
  exchange-rates between, 254, 255, 256
  national, 244
  prices of, in terms of each other, 254
customs and excise, 76

dairy farm, illustrating effects of factor
  proportions, 28

Index

debt
  acknowledgments of, excluded from
    'real capital', 8
  government's, management of, 227, 237
  national, not a burden on posterity, 239
deficit
  in Government Budget, 227, 233
  in Government Budget, monetary
    accompaniments of, 228, 229, 230
demand
  and exchange value, 11
  and 'inferior goods', 16
  and net investment, 167
  as a function of income, 253
  as function of price, 23, 57, 253
  effective, 164, 165, 166, 167, 169, 241
  effective, Government's power to aug-
    ment, 232, 241
  law of, 14, 15
  law of, and human nature, 17
  law of, and price mechanism, 18
  limited by price, 21
  play of, in foreign currency market, 254
  price, and marginal efficiency of capital,
    155, 156
  price of equipment, 145–50, 153, 155
  price, personal, 153, 154
  price, personal, diversity of, 155
deposits, in the banks, 98
depreciation
  allowance for, 71, 79, 80, 81
  and reckoning of national income, 77
  of durable goods, 70, 71, 72
difference
  and marginal utility, 4
  or marginal quantity, 31
diminishing marginal productivity, 27
diminishing marginal utility, law of
  and diminishing marginal productivity,
    27
  and prices, 15, 18
  elaborated, 12
  explained, 3, 4
Discount Houses, and bills of exchange, 203
discounted value, of future instalments,
  146, 147, 149
discounting, notion of, 148
diseconomies of large scale, 126
distribution, or sharing of income, 99
disutility, of work, 103
durable goods
  and efficiency of production, 214
  depreciation of, 71

econometrics, combines realism, measurement and theory, 44

economic processes, mutual support of, 85
economics, the typical problem of, 50
economies of large scale, 126
Edgeworth, F.Y., and contract zone, 107
  108, 109
efficiency
  economic, 26
  economic, and factor proportions, 27, 39
  economic, and marginal physical pro-
    duct, 31
  economic, and prices, 30
  economic, and relation to technical, 30
  economic, maximised by equilibrium of
    the industry, 55
  technical, 26, 30
elastic supply, of factor of production, and
  rent, 114
elasticity
  infinite, and perfect competition, 58, 61
  is a ratio, 59, 60
  of demand, 58, 59, 61, 252
  of demand for imports, effects of, 255, 260
  of supply of exports, effects of, 255, 260
  unit, 59, 60, 61
  unit, and firm's revenue, 60
employment, level of, how determined, 167
endowment, of a region with resources, 243
equation
  meaning and nature of solving operation,
    49
  showing uses of product i, 46
equilibrium
  and absence of saving, 63
  and constant returns to scale, 129
  and differing rates of adjustment, 267
  and profit, 131
  and wages, 101, 102, 104
  as an optimum position, 62
  defined, 60
  general, 62, 63, 66, 102, 127, 267
  general, and income distribution, 127,
    129
  general, and interdependence of econo-
    mic quantities, 66, 86
  general, compared to centipede, 267
  general, conditions of, 63
  general, determinacy of, 66, 67, 86
  general, implications of, 66, 123
  hours of work, 64
  in international trade, and currency
    exchange-market, 256
  long-period, 54
  long-period of firms and industries, 64
  of perfectly competitive industry, 55, 102
  of the consumer, 63
  of the firm, 52, 60, 65

Index

equilibrium (*cont.*)
of the industry, 54, 55, 60, 65
of the industry, conditions for, 55
of the whole economy, 66, 102
partial, 267
equi-marginal productivity
and divisibility of means of production, 37
explained, 29
equipment-to-output ratio (capital-out-put ratio), 178, 179
ex ante
income, 163, 168, 173
investment, 166, 168, 173
saving, 166, 168, 173
viewpoint, 160, 175
ex post
income, 173
investment, 173
saving, 173
viewpoint, 160, 175
exchange
and equilibrium, 60
equalisation account, 258, 259
indirect, 33
inseparable from specialisation, 32, 246
medium of, 33
exchange-market, working of, 255
exchange-ratios, determinate amongst real goods, 87
exchange-ratios (rates), of international currencies, 254, 255, 256, 257, 258, 259
expectations
and relation between investment and saving, 160
uncertainty of, 144
expenditure
government's, must be considered in estimating net effect of taxation, 226
restricted in budget, 2
export, of capital, 250, 252, 256
export surplus
and currency exchange-rates, 256
and effect on demand for currencies, 254
and export of capital, 250
and the multiplicand, 173, 174
how reducible, 256, 268
meaning of, 250
factor-income, and commodity taxes, 77
factor-market, perfect competition in, 37
factor(s) of production
allocated by price-system, 22
and economic efficiency, 26
as mutual substitutes, 7
best proportions of, depend on their prices, 39

collaboration of, 7
demand for, 110
diminishing returns to, 124
distinct from categories of resources, 8
enterprise as, 119
homogeneity of, 8, 9
indivisible, 37, 38, 65
lumpy, 37, 38, 65
market for, perfect competition in, 37
meaning, 6, 7
movement impeded between regions, 243
owners of, are also consumers, 35
patterns, proportions, in which combined, 7, 9, 38, 243
price of, as function of quantity used, 36
pricing of, and income distribution, 122, 132
proportions of, and comparison with household budget, 27
proportions of, distorted by lumpy factor, 38
use of cheapest, benefits everybody, 35
Fiduciary Issue, controlled by Parliament, 200
final demand for a product, meaning of, 50
final demands for all products, requirement of any one product dependent on, 47
firm(s)
and the money circulation system, 68, 83
as tax gatherers, 84
buys factors and sells goods, 35
in monopolistic or imperfect competition, 57
pay out income, 72
receive outlay of consumers and of other firms, 72
serves general interest in seeking own profit, 35
streams of goods converge upon and spread from, 68
fiscal policy, meaning of, 227
Fisher, Irving, 96
flow
defined, 3, 4,
increase of, 3, 4
freedom of entry into an industry, and paradox of profit, 60
function
connecting price and output, 57
increasing, 22
mathematical, meaning of, 12

GNP, 77
gold
and international trade, 256

Index

gold (cont.)
external drain of, and banking system, 259
no longer the basis of the money stock, 205
standard, meaning of, 258
goods
as store of services, 2
consumers', 78
gratify wants, 2
producers', 78
some not physical, 2
government
and economic circulation, 83
revenue, 83
gross national product (GNP), 77
growth
instability of, 180
regular, 268
warranted, in Harrod's dynamic theory,
178, 179
growth economics, and resources, 9

Harrod, Sir Roy
and the balancing of the effects of
investment, 176
and the instability of growth, 180
and warranted growth, 178, 179
combined the Multiplier and the
Accelerator, 178
his dynamic theory, 176 and following
his theorem a tool for the applied economist, 180
Hayek, F. A., and structure of the stock of
equipment, 212
Hercules and the Tortoise, 171
hotel, as example of lumpy factor, 38

import duty, effect of, 263
import surplus
and drain of foreign currencies, 259
and drain of gold, 259
how reducible, 260
tariffs intended to eliminate, 262
imputation, and distribution of income, 100
income(s)
and balance of payments, 260
and commodity taxes, 77
and demand, 16
and desired stock of money, 93
and equilibrium hours of work, 64, 103
and GNP, 77
and map of economic flows, 69
and price as distributor of given supply,
20
and prices of productive services, 100
and velocity of circulation of money, 96
disposable, 136

disposable, and saving, 137, 138, 139,
142, 232
ex ante, 163, 168, 169
expected, 163, 165
flowing from firms to individuals, 73,
78, 80
left unspent, 74, 81
marginal utility of, 103
matched by outlay, 69, 70
national, difficulty of reckoning, 77
production as sole source of, 100
redistribution of, by taxation, 226
reflecting real process of production, 80
saving out of aggregate, 141
sharing of, 99, 100, 122–32
sharing of, and leverage given to tastes, 27
sharing of, and size of aggregate saving-
flow, 138
sharing of, engrossed early economists,
131
shown in square table, 79, 80, 83
transfer of, 84
transfer of, by interest paid out of taxes,
236
index number
and value of money, 91
explained, 90
weighting of, 90
India, density of population, 8
indivisibility
and economies of large scale, 126
and the 'adding-up problem', 126
defined, 38
industry, equilibrium of, 55
'infant industry' argument, for tariffs, 264
'inferior' goods, 16
inflation
and taxation, 234
evils of, 233
government action against, 234
through too-rapid growth, 180
input-output analysis
and fixed co-efficients of production, 45
and notion of *sector*, 45
assumes that input-proportions are fixed,
45
invented by Leontief, 45
purpose of, 45
interdependence
and simultaneous equations, 66
of all economic quantities, 66, 220
interest, rate of
and Austrian theory of capital, 216
and demand-price of machines, 143
and inducement to invest, 148, 151, 207,
211

Index

interest, rate of (*cont.*)
 and marginal efficiency of capital, 157, 159
 and present value of future sums, 147, 148, 149
 and price of deferred sums, 183, 184, 185
 and the balance of payments, 253
 as a proportionate time-rate of growth, 185
 beliefs about future movements of, 186
 Central Bank's control of, 238
 central importance accorded to, 197
 consensus of opinion must cause movement of, 186
 determined on securities market, 185, 186, 189, 190
 formerly explained by capital theory, 211
 how reckoned, 182
 influence of size of money stock on, 194, 207, 253
 is price of liquidity, 88
 leverage of, on present value, 151
 normal range of variation of, 191, 210
 on government debt, 236
 origin of, 196
 reciprocal of, and maximum effect on discounted value of deferred sum, 150
 unstable, except when there are two opinions, 190
international trade
 defined, 243 244
 object of the theory of, 264
intervention, of government in economic life, 239, 240
inventories, changes in, are a form of investment, 142
investment
 adds to both demand and supply of means of production, 176
 and profitability, 177
 and saving, 160, 161, 172
 by means of an export surplus, 250
 defined, 176
 ex ante, 166, 168
 ex post, 170
 gross, 158
 has *two* effects, 176
 inducement for, found in growth of output or technical advance, 177
 in durable equipment, 144
 influenced by interest-rate, 207
 net, 158, 162
 net, and demand for goods, 164, 167
irredeemable securities
 called Consols, 195
 ease of reckoning yield of, 195

Japan, shortage of land in, 8

Kahn, Richard, and the investment multiplier, 172, 175, 210, 252
Keynes, John Maynard, 97
 and central importance of interest-rate, 197
 and ideas derived from Wicksell, 212
 and liquidity preference, 186
 and propensity to consume, 136, 138, 230
 and Stock Exchange 'Bulls' and 'Bears', 186, 187
 and the general level of prices, 206
 and the investment multiplier, 172, 175, 210, 252
 and under-employment equilibrium, 269
 terms introduced by, 140

labour
 as category of productive resources, 7, 9
 defined, 7
land
 a pure gift of nature, 111
 as category of productive resources, 7, 9, 111
 cannot be increased, 112
 defined, 7
 distinct from capital, 8
 distinguished from equipment, 113
 inelastic supply of, and rent, 114, 117
language, algebraic
 subscript conventions of, 47
Leontief scheme
 and choice of bill of goods for final use, 50
 and fixity of technical co-efficients, 45, 49
 and one-one correspondence of sectors and products, 49
 essential simplicity of, 49
 excludes price effects, 45, 50
Lilliput
 costs of producing food and fuel in, 244, 245
 wages and rent in, 244, 245
Lindahl, Erik
 and sequence analysis, 269
 and Swedish expectational school, 160
liquidity
 and transactions motive, 187
 market value of, measured by interest-rate, 178
 meaning of, 178
 obtained at sacrifice of interest, 184
liquidity preference, and government borrowing, 237
loan, meaning of, 184
long period, meaning of, 56

Index

luck, a factor of production, 119
lumpiness, of factor of production, and prime costs, 42

manipulation, mathematical
reveals but does not increase information, 48
marginal cost
and exchange value, 11
and general equilibrium, 130
and price, 22
equal to average cost where the latter is lowest, 43, 65
equal to price where net revenue a maximum, 43
equal to supply-price, in perfect competition, 152
explained, 10, 11
illustrated, 22
in short period, 40
varies with output, 11, 152
marginal disutility of work, 103, 104
marginal efficiency of capital
and uncertainty, 155
as function of output of investment-goods, 155, 156
as suppositious interest-rate, 154
difficulties of the concept of, 157
equalised over all types of equipment, 155
schedule of, 158
marginal physical product
and rent, 113
defined, 30
of a factor, uniform under ideal conditions, 101
value of, and wages, 101, 123
value of, distinguished from marginal value product, 114
marginal pound, spent on various factors, and their productivities, 102
marginal productivity (-ies)
and income distribution, 123, 246
diminishing, 27, 30
high for a scarce factor, 246
meaning in imperfect competition, 105
proportion to prices, 29
marginal propensity to consume
and convergence, 171
and progressive taxation, 230, 231
and the Kahn-Keynes multiplier, 169
idea introduced by Keynes, 140
marginal propensity to save, reciprocal of, equals the Kahn–Keynes multiplier, 172, 176
marginal quantity, defined as difference, 31

marginal revenue
and equilibrium of firm, 40
and general equilibrium, 130
and price, 40
marginal utility (-ies)
and household budget, 14, 15
explained, 3, 4, 5
law of diminishing, 4, 12, 15
of earnings, 103, 104, 110, 111
proportional to prices, 15, 18, 29
weighted, and consumer's equilibrium, 64
marginal value product (marginal product of value, marginal revenue product)
distinguished from value of marginal physical product, 113, 114
explained, 106
Marshall, Alfred
and 'bit at a time' method, 53, 268
and Cambridge version of Quantity Theory of Money, 93
and profit, 118
and quasi-rent, 117
matrix notation, advantage of, 49
matrix, or square array of entries
defined, 48
serves accounting coherence, 48
models
expectational, 266, 269
non-expectational, 266
process, 266
purpose of devising, 265, 266
situation, 266
static equilibrium, 266
money
and determinateness of general equilibrium, 86, 87
and putting off decisions, 20, 188
as general purchasing power, 82
as medium of account, 33, 34, 81, 85, 87
circulation system of, compared to river basin, 85
created by banks, 197, 198
deposited with a bank, not available to be lent, 81
desired stock of, 92, 93
expressing price, 19
expressing scarcity, 1
legal tender, 199, 201
prices, general level of, 87, 88
purchasing power of, 88
quantity of, and open-market operations, 202
quantity of, how controlled, 97, 201, 202, 204, 205
quantity of, regulated by a 'feed-back', 205

Index

money (*cont.*)
  quantity of, stock of, 78, 82, 91, 92, 95, 96, 97, 81, 201, 202, 208, 259
  reflecting 'real' processes, 80
  reserves of, 81
  reservoirs of, 78
  streams of, representing incomes and expenditures, 68
  value of, 88, 182
  velocity of circulation of, 91, 92, 94, 97
monopolist
  firm identical with industry, 61
  sole seller of some commodity, 61
monopolistic competition
  and seller's control of price, 105
  or imperfect competition, 57
  price a function of output under, 105
monopolistic competitor, must lower price to sell more, 57, 105
monopoly
  and income distribution, 130
  exists when product is distinct, 105
multiplicand
  and government expenditure, 174, 175
  components of, 173, 174
  export surplus an item of, 262
  items of, 175, 180
multiplier
  combined with the accelerator in Harrod's dynamic theory, 178
  foreign trade, 262
multiplier, investment
  alternative formulation of, 180
  as a link between money stock and prices, 207
  definition of, 173, 175
  in equilibrium, 172, 176
  invented by R. F. Kahn and J. M. Keynes, 172, 175
Myrdal, Gunnar
  and sequence analysis, 269
  and the *ex ante– ex post* distinction, 160

national income, as collection of flows of goods, 7
net revenue
  and firm's best output, 41
  at a maximum where marginal cost equals price, 43
  endeavour to maximise, serves general interest, 41
  when at a maximum, firm in equilibrium, 52
  zero when the industry in equilibrium, 54

notes
  as means of keeping account, 33
  quantity of, controlled through Bank of England, 98
  quantity outside banks, increases with increase of national income, 199

objective function, in activity analysis, 51
obstacle race, international trade compared to, 254
oligopoly, and income distribution, 130
open-market operations, of Bank of England, 202
outlay
  flowing from individuals to firms, 73, 78, 80
  matches income, 69, 70
  reflecting real process of consumption, 80
  shown in square table, 79, 80
output
  and constant returns to scale, 128
  and direct or prime costs, 50
  and general equilibrium, 65
  and minimum average cost, 128
  and overhead expenses, 50
  and production-function, 124, 127
  and rise of product price, 52
  defined, 22, 152
  demand as function of, 57
  ex ante, 164
  in relation to growth of wealth, 161
  marginal cost an increasing function of, 22
  of dairy farm, 28
  price as function of, 57, 61, 105
  rule for producing at least cost, 29
  test by which firm selects, 37, 41
  total cost of, 42
overhead expenses
  and economies of large scale, 126
  explained, 42

palisade, planning compared to, 241
planning, centralised, 241
poverty, relieved by government, 226
present value
  and marginal efficiency of capital, 155
  of future instalments of money, 146, 147, 149, 185
price(s)
  a ratio, 19
  adjusts supply to demand, 20, 21, 22, 23, 153, 232
  and aggregate effective demand, 235
  and chain of events, 19
  and diminishing marginal utility, 15

Index

price(s) (*cont.*)
  and economic efficiency, 30, 31
  and elasticity of demand, 58, 59, 60, 61, 252
  and marginal cost, 22, 43, 52
  and profit, 118
  as a warning system, 41
  as means of measuring mixed collections of goods, 69
  balances cost and desire, 22
  by rising, curtails demand, 22
  by rising, elicits larger output, 22, 52, 53, 153
  can be chosen by monopolist, 105
  demand-, 145–50, 153, 154, 155, 160
  distributes a given supply, 20, 21, 22
  equilibrium, 23, 253
  general level of, 87, 88, 89, 90, 91, 94, 95, 96, 97, 206, 208, 232, 233, 240
  in terms of money, 19, 86
  indeterminate, inbilateral monopoly, 107
  index number of, 90, 91
  like boats on a lake, 22
  of currencies in terms of each other, 254, 255
  of substitutes and complements, 17, 18
  output as function of, 23, 57, 61, 105
  percentage or proportionate change of, 58, 60
  reduced by addition of new firms to the industry, 54
  supply-, 152, 153, 154, 155, 156
  taken out of firm's control by perfect competition, 35, 36, 40, 53, 54
price-mechanism, price-system
  and law of demand, 18
  meaning of, 21
primary inputs, 51
product *i*
  total demand for, dependent on final demands for all other products, 46
  total demand for, dependent on outputs of all other products, 46
product, non-homogeneous, 56
production
  defined, 24
  function, 124
  function, giving constant returns to scale, 124, 127
  function, 'linear and homogeneous', 127
  is value added, 162
  roundabout process of, 213
  total value of, 25, 134, 162
  total value of, as sole source of incomes, 100, 162, 163

production possibility schedule, meaning of, 246
profit(s)
  and inventions, 118
  and time-gap between input and sale, 120
  and uncertainty, 120, 121, 130, 131, 151
  as a reward, 120
  as a vector, 122
  as an inducement, 120
  as element of competitive mechanism, 118
  attract new firms to an industry, 54, 118 130
  depend on tastes and distribution of resources, 27
  discounted, 154
  expected, 163
  expected, and choice amongst courses of action, 121, 122
  expected, and investment, 145, 151, 154
  expected, as a scalar quantity, 121
  firm's endeavour to maximise, leads to economical production, 35
  helps allocate resources, 118
  in Marshallian economics, 118, 119, 120
  paradox of, 60
  power to make, disregarded for distant future, 148, 151
  realised and expected, 119
  recorded, 121
  reduced by addition of new firms to the industry, 54
  uncertainty of, and freedom of entry, 130
  zero in general equilibrium, 65
propensity to save, 177, 178, 179
proportionate time-rate of growth of debt, defines an interest-rate, 185
protection, of an industry by a tariff, 264
public finance, scope of, 227

Quantity Theory of Money, 96
quasi-rent, and Alfred Marshall, 117

radar, price as, 19
rent
  and inelastic supply of factor, 114
  and marginal value product, 114
  defined, 112
  double purpose served by, 115
  idea not important from viewpoint of firm, 117
  of ability, 112
  of differential fertility, 116
  origin of, 113
  taxation of, 117
  two essentials of, 116

resources
  as unripe consumers' goods, 6
  categories of, 7
  classified into factors of production, 6, 7
  distribution of, and equilibrium, 63
  economised by price, 22
  least sacrifice of achieved by price system, 41
  meaning of, 5
  versatile, 25
  wasteful use of, and price, 41
revenue
  average, 53
  marginal, and maximisation of net revenue, 40, 41, 43
  marginal, defined, 40
  marginal, equal to price in competitive equilibrium, 40
  net, and determination of wages, 102
  net, and general equilibrium, 66
  net, endeavour to maximise serves general interest, 41
  net, when above zero attracts new firms, 53, 54, 55
  of firm, defined, 40
  systems for collecting, 221
  tariffs intended to gather, 261
  total, 41, 43, 52, 53, 55
Ricardo, David
  and effects of increase in money stock 206
  and rent, 116
risk allowance, and inducement to invest, 151
river-gorge productive system compared to, 205, 206, 208, 209

save, propensity to, 177, 178, 179
saving
  and disposable income, 136
  and net investment, 160, 161, 165, 172
  and taxation, 230, 231
  as a proportion of general output, in Harrod's dynamic theory, 177
  by citizens of Lilliput, 249
  ex ante, 166
  flow of, depends on distribution of income, 141
  meaning of, 177
  through government action, 140, 141
saving-and-lending
  reflecting real process of augmenting equipment, 80
  stream of, 74, 75, 79
  stream of, drawn off by government, 76
scar of old wounds, national debt compared to, 239

scarcity
  and dismal science, 1
  and equilibrium 61
  and fewness, 10
  and role of prices, 20, 41
  defined, 4
  necessary conditions for, 11
  of labour, results in high wages, 246
  of land, results in high rents, 246
service(s), tangible goods a store of, 2
shares, in a firm, 82
short period, defined, 40
signatures, on banknotes to calculate velocity, 93, 94
slices, growing at compound interest, 182
Smith, Adam, 31
specialisation
  Adam Smith on, 31
  amongst regions and nations, 243, 246, 263
  and need for exchange, 32
  by product and by process, 32
  consequences of, 32, 34
  international, obstructed by tariffs, 263
State Servants, source of incomes for, 219, 220, 224
static analysis, time excluded from, 110
stationary state, defined, 72
stock
  defined, 3
  replenished by production, 5
substitutes
  amongst factors of production, 29, 101
  and complementary goods, 17
  perfect, and homogeneity, 8, 57
supply
  and maginal efficiency of capital, 155
  increase of, elicited by rise of price, 52, 53, 152
  price, of machines, 153, 155, 156
surplus, in Government's Budget, 227, 233, 234

tariff(s)
  arguments for and against, 262, 263, 264, 265
  meaning of, 260, 261
  purposes of, 261, 262, 263, 264, 265
tastes, given leverage by income, 104
tax(es)
  and the economic circulation, 83
  direct, 76, 83, 84, 220, 224
  disincentive effect of, 234
  income, 76
  on commodities, 76, 84, 220, 224
  on commodities, regressive effect of, 224
  progressive, 222, 224

Index

tax(es) (*cont.*)
  progressive, and effect on employment, 230, 231
  purchase, 76
  reason for levying, 220
taxation
  and incentive to produce, 221
  and size of saving-flow, 139
  and the multiplicand, 174
  as part of individual's outlay, 76
  best system of, 221
  disincentive effect of, 230
  four requirements for a good system of, 221, 225
  progressive, 222
  progressive, disincentive effect of, 222, 223
  proportional, 222
  regressive, 223
terms of trade
  altered by a tariff, 263, 264
  meaning of, 262
time
  and definition of flow, 3
  and the nature of capital, 212
  in models of economic systems, 266, 267, 268
total discounting rate, and uncertainty, 151

uncertainty
  absent from static analysis, 131, 132
  and currency exchange-rates, 261
  and income distribution, 129
  and marginal efficiency of capital, 157, 158
  as explanation of rate of interest, 184
  causes unemployment, 240
  is basis of profit, 120, 121
  lender's, 193, 194, 196
  universal effect of, 197
under-developed countries, 8, 9
unemployment, through too-slow growth, 180
utility
  equivalent to contentment, satisfaction, 4
  law of diminishing marginal, 4, 12, 15
  marginal, and household budget, 14, 15
  marginal, proportional to prices, 15
  marginal, weighted, and consumer's equilibrium, 64

value
  added, 24, 162
  and cost, 11
  and distribution, theory of, 131

as measure of economic significance, 69
capital, risk of loss of, and interest-rates 192
due to man rather than nature, 113
economic, production of, 24
in exchange, 10
of money, 91
variable quantity(-ies), mutual dependence of, 85, 122
velocity of circulation
  and Fisher theory, 97
  of money, 92, 94
Voltaire, 2

wage(s)
  and rise of general price-level, 233
  dependent on number of workers per acre, 246
  equal to marginal product of value, 246
  hours of work dependent on, 103, 111
  weekly payment of, and velocity of circulation, 97
wage-rate, brings supply of and demand for labour to equality, 103, 104
wants
  and inter-personal comparison, 20
  are for a flow of goods, 3, 5
  diversity of, 2
  'once-for-all', 3
warranted growth
  in Harrod's dynamic theory, 178
  defined, 179
wealth, real, accumulation of, 8
Wealth of Nations, 31
web or network of activities constitutes general production, 44, 45
weight(s), weighting, of index number, 89, 90
Wicksell, Knut
  and sequence analysis, 269
  and Swedish expectational school, 160, 199, 211
Wicksteed, Philip, and theory of income distribution, 132
wine, maturing of, 213

yield
  of different maturities, pattern of, 195, 196
  of fixed-interest securities, 189, 192, 193, 194
  of fixed-interest securities, influence of share prices on, 193

Zeno, Paradox of, 171